Generalizing from Educational Research

T4-AHH-357

Beyond Qualitative and Quantitative Polarization

Edited by

Kadriye Ercikan
University of British Columbia, Canada

and

Wolff-Michael Roth
University of Victoria, Canada

Routledge
Taylor & Francis Group

NEW YORK AND LONDON

First published 2009
by Routledge
270 Madison Ave, New York, NY 10016

Simultaneously published in the UK
by Routledge
2 Park Square, Milton Park, Abingdon, Oxon OX14 4RN

Routledge is an imprint of the Taylor & Francis Group, an informa business

© 2009 Taylor & Francis

Typeset in Sabon and Gill Sans by EvS Communication Networx, Inc.
Printed and bound in the United States of America on acid-free paper by Walsworth Printing
Company, Marceline, MO

Library of Congress Cataloging in Publication Data
Generalizing from educational research / edited by Kadriye Ercikan and Wolff-Michael Roth.
p. cm.
Includes bibliographical references and index.
1. Education—Research—Methodology. I. Ercikan, Kadriye. II. Roth, Wolff-Michael, 1953–
LB1028.G398 2008
370.72—dc22
2008027765

ISBN 10: 0-415-96381-8 (hbk)
ISBN 10: 0-415-96382-6 (pbk)
ISBN 10: 0-203-88537-6 (ebk)

ISBN 13: 978-0-415-96381-7 (hbk)
ISBN 13: 978-0-415-96382-4 (pbk)
ISBN 13: 978-0-203-88537-6 (ebk)

Contents

Preface   ix

1   Introduction   1
    WOLFF-MICHAEL ROTH AND KADRIYE ERCIKAN

SECTION I
Generalizing Within and Beyond Populations
and Contexts   9
    Overview

2   Generalizability Theory and Its Contribution to the
    Discussion of the Generalizability of Research Findings   13
    RICHARD J. SHAVELSON AND NOREEN M. WEBB

3   The Testing of English Language Learners as a Stochastic
    Process: Population Misspecification, Measurement Error,
    and Overgeneralization   33
    GUILLERMO SOLANO-FLORES

Section I Highlights   46

SECTION II
Combining and Contrasting Qualitative and
Quantitative Evidence   49
    Overview

4   Generalization from Qualitative Inquiry   51
    MARGARET EISENHART

5   On Qualitative and Quantitative Reasoning in Validity   67
    ROBERT J. MISLEVY, PAMELA A. MOSS, AND JAMES P. GEE

6   Generalizability and Research Synthesis   101
    BETSY J. BECKER AND MENG-JIA WU

    Section II Highlights   117

SECTION III
How Research Use Mediates Generalization   123
    Overview

7   Generalizability and Research Use Arguments   127
    LYLE F. BACHMAN

8   Repetition, Difference, and Rising Up with Research in
    Education   149
    KENNETH TOBIN

9   Critical Realism, Policy, and Educational Research   173
    ALLAN LUKE

    Section III Highlights   201

SECTION IV
**Rethinking the Relationship Between the General and
the Particular**   207
    Overview

10 Limitations in Sample-to-Population Generalizing   211
    KADRIYE ERCIKAN

11 Phenomenological and Dialectical Perspectives on the
    Relation between the General and the Particular   235
    WOLFF-MICHAEL ROTH

    Section IV Highlights   261

12 Discussion of Key Issues in Generalizing in Educational
    Research   265
    EDITED BY KADRIYE ERCIKAN AND WOLFF-MICHAEL ROTH WITH
    CONTRIBUTIONS FROM LYLE F. BACHMAN, MARGARET EISENHART,
    ROBERT J. MISLEVY, PAMELA A. MOSS, GUILLERMO
    SOLANO-FLORES, AND KENNETH TOBIN

    Contributors   295
    Index   299

Preface

In 2007, we (the editors) invited some colleagues who had been working, explicitly or implicitly, on the problem of generalizing in educational research to contribute to a book on the topic. These are colleagues who look at assessments as evidentiary reasoning and at validity from different perspectives including situative and hermeneutic, who discuss utility of information from research as an integral part of validity of generalizing from small-scale studies, or who think about the validity of assessment interpretations for special populations such as English language learners. For these colleagues, generalizability theory as a measurement theory deals explicitly with such factors and the degree to which they affect generalizing from assessment results. Their contributions to this volume focus on different forms of generalizing, for example, across individuals versus across time or across several research studies, such as in the case of meta-analysis; or they focus on the relationship between the particular and the general.

In 2007, when we put together a proposal for a symposium for the American Educational Research Association Annual Meeting on the issues discussed in this book, even though we believed the topic would be of interest to all educational researchers, Division D (Measurement and Research Methodology) seemed to be the most appropriate to which to submit our proposal. The next step in the submission process was to decide to which section of Division D to submit it. The point here is that our proposal submission faced the polarization and boundaries that currently exist in conceptualizations of research methods and in our disciplines in general. Division D has three sections, one dedicated to measurement, another to quantitative research, and a third to qualitative research. Our proposal cut across interests of all three sections, whereas one of the primary goals of the symposium—and this book—was to break down boundaries such as those that currently exist in Division D. Similar boundaries exist in our journal foci and in specializations in the association of generalization (or lack thereof) to types of data and data summarization techniques. These boundaries do not serve education or education research well. Our intention in this book is to move education research in the direction of prioritizing research questions and knowledge creation using many and multiple modes of research and go beyond simplistic divisions of research types.

Chapter I

Introduction

Wolff-Michael Roth and Kadriye Ercikan

A fundamental presupposition in cultural-historical activity theory—an increasingly used framework for understanding complex practical activities, interventions, and technologies in schools and other workplaces (e.g., Roth & Lee, 2007)—is that one cannot understand some social situation or product of labor without taking into account the history of the culture that gave rise to the phenomenon. This book, too, can be understood only within the particulars of some fortunate events that brought us, the two editors, together in quite unpredictable ways. From this coming together emerged a series of collaborative efforts in which we, normally concerned with teaching quantitative and qualitative methods, respectively, began to think about educational research more broadly and transcending the traditional boundaries around doing inferential statistics and designing (quasi-) experiments and doing various forms of naturalistic inquiry.

Some time during the early part of 2004, King Beach and Betsy Becker approached the two of us independently inviting us to co-author a chapter for a section in a handbook of educational research that they edited. Kadriye works in the program area of measurement, evaluation, and research methodology and focuses on psychometric issues; Michael, though trained as a statistician, teaches courses in interpretive inquiry. Despite or perhaps because of the apparent differences, we both tentatively agreed and, soon thereafter, met when Michael participated at a conference in Vancouver, the city where Kadriye's university is located. During the subsequent months, we interacted both on the phone, via e-mail, and through our mutual engagement with each other's texts and contributions to the joint endeavor. The collaboration as process and our final product on "Constructing Data" (Ercikan & Roth, 2006a) both provided us with such a great satisfaction that we soon thereafter decided to work together on another project, this time dealing with one of the issues that had emerged from our collaboration: the apparent opposition of "quantitative" and "qualitative" approaches in educational research, which in the past has lead to insurmountable conflicts and paradigm wars. We, however, had felt while writing the handbook chapter that there are possibilities for individuals such as ourselves with different research agendas and methods to interact collegially and productively. We decided to grabble with the question, "What good is polarizing research into qualitative and quantitative?" and to report the outcome of our collaborative investigation to a large audience of educators (Ercikan & Roth, 2006b).

In the process of working on the question, we came to argue against polarizing research into quantitative and qualitative categories or into the associated categories of subjective and objective forms of research. We demonstrated that this polarization is not meaningful or productive for our enterprise, educational research. We then proposed an integrated approach to education research inquiry that occurs along a continuum instead of a dichotomy of generalizability. We suggested that this continuum of generalizability may be a function of the types of research questions asked; and it is these questions that ought to determine the modes of inquiry rather than any a priori questions about the modes of inquiry—which drives the "monomaniacs" (Bourdieu, 1992) of method, which build entire schools and research traditions around one technique.

As during our first collaborative venture, we emerged from this experience both satisfied to have conducted a conversation across what often is perceived to be a grand divide and to have achieved a worthwhile result. Not soon after completion, we began talking about a special issue in a journal that would assemble leading scholars in the field discussing the issues surrounding generalization in and from educational research. But it became quite clear in our early discussions that the format of a journal issue would be limiting the number of people we could involve and the formats that the individual pieces could take. It also would limit us in producing the kind of coherent work that we present in this book, where chapters are bundled into sections, with an all encompassing narrative that provides linkages between chapters and starting points for further discussion. Our motive for this book, elaborated in the following section, was to have our contributors think about questions arising for them in the endeavor to generalize from educational research with the aim of going beyond the dichotomous opposition of quantitative and qualitative research method.

Beyond the Quantitative–Qualitative Oppositions

The discussion concerning the generalizability was sharpened with and in the debate between what came to be two camps, those doing statistics and denoting their work as "quantitative" and those doing other forms of inquiry denoted by the term "qualitative" or "naturalistic."

The discussion was polarized, among others, in Yvonna Lincoln and Egon Guba's (1985) *Naturalistic Inquiry*, where the "naturalist paradigm" was presented to be the polar opposite to "positivist paradigm." Accordingly, naturalists were said to have difficulties with the concept of external validity, that is, the generalizability of research-generated knowledge beyond the context of its application. The *transferability* of findings made in one context to some other context was taken to be an empirical matter rather than one that could be assumed based on statistical inference, even with its safeguards of estimating the probability of type I and type II errors. The classical position assumed that given high internal validity in some sample A and given the sample is representative of the population P, then findings made in the sample A could be generalized to the population P as a whole, and, therefore, to all other samples that might be taken from it.

The so-called naturalists rejected this form of generalization. One of the main points of the rejection is grounded in the very idea of a population. Guba and Lincoln remind their readers that inferences about populations can be improved with the specification of "homogeneous strata." But this in fact constitutes a specification of context and contextualization of knowledge. This therefore raises the issue about the extent to which something found in some inner-city school district in Miami can be used to inform teaching and learning in inner-city Philadelphia or New York, i.e., the three cities where one of our chapter authors, Kenneth Tobin, has conducted detailed studies of teaching and learning science. Concerning teaching, we know from detailed ethnographic work that a Cuban-African American science teacher highly successful in inner-city Miami was unsuccessful in his own account teaching science to "equivalent" students in inner-city Philadelphia. But the same teacher, much more quickly than other (novice) teachers, became a highly effective teacher in this for his new environment. Thus, his practical knowledge of teaching science to disadvantaged students turned out to be both transferable and non-transferable.

The discussion concerning the generalizability of educational research in the United States has heated up again during the George W. Bush era, when policy makers declared that experimental design constituted the "gold standard" of (educational) research. All other forms of research generally and "qualitative research" more specifically, were denigrated as inferior. In this book, we invited well-established and renowned researchers across the entire spectrum of educational research methods to weigh in on the question concerning the extent to which educational research can be generalized and transported (transferred) to other contexts.

Generalization and generalizability are gaining more importance with increased levels of scrutiny of value and utility of different types of educational research by funding agencies, the public, educational community and researchers themselves. These aspects of educational research have come to define the utility and quality of research in education and have also come to further polarize conceptualizations of educational research methods (Shaffer & Serlin, 2004). In light of the present political debates about the usefulness of different kinds of research (e.g., the "gold standard"), the issue of generalizability is often entered into the discussion as a criterion to argue for one form of research as superior over another. Typically, the scholarly (and political) discussion of degrees of *generalizability* is inherently associated with statistical (i.e., "quantitative") approaches and commonly questions the generalizability of observational (i.e., "qualitative") approaches. Unlike often assumed, we argued in our *Educational Researcher* feature article that a quantitative–qualitative distinction does not correspond to a distinction of the presence and absence of generalizability (Ercikan & Roth, 2006b). Rather, there are "qualitative" forms of research with high levels of generalizability and there are "quantitative" forms of research with rather low levels of generalizability. In addition, we argued and demonstrated that research limited to polar ends of a continuum of a variety of research methods, such as experimental design in evaluating effectiveness of intervention programs, in fact can have critically limited generalizability to decision making about sub-groups or individuals in intervention contexts.

One of the central issues may be the usefulness of different types of data and descriptions useful to different stakeholders in the educational enterprise. Thus, the following graphical representation that a researcher may have constructed to correlate the performance on a pre-test with scores indicating a particular learning outcome. Whereas the pretest might be consistent with published research and therefore reproduce

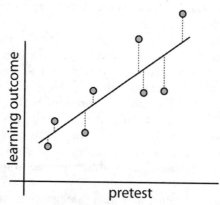

Figure 1.1 Correlation between pretest and learning outcomes.

existing (statistically reliable) relationships with the learning outcome variable, knowing the correlation actually helps a classroom teacher very little. The teacher, to design appropriate instruction for individual students, is interested precisely in the variation from the trend, that is, she is interested in the variation that in statistical approaches constitutes error variance. That is, to properly inform this teacher on what to do in her classroom, we need to provide her with forms of knowledge that are simultaneously sufficiently general to provide her with trends and with forms of knowledge that are sufficiently specific to allow her to design instructions to the specific needs expressed in the variation from the trend.

This book is designed to address these issues in a comprehensive way, drawing on the expertise of leading, well-known researchers in the fields traditionally characterized by the adjectives qualitative and quantitative research. The purpose of this book is twofold: (a) to work out and present an integrated approach to educational research inquiry by aiming at a continuum instead of a dichotomy of generalizability, how this continuum might be related to types of research questions asked and how these questions should determine modes of inquiry; (b) to discuss and demonstrate contributions of different data types, and modes of research to generalizability of research findings and limitations of research findings in research that utilizes a single research approach.

Arguing against single-method research but for generalization, Pierre Bourdieu (1992) portrays analogical reasoning to be one of the powerful instruments of research. Analogical reasoning allows researchers to immerse themselves in the particularities of their cases without drowning in them—a familiar experience to many novice researchers. As Bourdieu elaborates, analogical reasoning realizes generalization

> not through the extraneous and artificial application of formal and empty conceptual constructions, but through this particular manner of thinking the particular case which consists of actually thinking it as such. This mode of thinking fully accomplishes itself logically in and through the comparative method that allows you to think relationally a particular case constitutes as a "particular instance of the possible" by resting on the structural homologies that exist between different fields ... or between different states of the same field. (p. 234)

In the course of this book, we work toward such a conception of generalization in educational research, as outlined in more or less the same form in the chapter by Wolff-Michael Roth, who takes a similar dialectical perspective as Bourdieu though grounded in and arising from a different scholarly context.

Most importantly, this book not only is about generalizing from educational research but also is and arose from the self-questioning accomplished researchers engaged in when we asked them to address the question at the heart of this book. We emerge from this work with a sense that there is a lot of recognition for the different problems arising from different forms of inquiry, a mutual respect, and a desire to continue to contribute to resolving the hard question: how to make research relevant to all stakeholders in the educational enterprise.

Structure and Content

This book consists of 11 chapters clustered into four sections: "Generalizing Within and Beyond Populations and Contexts," "Combining and Contrasting Qualitative and Quantitative Evidence," "How Research Use Mediates Generalization," and "Rethinking the Relationship Between the General and the Particular." Each section begins with an overview text presenting and contextualizing the main ideas that gather the chapters in the section. Each section is completed by concluding comments by the editors that highlight issues covered in the section. At the end of the four sections is a discussion chapter of a set of key issues that cut-across all the chapters. These discussions among the contributing authors and the editors are targeted to addressing three key questions:

1. How do you define "generalization" and "generalizing"? What is the relationship between audiences of generalizations and the users? Who are the generalizations for? For what purpose? Are there different forms and processes of generalization? Is it possible to generalize from small scale studies?
2. What types of validity arguments are needed for generalizing in education research? Are these forms of arguments different for different forms of generalization? Can there be common ground for different generalizability arguments?
3. Given that "qualitative researchers" may count objects and members in categories and even use descriptive statistics: Do "qualitative" and "quantitative" labels serve a useful function for education researchers? Should we continue to use these labels? Do you have suggestions for alternatives, including not having dichotomous label possibilities?

The purpose of the discussion chapter is to highlight the salient issues arising from the chapters and to move our understanding to the next higher level given that each chapter constitutes a first level of learning. Taken as a whole, the introduction, overviews and highlights and the discussion chapter constitute the main narrative of this book in which the individual arguments are embedded. This main narrative, to use an analogy, is like the body of a pendant or crown that holds together and prominently features all the diamonds and other jewels that make the piece of jewelry.

References

Bourdieu, P. (1992). The practice of reflexive sociology (The Paris workshop). In P. Bourdieu & L. J. D. Wacquant, *An invitation to reflexive sociology* (pp. 216–260). Chicago: University of Chicago Press.

Ercikan, K., & Roth, W.-M. (2006a). Constructing data. In C. Conrad & R. Serlin (Eds.), *SAGE handbook for research in education: Engaging ideas and enriching inquiry* (pp. 451–475). Thousand Oaks, CA: Sage.

Ercikan, K., & Roth, W.-M. (2006b). What good is polarizing research into qualitative and quantitative? *Educational Researcher, 35*(5), 14–23.

Lincoln, Y. S., & Guba, E. G. (1985). *Naturalistic inquiry.* Newbury Park, CA: Sage.

Roth, W.-M., & Lee, Y. J. (2007). "Vygotsky's neglected legacy": Cultural-historical activity theory. *Review of Educational Research, 77,* 186–232.

Shaffer, D. W., & Serlin, R. C. (2004). What good are statistics that don't generalize? *Educational Researcher, 33*(9), 14–25.

Section I

Generalizing Within and Beyond Populations and Contexts

Overview

Educational research relies on deconstructing[1] data about constructs such as student learning, classroom climate, and student attitudes to develop and gain insights about the education process and to inform policy and practice. Measurements such as tests, classroom observations, or interviews may facilitate this data construction effort. Most theoretical constructs education research focuses on cannot be directly observed. For example, student knowledge and skills cannot be directly observed, and what students say, do, and produce in testing situations are used to make *inferences* about these knowledge and skills. This is where much research falls short because inferences are not always supported or necessary. Thus, for example, conceptions and conceptual change researchers recognize that (a) students do not respond to instruction and (b) teachers do not take up the theory. This may not surprise some because teachers do not observe these constructs but come face to face with student talk. If we were to theorize talk-in-situation, changes therein, and teaching strategies we might obtain results that teachers can actually use.

Capturing of classroom interactions and processes through videotaping are also used to make inferences about certain target constructs such us teacher promotion of interactivity, student interest, and engagement. For data such as scores from tests to be used in a meaningful way in research, the scores need to be accurate indicators of the constructs of interest.[2] Validity of interpretations of test scores, defined as meaningfulness and appropriateness of interpretations of test scores, has played a centerpiece role in discussions of quality of research findings. Validity of interpretations of scores depends on key characteristics of tests. These include the degree to which the content covered in the test is representative of the content domain the researcher is interested in measuring. Other test characteristics are related to critical aspects of validity of interpretations. They include the questions whether tests provide consistent scores across time, raters, and test forms; whether test items are capturing student true knowledge and skills; and whether test items depend on the format of the test items, whether they are free of culture bias. Generalizability theory (G-theory) is a statistical way of examining possible errors made in constructing the data for the research through measurement.

The most commonly understood notion of making generalization in educational research is that it denotes the making of inferences based on research in a specific context and sample to a broader set of contexts and population of subjects. Educational research defines generalizability of research findings as "external validity" (Cronbach, 1987). In other words, generalizability refers to the degree to which research claims can be extended to contexts and populations beyond those in the study itself. Even though external validity or generalizing are key components of educational research, there is not a systematic way of examining and evaluating generalizability of research findings. This problem leads to inappropriate evaluation of research generalizability based on superficial aspects of research such as sample size (small-scale versus large-scale) and methodology (statistical versus interpretive).

Generalizing and validity of inferences to a broader context are key to assessment and measurement in education. Therefore, educational measurement has systematic ways of investigating this generalizability of findings based on measurements. In particular, researchers in the area of measurement developed a statistical modeling approach to examining and estimating the degree to which inferences from test scores can be generalized beyond the testing contexts. Measurement of students' knowledge and skills are made based on a limited set of test questions and formats. Generalizability theory helps us understand to what extend scores created through measurements can be generalized beyond the set of questions and formats and to what extent the measurements represent true knowledge, abilities, and constructs that researchers are interested in. The authors assembled in this first section focus on generalization in educational research by applying the principles of G-theory to systematically think through the range of factors that may affect efforts of generalizing from educational research. The chapters in this section describe generalizability of data and how this generalizability is related to findings in research to other populations and contexts.

In their chapter entitled "Generalizability theory and its Contribution to the Discussion of the Generalizability of Research Findings" Rich Shavelson and Noreen Webb describe how Generalizability theory is related to the more general issue of generalizability of research findings. Shavelson and Webb's chapter on Generalizability theory sets us up for the subsequent chapter entitled "The Testing of English Language Learners as a Stochastic Process: Population Misspecification, Measurement Error, and Overgeneralization." In this chapter, Guillermo Solano-

Flores discusses the contribution of Generalizability theory as a theory that allows examination of sampling issues in the testing of English Language Learners (ELLs). Testing is one of the primary ways of constructing data in educational research. This research highlights the factors that might affect the inferences made based on data constructed through testing and therefore generalizability of research findings based on such data. The complexity of factors identified as relevant to the validity of test scores is a good reminder of the diversity and multiplicity of factors that affect the validity of inferences and the factors we need to consider when we examine generalizability of research findings. Previous research identified some inappropriate interpretations, generalizations, based on ELL test score data. Previous research indicates that the low test scores of ELLs often are interpreted as evidence of deficits or even disorders. For example, Richard Durán (1989) has reported that the language gap in testing has been a major contributor to the disproportionate numbers of Hispanic ELLs diagnosed as "mentally retarded" when IQ test scores were used. One study of Hispanic ELLs in Riverside, California, found that the Hispanic students, who constituted less than 10% of the school population at that time, comprised 32% of the students identified as mentally retarded (Rueda & Mercer 1985). For most of these students (62%) such decisions were based solely on low IQ scores.

Notes

1. Where, following philosophers such as Martin Heidegger and Jacques Derrida, we understand "deconstructing" to mean both taking apart (Ger. "abbauen") and preserving (Ger. "aufheben").
2. As the contributions to part C show, beyond accuracy lies the question of appropriateness and intelligibility to the target audiences.

References

Cronbach, L. J. (1987). *Designing evaluations of educational and social programs*. San Francisco: Jossey-Bass.

Durán, R. P. (1989). Testing of linguistic minorities. In R. Linn (Ed.), *Educational measurement* (3rd ed., pp. 573–587). New York: American Council of Education, Macmillan.

Rueda, R., & Mercer, J. (1985). *A predictive analysis of decision-making practices with limited English proficient handicapped students*. Paper presented at the Third Annual Symposium for Bilingual Special Education, Evaluation, and Research, University of Colorado and Council for Exceptional Children, Northglenn, CO.

Chapter 2

Generalizability Theory and Its Contribution to the Discussion of the Generalizability of Research Findings

Richard J. Shavelson and Noreen M. Webb

What's in a name? That which we call a rose By any other word would smell as sweet.

From *Romeo and Juliet* (II, ii, 1–2)

What's in a name? For Romeo Montague and Juliet Capulet who meet and fall in love in Shakespeare's romantic tale ... and for us ... it turns out to be nothing—Romeo by any other name is Romeo ... and everything—Romeo is a Montague and Juliet a Capulet, members of two relentlessly warring families. In the end, their love cannot transcend family hatred and they pay the ultimate price with their lives.

Our situation is not quite so dire. So what's in a name—oh say, "Generalizability Theory?" Nothing, it's just a name of a psychometric theory and by any other name, such as "Dependability Theory," it would be the same theory. And everything—how could a book entitled, *Generalizing from Educational Research*, not include a chapter entitled, "Generalizability Theory," regardless of the theory's content?

Now that's the question we asked ourselves when invited to contribute to this book. Our response at first was, "nothing!" The theory is not about the generalizability of research findings. Upon reflection and by analogy, however, we decided, "everything!" Well, not quite everything. Nevertheless, some of the central ideas in this arcane psychometric theory might be applied to the design of research with consequences for the generalizability of research findings. Hence we agreed to write this chapter.

Introduction

Decisions and Generalizability

When designing and carrying out empirical studies, researchers make decisions about who to study, what to study, what data to collect, and how data will be collected and analyzed. All of these decisions have implications for the generalizability of research findings. These implications are often discussed as aspects of validity. For example, we often speak of validity of measurements, the extent to which we can generalize from scores on one measure to scores on different measures of the same or a different domain, at the current time or at a point in the future. Or we may speak of population validity, such as the extent to which research findings can be generalized from the particular sample studied to a larger (or different) population of interest. Or we may speak of ecological validity, such as the extent to which the research findings can be generalized beyond the particular environmental conditions studied to another set of conditions. Limitations arising from the researcher's decisions about the measurements to take, the population to study, and the conditions to be implemented and/or studied are often addressed in perfunctory manner in reports of findings, and may not always be recognized by researchers themselves.

Contribution of Generalizability Theory to Research Generalization

We believe that Generalizability theory, originally developed as a comprehensive approach to assessing measurement consistency—i.e., *reliability*—provides a way of making these validity issues explicit. In this paper, we show how using the lens of "G-theory" to address these validity issues can help researchers identify sources of limitations in the generalizability of their research findings (e.g., features of the measurements, the population studied, the particular instantiation of conditions in a study) and, furthermore, how G-theory provides a means of systematically investigating the extent to which these factors limit research generalization.

In a nutshell, Generalizability theory is a statistical sampling theory about the dependability or reliability of behavioral measurements. In G-theory, a person's score on a measurement (e.g., science test) is considered to be a sample from an indefinitely large universe of scores that person might have earned on combinations of other test forms, on other occasions, scored by other raters. Reliability, then, is an index of just how consistently we can generalize from the sample of measurements in hand to the universe of interest. That is, it is an index of how accurate the inference is *from* a person's score on this particular form of the science test given on this particular occasion as scored by this particular rater *to* this person's average score earned if she had taken all possible test forms on all possible occasions scored by all possible raters. G-theory, then, views reliability as the accuracy with which we can generalize from a sample (a single test score) to the universe of interest defined by the average score over all possible forms, occasions and scorers.

It seems to us that the question of generalizing education research findings from a sample of measurements in hand to a larger universe of interest can, at least in part and for some purposes, be conceived in a similar way. How well can we generalize from the sample of measurements in hand to a broader domain? We believe that the kind of reasoning that underlies G-theory would at least be heuristically useful in thinking about the design of research for certain kinds of inferences, whether we are speaking about large statistical samples or small case studies.

In what follows, we sketch G-theory in a bit more conceptual detail, leaving aside completely the statistical developments (see G-theory references above). We believe that notions underlying G-theory such as the "universe of admissible observations," "universe of generalization," "random and fixed facets," and "crossed and nested designs" have much to say about the design of research. Once we have laid out these fundamental notions, we then draw parallels from G-theory to generalization in education research.

Some Fundamental Ideas from Generalizability Theory

In G-theory a behavioral measurement (e.g., a test score) is conceived as a sample from a *universe of admissible observations*. This universe consists of all possible observations that decision makers consider to be acceptable substitutes (e.g., scores sampled on occasions 2 and 3) for the sample observation in hand (scores on occasion 1). A measurement situation, then, can be characterized by a set of features such as test form, test item, rater, or test occasion. Each characteristic feature is called a *facet* of a measurement. A universe of admissible observations, then, is defined by all possible combinations of the levels of the facets (e.g., all possible items combined with all possible occasions).

Generalizability Study

A generalizability (G) study is like a "pilot study" that is designed to isolate and estimate as many facets of measurement error in the universe of admissible observations as is reasonably and economically feasible. The study includes the most important facets that a variety of decision makers might wish to generalize over (e.g., items, forms, occasions, raters). This explicit, full formulation of the universe, some or all of which a particular decision maker might generalize to, might prove useful to researchers concerned about research generalization. In some senses, making explicit the universe of admissible observations provides

a vision of what ultimately research such as the particular study in hand
is intended to tell its audiences about.

To be concrete, suppose that, in studying science achievement the universe of admissible observations is defined by all possible combinations
of items, raters and test occasions that a variety of decision makers would
be equally willing to interpret as bearing on students' science achievement. Ideally, a G-study would include all three facets (item, rater, test
occasion). For example, a random sample of students would be tested on
3 test items randomly sampled from a large domain of such items and 3
randomly sampled raters would score their performance on 2 randomly
selected occasions (see Table 2.1). Depending on which multiple-choice
alternative was selected the student could earn an item score ranging
from 1 to 5 points. The test was administered twice over roughly a two-
week interval.

In this G-study, student (person) is the *object of measurement*[1] and
both item and occasion are *facets* of the measurement.[2] The test items
and occasions in the G-study constitute a sample from all possible items
and occasions that a decision maker would be equally willing to interpret as bearing on students' science achievement. To draw a parallel to
research generalization, note that: (a) the object of measurement corresponds to the population to which a researcher wishes to generalize,
(b) the facets correspond to the treatment conditions and (say) organizational contexts to which she wishes to generalize, and (c) the item sample
corresponds to the universe of science content, knowledge and skills to
which the researcher wishes to generalize.

To pinpoint different sources of measurement error, G-theory estimates the variation in scores due to each person, each facet, and their
combinations (interactions). More specifically, G-theory estimates the
components of observed-score variance contributed by the object of

Table 2.1 Person × Item × Occasion G-Study of Science Achievement Scores

| Person | Item | Occasion | | | | | |
| | | I | | | II | | |
		1	2	3	1	2	3
1		3	1	5	4	3	4
2		4	1	4	4	2	3
3		2	3	3	3	2	4
...							
p		4	5	4	4	4	2
...							
n		2	4	4	3	4	3

measurement, the facets, and their combinations. In this way, the theory isolates different sources of score variation in measurements. In a similar manner, research generalization might attend to estimating the "effects" of person, treatment and content sampling.

To be concrete about estimating effects, continuing with the science test example, note that the student is the object of measurement and each student's observed score can be decomposed into a component for student, item, occasion, and combinations (interactions) of student, item, and occasion. The student component of the score reflects systematic variation in their academic ability, giving rise to systematic variability among students (reflected by the student or person variance component). The other score components reflect sources of measurement error. For example, a good occasion (e.g., following a school-wide announcement that the student body had received a community award for reducing environmental hazards based on their science experiments) might tend to raise all students' achievement, giving rise to mean differences from one occasion to the next (indexed by the occasion variance component). And the particular wording of an item might lead certain students to answer incorrectly compared to other students, giving rise to a non-zero person x item interaction (p x i variance component).

Decision Study

The Decision (D) study uses information from the pilot study—the G-study—to design a measurement procedure that minimizes error for a particular purpose. In planning a D-study the decision maker defines the *universe of generalization*, which contains the facets (and levels of them) over which the decision maker proposes to generalize. A decision maker may propose to generalize over the same facets (and levels of them) as in the universe of admissible observations (e.g., item, occasion, rater). Another decision maker, however, may propose to generalize less broadly than the universe of admissible observations because of time, cost, or particular interest (e.g., a decision maker is only interested in students' spring science achievement). That is, a decision maker may propose to generalize over only a portion of the universe of admissible observations. In this case, the universe of generalization is a subset of the universe of admissible observations—the set of facets and their levels (e.g., items and occasions) to which the particular decision maker proposes to generalize.

What the particular decision maker would ultimately like to know about a student is his or her *universe score*—defined as the long-run average of that student's observed scores over all observations in the decision maker's universe of generalization. The theory describes the dependability ("reliability") of generalizations made from a person's observed score on a test to the score he or she would obtain in this universe of generalization—to his or her *"universe score."* Hence the name, "Generalizability Theory."

A decision maker's universe of generalization (and hence the design of the D-study) may be narrower than the universe of admissible observations for a variety of reasons. Consider a universe of generalization restricted to one facet, say, items. In this case, multiple items would be used but only one test occasion (e.g., the spring test administration) would be used in the D-study and generalization would not be made from the spring test scores to scores that might have been obtained on another occasion. Some decision makers may choose to hold constant occasion (spring testing) because they would like to know how many items are needed on the science achievement test to produce a trustworthy sample of a student's spring science achievement. Other decision makers may be interested in generalizing over occasions but decide to restrict attention to one test occasion because it turns out to be too expensive or time-consuming to obtain scores from multiple occasions in the D-study. Or the G-study may show that you would need to have too many occasions for decent generalizability and the decision maker throws up his arms and says, "Forget about generalizing across occasions!"

From a research generalization perspective, G-theory's lesson might be its insistence on clarity between the universe of admissible observations—perhaps a comprehensive ideal—and the practical reality of resource constraints—the universe of generalization. Being explicit about the differences between these two universes might make clear to researchers and more general audiences the extent and limits of research generalization.

Generalizability and Decision-Study Designs

Generalizability theory allows the decision maker to use different designs in G- and D-studies because the two types of studies have different goals. G-studies attempt to estimate as many variance components as possible in the universe of admissible observations so as to be useful to decision makers with different goals. D-studies attempt to meet decision makers' goals while economizing on facets to get the biggest bang (reliability!) for a constrained buck. Again, this explicit representation of universes might prove useful to research generalization.

Designs with Crossed and Nested Facets

Typically in a G-study, a *crossed* design is used. In a crossed design, all students are observed under each level of each facet. This means that, in our example, each student responds to each science-test item on each occasion. The crossed design provides maximal information about the components of variation in observed science scores. In our example, seven different variance components can be estimated—one each for the main effects of person, item, and occasion; two-way interactions between person and item, person and occasion, and item and occasion; and a residual due to the person x item x occasion interaction and random error.

Information from the G-study, in the form of variance components, can be used to design a D-study by projecting the impact of changing the number of levels of a facet on the reliability of the measurement. Consider the case of the decision maker choosing to hold constant occasion (spring testing) and seeking to know how many items are needed on the science achievement test to produce a trustworthy sample of a student's spring science achievement. It is well known that the sampling variability of test items, especially in interaction with the object of measurement, person (p x i), is very large. By focusing on the facet, item, the decision maker can determine the number of test items needed to reach some level of reliability, say 0.80 (on a scale ranging from 0 to 1.00).

When more than one facet is a major source of measurement error the decision maker might want to project the tradeoff in reliability by varying the number of items *and* the number of occasions. When more than one facet is considered in a D-study—e.g., the decision maker is interested in students' science achievement any time from March to June—information from the G-study can be used to evaluate the tradeoff of increasing items on the test or the number of test occasions.

Finally, the decision maker might be concerned with the amount of testing time, especially if the test were to be given on two occasions. In this case, she might consider testing a different subset of science items on each of two different occasions. In this last example, and as is common in D-studies, we say that test items (subtests) are *nested* within occasions—items 1 to 20 are administered at occasion 1 and items 21 to 40 are administered at occasion 2. With this nested design, the decision maker can hold total testing time constant, while administering a broader array of items (40 items) than if the same 20 items were administered on both occasions (a *crossed* design).

While G-studies typically employ or should to the extent feasible employ crossed designs in order to estimate each and every possible source of variation in a student's test score, D-studies may profit by using nested designs which are economical and efficient and can be used to increase the levels of a particularly cantankerous facet[3] within reasonable cost constraints. The parallel to research generalization, it seems to us, is for researchers to decide on which of a variety of designs would meet requirements for inferring to their universe of generalization while maximizing the power of their statistical tests.

Designs with Random and Fixed Facets

G-theory is essentially a random effects theory—inferences are drawn from a random sample in hand to what is the case in an indefinitely large, carefully defined universe of possible observations. Typically, a random facet is created by randomly sampling levels of a facet.[4]

A fixed facet (cf. fixed factor in analysis of variance) arises when the decision maker: (a) purposely selects certain levels of the facet and is not interested in generalizing beyond them, (b) finds it unreasonable to generalize beyond the levels observed, or (c) when the entire universe of levels is small and all levels are included in the measurement design. A fixed facet, then, restricts the decision maker's *universe of generalization*. G-theory typically treats fixed facets by averaging over the levels of the fixed facet and examining the generalizability of the average over the random facets. When it does not make conceptual sense to average over the levels of a fixed facet, a separate G-study may be conducted within each level of the fixed facet.

To see how fixing a facet might work, consider a study of teaching behavior in which elementary teachers are observed teaching mathematics and reading. These are two subjects in a potentially broad array of subjects that might be taught in elementary school. Because we believed that teaching behavior in mathematics and reading may not be generalizable to teaching behavior in other subjects, we considered "subject" to be a fixed facet in the *universe of generalization*. Moreover, we reasoned that teaching mathematics is considerably different from teaching reading. As a consequence, we conducted separate D-studies for mathematics and reading scores.

Designs and the Object of Measurement

The discussion up to this point has treated person as the object of measurement. However, the focus of measurement may change depending on a particular decision maker's purpose, as described in the *principle of symmetry:* "The principle of symmetry of the data is simply an affirmation that each of the facets of a factorial design can be selected as an object of study, and that the operations defined for one facet can be transposed in the study of another facet" (Cardinet, Tourneur, Allal, 1981, p. 184). In a persons (p) x items (i) x occasions (o) design, whereas persons may be the focus of measurement for evaluators wishing to make dependable judgments about persons' performance, items may be the focus for curriculum developers wishing to calibrate items for use in item banks. In the latter case, individual differences among persons represent error variation, rather than universe-score variation, in the measurement.

Moreover, the object of measurement may be multifaceted, for example, when educational evaluators are interested in scholastic achievement of classes, schools, and districts, or in comparisons across years. Or the focus may be on items corresponding to different content units in which the universe-score of interest is that of items (i) nested within content units (c). Or objects of measurement may be defined according to attributes of persons, such as persons nested within geographic region, gender, or socio-economic status. We treat the concept of multifaceted populations more fully below.

From a research generalization perspective, we see two related lessons from G-theory. The first lesson is that generalization depends on how the object of measurement is sampled, how treatment and context are sampled, and how the outcome measurements are sampled. We see great attention paid to sampling the object of measurement but little attention paid to sampling treatments/contexts or measurements in substantive research. Yet such sampling has a great deal to say about the credibility of generalization from treatments/contexts or achievement tests in hand and the broader universe of generalization. The second related lesson is that, as we will show below, treatments/ contexts are often implicitly sampled (not fixed) and yet such sampling is not taken into account in research generalization.

Generalizability Theory and Validity

G-theory has focused on estimating multifaceted measurement error and reliability. It extended traditional reliability theory by going beyond separate estimates of reliability: internal consistency ("Cronbach's alpha"), test-retest, and alternate or parallel forms, inter-rater reliability. G-theory includes as *typical facets* of a measurement within in an overarching framework—items (alpha), occasions (test-retest), forms (alternative forms) and raters (inter-rater). The theory then statistically estimates the contribution of these facets individually and in combination with each other and the object of measurement—to estimate the (in)consistency of measurement simultaneously.

If we move beyond the typical measurement facets associated with reliability of test (and other) scores—item, form, rater, occasion—to include facets such as type of test (multiple-choice, short answer, performance assessment), we have moved outside the traditional boundaries of reliability and generalizability theory into areas of validity. In particular, in this case, we have moved to convergent validity, asking, "To what extent do different measurement procedures purported to measure the same attribute converge and give the same 'picture'?" Or, "To what extent do the sample of test items generalize to the broad content domain?" an issue of content validity. That is, "To what extent do the results of a particular measurement procedure generalize to NAEP science standards including physical, life and Earth/space science content?" Finally, how much variation is introduced into a measurement when the time between occasions is extended from (say) a few weeks where a student is assumed to be in a "steady knowledge state" to occasions months or even years away? In this case, a question of "predictive validity" has been raised.

We find it helpful to distinguish between reliability facets (r-facets of, for example, items, occasions, forms, raters) and validity facets (v-facets of, for example, different measurement procedures, different test content, and different time scale). However, we acknowledge that at times the distinctions between r- and v-facets may be fuzzy. For example, how much time needs to elapse between testing occasions for us to consider occasions to be a v- rather than an r-facet? Ultimately, we would like to know a student's universe score defined as the average of her scores on an indefinitely large universe of admissible observations defined *by all combinations of r- and v-facets.*

The reliability-validity trade-off paradox can be seen here. To maximize reliability for a D-study, we would like to restrict the universe of generalization holding constant certain r-facets and taking a large sample from one or two important r-facets. But by restricting the universe of generalization for a reliability study we have severely restricted the universe of admissible observations of concern in a validity study. The question, then, is how well can we generalize from our restricted test score to the score a student would earn on tests generated by all possible combinations of r- and v-facets in the universe of admissible observations? The dilemma confronted by G-theory is well known in research generalization. It is the trade-off between internal and external validity.

Having laid out some of the rudimentary ideas in G-theory, we now turn to the task of drawing implications for the design of educational research. Our goal is to identify design considerations from G-theory that might improve the generalizability of education research findings.

An Example Study: Behavior and Learning in Cooperative Groups

The topic of this book and that of G-theory are about drawing inferences or generalizing from a sample or person to a larger population of people and/or from a sample of measurements in hand to a larger universe of conditions of interest. Where G-theory and research generalizability differ is in focus. G-theory is concerned about the dependability and validity of measurements, whereas educational research is about (a) describing situations, (b) testing conjectures about functional and causal effects, and (c) testing conjectures about mechanisms underlying those effects. In what follows, we use a concrete experimental study to discuss four issues pertaining to generalizability of measurements and research generalization: (a) dependability (reliability) of the measurements, (b) validity of the measurements, (c) generalizing from the population studied, and (d) generalizing from the research conditions investigated.

Cooperative peer-directed learning is used in classrooms around the world to increase academic achievement and interpersonal skills. Not all cooperative group experiences lead to increased achievement and improved social relations, however. The effectiveness of group work depends on the nature of students' behavior in groups, including, for example, actively participating in discussion, or giving elaborated explanations instead of correct answers. Recognizing that students do not automatically engage in these beneficial activities, researchers have designed and tested programs to enable students to work together more effectively.

In one such program, Gillies and Ashman (e.g., 1998) trained Australian middle-school students in small-group procedures and interpersonal behaviors believed to promote group learning and cooperation (e.g., dividing activities into small manageable tasks, listening to others, providing constructive feedback, sharing tasks, resolving disagreements amicably). One of their experimental studies compared trained and untrained students' behavior and learning in a 12-week social studies unit on the British exploration of Australia in 10 classrooms ($N = 192$) from 8 public schools in the Brisbane, Australia, metropolitan area. Students were stratified on ability and randomly assigned to heterogeneous small groups that were, in turn, randomly assigned to conditions (trained vs. untrained) within classrooms. Students then worked in groups for three 1-hour sessions per week on such activities as discussing ways of preserving food on long sea voyages. Analyses of videotapes of group work showed that students in trained groups were more cooperative and helpful, gave more explanations, and were more inclusive of others than students in the untrained groups. Furthermore, trained students outperformed untrained students on the achievement measure administered at the end of the curriculum unit.

Issues of Reliability and Validity in the Exemplary Study

In this section, we use Ashman and Gillies' study (1997) as a starting point for the discussion of generalizability theory and research generalization. Here the overlap between G-theory and Research Generalization is most obvious to us—in both cases we are interested in the dependability of what we measure and the extent to which we can generalize from sample in hand to a broader universe of outcome score interpretations.

For each outcome of interest in Ashman and Gillies' study, such as students' achievement and cooperative behavior, we can conceive of a universe of admissible observations characterized by *reliability* facets and *validity* facets. As will be seen in more detail below, reliability (r-) facets are sources of variability that influence the consistency of scores that might be obtained by repeated administrations of tests like those in the Gillies and Ashman study (for measuring student achievement) or by repeated observations of small groups (for measuring cooperative behavior) under the observation conditions used in the study. Validity (v-) facets, on the other hand, correspond to different ways of obtaining information about student achievement (e.g., multiple-choice tests or performance assessments) or cooperative behavior (videotapes vs. on-site time-sampled observations). V-facets are of concern when making generalizations from the type of test or observation procedure used in Gillies' study to other tests that might have been used. In the following sub-sections, we show how generalizability theory can be applied to reliability and validity issues.

Reliability Issues: Dependability of measurements

Reliability facets are the typical measurement facets associated with reliability. In measuring student achievement in Gillies and Ashman's program, these might be test form, occasion, and rater. In this case, dependability (reliability) of achievement scores pertains to the consistency of scores across administrations of multiple forms of the test, on multiple occasions, and with multiple raters scoring student responses. A three-facet G-study (*student x test form x rater x occasion* design)[5] would provide information about variability of student performance across test forms, raters, and occasions, which then could be used to make decisions concerning the number of each needed for dependable measurement of student achievement in the British exploration of Australia.

With respect to measuring students' cooperative behavior (e.g., unsolicited explanations), the consistency of scores (reliability) may be affected by rater and occasion facets. In this case, dependability of behavior scores pertains to the consistency of scores across multiple observations that might be obtained by videotaping groups on multiple occasions and using multiple raters to evaluate behavior on each occasion. A two-facet G-study (*student x rater x occasion* design) would provide information about variability of student behavior across raters and occasions, which then could be used to make decisions concerning the number of each needed for dependable measurement of students' cooperative behavior.

In designing a G-study of student achievement or cooperative behavior, special attention needs to be paid to *specifying* the conditions of the facets: What are the possible items that might comprise each test form? What are characteristics of possible raters? What occasions might be considered? We must equally attend to how levels of the facets will be *sampled* in the G-study: How are items on a particular test form selected? Are the items in one test form considered exchangeable with other possible test forms? Or, how are raters selected? Are the raters selected representative of any raters who might be suitable?

Validity Issues

The achievement test used in Ashman and Gillies' (1997) study addressed one content area in sixth-grade social studies (the British exploration of Australia) and used one particular item format (essay). In making interpretations about student learning outcomes in their study, Ashman and Gillies may not want to restrict conclusions about the effectiveness of cooperative training to scores from tests with that particular item format or particular content area. They may wish to generalize from the scores on their test to other content areas (e.g., exploration of the Americas) and to other test item formats (e.g., short answer, multiple choice). The validity facets in their universe of admissible observations for measuring student achievement in social studies, then, may include item format and content area.

Similarly, in making interpretations about cooperative behavior, Ashman and Gillies may wish to be able to generalize from behavior scores based on Likert-type scale ratings of videotapes of group work (1 = almost never occurred to 5 = almost always occurred) to other scale types (e.g., frequency or duration of behavior) and other observation methods (e.g., on-site time-sampling using behavioral checklists). The validity facets in their universe of admissible observations, then, may include scale type and observation method.

Just as a G-study can be designed for reliability facets, a G-study can encompass validity facets. A G-study of student *achievement* with item format and content area as facets would provide information about the variability of performance across these facets. A G-study of *cooperative behavior* with scale type and observation method as facets would provide information about the variability of cooperative behavior across scale types and observation methods. The results of these G-studies would show the limits of inferences from, for example, one content area to another. Large variability in scores across content areas suggests that inferences from scores on a test on the British exploration of Australia may not generalize to inferences from scores on a test on the exploration of the Americas.

As is the case for reliability facets, special attention needs to be paid to specifying the possible levels of the validity facets (e.g., what content areas comprise the domain of British exploration of Australia, or exploration in general, or social studies in general). Because the choice of levels of the validity facets used in a G-study influences conclusions that can be drawn about generalizability, it is important that the G-study represent the levels of the validity facets as fully as possible (e.g., including the full range of item formats or content domains that are represented in an investigator's universe of admissible observations).

Relationship between Reliability- and Validity-G-Studies

G-studies with reliability and validity facets are not as separate as they may seem. In designing a G-study with reliability facets (e.g., test form, rater, occasion), validity facets are implicitly represented, that is, they are "hidden." A G-study with test form, rater, and occasion as random reliability facets may focus on one content area (British exploration of Australia) and use one item type (essay). This G-study, then, uses one instance of each fixed facet (content area and item type), but does not provide information about generalizing to others.

Conversely, a G-study with validity facets may also have hidden reliability facets. A G-study exploring variation in scores across multiple content areas and item types, for example, may use one rater to score student performance and test students on one occasion. This G-study would not provide information about whether performance might vary across raters or occasions.

The larger issue is that *any* G-study invariably has hidden facets. For example, in a report of research on performance assessment in education and the military, Shavelson, Baxter and Gao (1993) showed that task-sampling variability was consistently quite large and that a large sample of tasks was needed to get a reliable measure of performance. However, Cronbach, Linn, Brennan, and Haertel (1997) questioned this interpretation, pointing out the hidden occasion facet. The importance of this challenge is that, if the occasion facet is actually the cause, adding many tasks to address the task-sampling problem would not improve the dependability of the measurement. Re-analyses of the data explicitly including occasion as a facet showed that part of the variability originally attributed to task sampling was, in fact, due to occasion sampling.

G-theory and our distinction between reliability and validity facets provides a framework for designing G-studies more broadly than is currently done. Importantly, designing a G-study with both reliability and validity facets encourages the investigator to define the facets and their levels explicitly (e.g., What specific content areas comprise the content facet? What test types comprise the test method facet?).

As we noted at the outset of this section, both G-theory and "Research

G" are concerned with the (limitation of) interpretation of measurements serving as outcomes in research, practice, or policy. Generalization from measurements in hand is limited by both measurement error (unreliability) and measurement validity. G-theory makes quite clear sources of unreliability and invalidity and estimates the effects of these sources on score interpretation. Such care in research generalization would be welcome.

Implications of G-Theory for Research Generalization

Our analysis of the distinction between the universe of admissible observations (theoretically what should be considered) and the universe of generalization (what the decision maker chooses to include) and of r- and v-facets in G-theory has direct implications for research generalizability, as we have attempted to point out along the way. Here we bring together and discuss these implications systematically rather than opportunistically as above.

The first implication of G-theory for Research G, not discussed further here, is that researchers must be careful to specify what they are and are not measuring as outcomes. Our analysis shows just how narrowly measures are typically defined and the limits to generalizing to the (say) achievement of interest.

The second implication, clear universe specification, has to do with specifying a sampling framework—a universe of admissible observations. Such a framework should include both the *population of students* (or other objects of measurement such as teachers, schools, etc.) and the *universe of conditions or situations* from which the "treatment" and "contexts" have been sampled.

Issues of specifying the population to which inferences are to be drawn are quite familiar if often neglected by the use of convenient samples, especially in small-scale randomized experiments. We simply note here that the intended population(s) to which inferences are to be drawn need to be specified explicitly. Deviations from a broader population should also be explicitly noted.

What may be somewhat of a surprise is that G-theory leads us to think of how "treatments" (e.g., teaching methods) are implemented as being sampled from a universe of possible ways in which the treatments could be implemented. Often we conceive of treatments as being implemented in a "fixed" way when in fact they may be implemented as samples from a finite universe. Moreover, our current conception of treatment implementation may ignore "hidden facets" that need to be explicated and limits of generalizability noted.

Generalizations about the Population

Just as the universe of admissible observations needs to be specified explicitly, clear specification of the population is essential for drawing samples and for drawing inferences from the sample to the population. Consider, for example, the sample of students, teachers, and schools used in Ashman and Gillies' (1997) study. The schools were located in low- to middle-socio-economic neighborhoods in the Brisbane, Australia metropolitan area in which 20% of children lived in welfare housing, 80% of workers were employed in blue-collar jobs, 25% of families had only one parent, and unemployment rates were high (10% or higher). The student population was mostly Caucasian, and achievement levels spanned a wide range. In these schools, peer tutoring was used quite extensively to enhance reading, spelling, and mathematics skills, and most students had experience working with others. Teachers typically received one or two days of professional development annually about peer tutoring, as well as visits from language arts and mathematics advisors who discussed the practicalities of different peer tutoring arrangements. The 8 schools (and the 10 teachers) participating in Ashman and Gillies' study were a representative (although not random) sample from this population (Gillies, personal communication, February 12, 2007).

This description suggests a multilevel, multidimensional characterization of the population. First are characteristics of students, including socio-economic status, race or ethnic background, achievement level, and previous experience with group work. Second are characteristics of teachers, including training in peer learning methods. Third are characteristics of schools and communities, including socio-economic status, support for peer-based learning methods, local geographic location (urban, suburban, rural), and global geographic location (e.g., Australia vs. the US).

Any of these characteristics might influence the generalization of the treatment effect (training vs. no-training) found in Ashman and Gillies' study. For example, might the effect of training (compared to no training) be smaller among racial or ethnic backgrounds which culturally support cooperation than among groups that emphasize competition and individual recognition? Might they be smaller in classrooms and schools in which students have support and experience with peer-directed learning methods, and teachers receive professional development concerning such methods than in classrooms and schools without such support for cooperative learning? G-theory explicitly addresses multilevel populations. The theory recognizes that a universe of admissible observations might include not only r-facets (which they called the "facet of generalization"—over items, raters, occasions) but also characteristics of the population such as students nested in genders or teachers (which they called the "face of differentiation"). At the very least, when conceptualizing a multi-faceted population, G-theory pushes us to be very explicit about the sampling from populations and the limits of research generalization that follow.

Generalizations about the "Treatment"

Referring to our example study, just as we have a universe of admissible observations for the measurement of outcomes of interest (here, student achievement and cooperative behavior), we can conceive of a universe of "treatment implementation"—different ways of implementing the treatment conditions. When implementing a cooperative learning program, for example, decisions must be made about the size and composition of small groups and about the nature of the work-group task.

Previous classroom research suggests that group composition (in terms of ability, gender, ethnic background, and race) influences group interaction and learning outcomes. Low-ability students receive more help and learn best in heterogeneous groups, and medium-ability students participate more actively and learn best in homogeneous groups. The impact of group composition on the experiences and outcomes of high-ability students is mixed and may depend more on the group dynamics that evolve in a particular group (e.g., whether students freely give and receive explanations, engage in positive or negative socio-emotional behavior) than on the grouping arrangement per se. Heterogeneous groups on gender and race have sometimes been found to disadvantage low-status students in participation and learning.

In their study, Ashman and Gillies formed small groups that were heterogeneous on ability and gender, reflecting the composition of the class. The question immediately arises as to the generalizability of groups so formed to other possible groupings. Suppose, for example, groups were heterogeneous in ability and homogeneous in gender? So we see that the choices made by Ashman and Gilles were actually choices from a finite range of potential group compositions. To what types of grouping practices might they generalize, or might a reader generalize?

Second, the nature of the task assigned for group work may influence both group cooperation and student learning. Students are more likely to participate actively in group work (e.g., sharing ideas and strategies for solving problems) when groups are given complex tasks with ill-structured solutions that require the combined expertise of the group members rather than well-structured tasks with clearly defined solutions that can be completed by one student. Cognizant of these findings, Ashman and Gillies assigned mostly open-ended activities to groups, such as recalling and generating ideas about ways of cooking, storing, and preserving food on long sea voyages. Again, we can conceive a range of such tasks and questions of generalizability then arise.

Whether the benefits of training found in Ashman and Gillies' study would accrue to students grouped in other ways or assigned other kinds of tasks is not known. Beyond the manipulations in Ashman and Gilles, we might ask: Would the training program (especially practice in interpersonal and collaborative skills) be particularly effective for the kinds of groups likely to suppress participation of some members (e.g., mixed-status groups) and less effective for groups that may tend to function well even without intervention (e.g., equal-status groups)? If so, the effects of the training program may appear stronger with some group compositions than with others. Compared to less structured tasks, would highly structured tasks produce muted collaboration in all groups, resulting in little difference in behavior and learning in trained and untrained groups?

We can conceive of a universe of treatment implementation, then, with facets corresponding to group composition and type of task, along with a generalizability-like study in which the treatment comparison (here, training vs. no training) is implemented with various group compositions and task types. In general, investigating variability of treatment implementation may lead to a more comprehensive study than is typically carried out, as researchers typically may not think of these generalization issues.

Concluding Comments

We began this chapter asking why a chapter on an arcane psychometric theory would be included in a book on research generalization. Actually, we were not all that surprised. We are often asked questions about G-theory that suggest that the questioner assumes G-theory is about research generalization. Nevertheless we did not see, at first blush, what G-theory could contribute to Research G. Nevertheless, we persuaded ourselves that there very well might be some lessons to be learned from G-theory that might inform research.

Once we went looking, we believe we found something. This revelation might not be surprising to those of you who have made it this far in the chapter but it may be to readers who skipped to the conclusion section: We assumed (and this is a big assumption) that research generalization was based on a statistical sampling argument as is G-theory. We suspect that not all those contributing to or reading this volume would agree with this assumption. Nevertheless, we believe that some of the "lessons" we briefly highlight might provide insight to other research generalization frameworks.

To get to the nub, what G-theory offers Research G is explicitness in specifying a sampling frame. In G-theory, in specifying the "universe of admissible observations" (including reliability and validity facets of that universe), we arrive at a rather complete conception and specification for a measurement procedure. Moreover, when we design a study in which data are collected for decision making, we can be explicit about how much the universe of admissible observations has been restricted by practical and policy interests, creating a universe of generalization. Similarly, we believe it is important for any research study to be explicit about its sampling frame—whether based on various random sampling procedures, or convenient sample procedures, or snowball sampling procedures, or extreme case samples. Just how much has the universe we would ultimately like to know about been restricted by practical and policy considerations and what is the extent of research generalization possible from the study?

We noted that in research, especially when formal sampling frames are constructed and implemented, a great deal of attention is given to sampling from the population—the subjects or objects of measurement to be included in the study. Moreover, and importantly, we noted how "treatments" (or "contexts") might not necessarily be fixed but rather constitute convenient or engineered samples from finite universes. That is, effects of "student grouping" on learning might be generalized from a study that used open-ended tasks with heterogeneous groups. Unknown, but implied in inference, is whether we can generalize from sample in hand to all possible tasks and ways of grouping students in classrooms. We encourage researchers to be explicit not only about what was included in the sampling frame but also about what was excluded and how the exclusion might limit research generalizations.

We also discuss how the notion of generalizability can be expanded beyond typical sources of measurement error used to address reliability issues (e.g., raters, test items, test occasions). We use a concrete example, a study of small heterogeneous groups receiving training in cooperative skills (vs. not receiving training) in history instruction, to illustrate how decisions made about *how* to measure (a particular observation procedure) and *what* to measure (specific content)—typically viewed as validity concerns—can be seen as sampling (even if implicitly) from universes of possibilities. Moreover, we showed that the particular ways in which the treatment is instantiated (e.g., composition of the small groups, the nature of the group-work task, content of the curriculum) represents a small sample from a fairly large universe of possibilities.

"What's in a name? That which we call a rose/By any other word would smell as sweet." (Shakespeare's *Romeo and Juliet* [II, ii, 1–2]). What's in a name—nothing but possibly a lot. While the link between G-theory and Research G was not obvious to us at the outset, we have convinced ourselves, and we hope some of you who made it this far, that G-theory has a lot, by analogy, to say about Research G. The former reminds us that clear specification of the universes of generalization—outcome measurements, objects of measurement, and treatment/contexts—is essential for interpreting measurements. The lesson for the latter, then, is an understanding of research generalization starts with the design of research and the sampling of measurements, objects of measurement, and treatments.

Acknowledgment

We wish to thank Mike Rose and Marsha Ing for their helpful comments on this paper. Of course we accept responsibility for errors of omission and commission.

Notes

1. In behavioral research, the person is typically considered the *object of measurement.*
2. To keep this example simple, we do not include rater as a facet.
3. For example, this may be item- or task-sampling variability, see Shavelson, Baxter, & Gao, 1993)
4. When the levels of a facet have not been sampled randomly from the universe of admissible observations but the intended universe of generalization is infinitely large, the concept of exchangeability may be invoked to consider the facet as random (Shavelson & Webb, 1981).
5. Whereas we identify four sources of variation in scores—student, test form, rater, and occasion—the first is the object of measurement and not a facet of error. Hence we speak of a three-facet design with student as the object of measurement.

References

Ashman, A. F., & Gillies, R. M. (1997). Children's cooperative behavior and interactions in trained and untrained work groups in regular classrooms. *Journal of School Psychology, 35,* 261–279.

Cardinet, J., Tourneur, Y., & Allal, L. (1976). The symmetry of generalizability theory: Application to educational measurement. *Journal of Educational Measurement, 13,* 119–135.

Cronbach, L. J., Linn, R. L., Brennan, R. L., & Haertel, E. H. (1997). Generalizability analysis for performance assessments of student achievement or school effectiveness. *Educational and Psychological Measurement, 57,* 373–399.

Gillies, R. M., & Ashman, A. F. (1998). Behavior and interactions of children in cooperative groups in lower and middle elementary grades. *Journal of Educational Psychology, 90,* 746–757.

Shavelson, R. J., Baxter, G. P., & Gao, X. (1993). Sampling variability of performance assessments. *Journal of Educational Measurement, 30,* 215–232.

Chapter 3

The Testing of English Language Learners as a Stochastic Process

Population Misspecification, Measurement Error, and Overgeneralization

Guillermo Solano-Flores

Obtaining dependable measures of academic achievement for students who have limited proficiency in the language in which they are tested is a formidable challenge for researchers and practitioners. Unfortunately, the trend of including English language learners (ELLs) in large-scale assessments has not been accompanied by effective approaches to minimize construct-irrelevant score variance due to language issues.

This chapter aims at providing a conceptual basis for examining the process of ELL testing from a comprehensive, systemic perspective that links the validity of academic achievement measures for ELLs and the capacity of assessment systems to properly test those students. More specifically, I contend that assessment systems are limited in their ability to produce valid measures of academic achievement for ELLs due to the fact that they use testing models that do not recognize or differentiate error due to multiple sources, including those that are part of assessment systems. Assessment systems have procedures for including ELL students in large-scale testing. Among these procedures are decision rules for classifying students into categories of English proficiency, deciding whether or when they should be tested, and the kinds of testing accommodations that should be made accessible to them in order to reduce the impact of limited English proficiency on their performance on tests. However, these procedures may not be entirely effective due to inaccurate measures of language proficiency, ineffective testing accommodations, and poor implementation. Thus, while the process of ELL testing is assumed to be a stable, dependable, and deterministic process governed by rules and well-specified procedures, in practice it behaves, to a large extent, as a stochastic process—a process in which its components behave as random variables.

A multidisciplinary perspective makes it possible to understand why ELL testing can be examined as a stochastic process. This multidisciplinary perspective integrates: (a) a general assessment framework; (b) a sociolinguistic perspective according to which ELL testing can be examined as a communication process between an assessment system and ELL populations; and (c) generalizability theory (see the previous chapter), a psychometric theory of measurement error. As we shall see, integrating these three theoretical perspectives allows adoption of a comprehensive, probabilistic view of the process of ELL testing.

General Assessment Framework

Knowing What Students Know (Pellegrino, Chudowsky, & Glaser, 2001) presents a simple, general conceptual framework for examining assessments. According to this conceptual framework, assessment can be thought of as a triad that includes cognition (the beliefs about the ways in which students develop competence on a domain), observation (the beliefs about the kinds of tasks that elicit from students responses that demonstrate their competence on that domain), and interpretation (a summary of patterns expected to be seen in data, given varying levels of student competence).

While such conceptual framework was not created especially for ELLs, with some stretch, it helps to identify three important aspects of their testing. We can redefine (and, in the case of the first component, rename) the three components as follows: (a) *cognition and language* refers to the implicit or explicit views of language, language development, and ELLs and, more specifically, to the ways in which those views influence the beliefs about the ways in which language affects the development of competence on a domain; (b) *observation* refers to the beliefs about the ways in which assessment tasks have to be developed, adapted, or administered to be able to elicit from ELLs responses that demonstrate competence in that domain; and (c) *interpretation* refers to the patterns across populations of ELLs that should be expected to be seen in assessment data, given varying levels of language proficiency and student competence.

These three categories allow examination of the wide variety of challenges in ELL testing and the limitations of current practices in this field. Discussing these serious challenges and limitations in detail is out of the scope of this chapter. Rather, Table 3.1 lists some examples with citations of related literature. Regarding cognition and language, many of the challenges for properly identifying and classifying ELLs derive from the tremendous heterogeneity of this population and the inability of assessment systems to recognize and deal with it. For example, each ELL has a unique pattern of bilingualism that results from a specific set of weaknesses and strengths in listening, speaking, reading, and writing skills in their first language (L1) and a specific set of weaknesses and strengths in those language modes in their second language (L2). At the same time, within the same broad linguistic group of native speakers of the same language, considerable language variation results from dialect

Table 3.1 Main Challenges and Limitations in ELLs Testing Practices

Cognition and language: Identification and classification of ELLs, population specification
Multiple strengths and weaknesses across language modes in L1 and in L2
Multiple patterns of language dominance
Home and cultural language influences
Multiple patterns of bilingualism across contexts
Multiple schooling histories and variation in the implementation of educational (e.g., bilingual programs in each school context)
Dialect variation
Inaccurate definitions of ELLs
Neglect of L1 in language development assessment practices
Flaws in the process of development of tests for measuring L2 development
Lack of approaches for assigning testing accommodations that are sensitive to individual students' needs
Inappropriate use of English as a foreign language standards in the development of L2 development tests
Views of limited English proficiency as a deficiency

Observation: Test development, adaptation, and administration
Alteration of constructs measured as a result of test translation or test adaptation
Failure of testing accommodation to address language
Failure of testing accommodations to address individual's needs
Inadequate or poorly implemented test translation review procedures
Linguistic misalignment of tests with local dialects
Inadequate skills among individuals who develop, adapt, or translate tests
Failure of testing policies to take into account the minimum time ELLs need to develop the academic language in L2 needed to learn at school and take tests

Interpretation:
Different dependability of achievement measures across school contexts within the same broad linguistic group of ELLs
Different dependability coefficients for ELLs and non-ELLs
Inconsistent implementation of testing accommodations across states, school districts, or schools

and from the ways in which register is used in the enacted curriculum. The issues listed show that, because of both the complexities of language and the lack of adequate theoretical support from current knowledge in the field of language development, bilingualism, and sociolinguistics, ELLs are inaccurately and inconsistently defined and classified and language proficiency and language development are insufficiently and inaccurately measured.

Regarding observation, the procedures used to develop, adapt, or administer tests for ELLs are limited in their effectiveness to address language or the fidelity of their implementation is questionable due to the vagueness with which these procedures are specified or to uncertainty on the qualifications of the individuals who implement them. The variety of instances of flawed testing practices is wide, from the adoption of

testing accommodations borrowed from the field of special education—
and which are irrelevant to language—to underlying misconceptions of
the nature of language.

Regarding interpretation, the major challenges derive also from the heterogeneity of ELL populations, and the inability of assessment systems to
view bilingualism not only as an individual condition but also as a social
phenomenon that involves communities. The dependability of measures
of academic achievement may vary considerably across ELLs and non-
ELLs and even within groups of ELLs. A critical mass of evidence on the
factors that shape the effectiveness with which certain testing practices
can be effectively used with any ELL population is yet to be developed.
Testing policy and legislation tend to prescribe blanket approaches that
may not contribute to valid testing. A question such as, whether ELLs
should be tested in English or in their native language appears to imply
that all ELLs are the same, regardless of their personal and schooling histories. Testing students in English may be appropriate for some students;
testing them in their native language may be appropriate for others.

Generalizability Theory

Generalizability (G) theory appears to be the only psychometric theory that allows development of testing models that are consistent with
the view of ELL as a communication process. For example, the theory
allows examination of language, dialect, and other language related
variables as sources of score variation. G-theory is a theory of measurement error which allows estimation of the sampling conditions needed
to make proper generalizations about students' knowledge in a given
domain based on a limited number of observations. G-studies examine
the amount of score variation due to the main and interaction effect of
two types of sources of score variation, student (the object of measurement) and facets (sources of measurement error). Typically, G-studies
include such facets as item, rater, and occasion. There is consistent evidence, obtained with monolingual populations, that a major challenge
to obtaining dependable scores is the instability of student performance
across items and across testing occasions. This instability is reflected as
a considerable proportion of measurement error due to the interaction of
student and item and the interaction of student and occasion.

Whereas the history of G-theory in the testing of ELLs is very short,
existing evidence suggests that it can be used as a powerful analytic tool
for examining the effectiveness of assessment systems in charge of testing ELLs (Solano-Flores & Li, 2006). Testing models can be generated
based on this theory that are consistent with theory in bilingualism, language development, and sociolinguistics. For example, G-theory allows

estimation of measurement error due to the fact that each ELL student has a unique set of strengths and weaknesses in English and a unique set of strengths and weaknesses in his native language.

In our studies on the use of G-theory in the testing of ELLs, we have given ELLs the same set of items in English and in their native language to examine the extent to which their performance varies across languages. We have observed that the main source of measurement error is the inter-action of student, item, and language, which indicates that each ELL student has a unique set of strengths and weaknesses in L1 and in L2, and that each item poses a different set of challenges in L1 and in L2.

We obtained similar results for samples of students tested in two dialects of L1. Moreover, we observed that dialect is as important as language as a source of measurement error. In a way, these results indicate that test items are not only samples of a universe of knowledge; they also are samples of language. Each item in a test contains a small sample of the features of the language in which it is administered.

We also have found that schools may vary considerably as to whether more dependable measures are obtained by testing students in L1 or in L2. Even within the same broad linguistic group (i.e., native speakers of the same language classified as belonging to the same category of English proficiency), the minimum number of items needed to obtain dependable scores by testing students in L1 or by testing them in L2 varies across schools.

It is important to note that the use of G-theory enables addressing language as a source of measurement error, not a difference between groups. Therefore, it allows examination of the technical quality of test scores without needing to compare ELL and non-ELL students' test scores. Also, it is important to note that this approach is more consistent with current views according to which bilingual individuals develop L1 and L2 as a single system rather than the sum of two separate languages. Thus, ELLs can be characterized as bilinguals (albeit incipient bilinguals) who use two languages according to multiple patterns of language dominance. This notion explains the strong interaction of student, item, and language observed in our G-studies.

Sociolinguistic Perspective

It is a surprising fact that ELL testing practices have focused on individual language proficiency and neglected the social dimension of language although testing is concerned with populations (or individuals with respect to populations). Due to such neglect, the process of testing has never been examined as a communication process. Recently (Solano-Flores, under review), I submitted the notion that ELL testing can be examined as a communication process from a sociolinguistic perspective. In this communication process, the ELL student and the assessment system interact. For example, the assessment system tests the students, ELLs respond to those tests, and the assessment system interprets those students' responses. How accurate are views of ELLs as users of English and their native languages and how appropriately the assessment system uses language to test the students and to interpret their responses ultimately influences the validity of scores.

The question, who is given tests in what language by whom, when and where acknowledges the fact that bilingualism is not only the condition of an individual who is able to use two languages with varying degrees of proficiency; bilingualism also refers to the behavior of bilingual communities whose use of one or another language (or both) is shaped by multiple contextual factors such as the topic of conversation, the interlocutor, the situation in which communication takes place, the emotions or affects expressed, and many more factors. This approach is compatible with modern views of language in education, according to which a given individual's competence in a language is multifaceted: "How a person uses language will depend on what is understood to be appropriate in a given social setting, and as such, linguistic knowledge is situated not in the individual psyche but in a group's collective linguistic norms" (Hakuta & McLaughlin, cited by Moschkovich, 2007, p. 122).

This sociolinguistic perspective allows examination of the effectiveness with which an assessment system communicates with ELLs according to six components in the process of ELL testing: *Who is given* (the characteristics of ELL students), *Tests* (the process of developing and adapting, and administering tests for ELLs, and the ways in which testing accommodations are provided to them), *In which language* (the language, dialect, and language modes in which tests are administered), *By whom* (the linguistic backgrounds and qualifications of the individuals who develop, adapt, administer tests for ELLs, or who provide them with testing accommodations), *When* (the number of occasions in which ELLs are tested and the time of their development of academic language in the language in which they are tested), and *Where* (the contexts in which ELLs are tested or are to be tested).

An important contribution of this sociolinguistic perspective is that it allows examination of language-related sources of measurement error rarely addressed or even recognized in ELL testing practices. These sources of measurement error can be studied with G-theory as facets. The actions encompassed by the *Tests* and the *By whom* components of the question illustrates this. Certain test development and adaptation procedures and test accommodations are used with the intent to reduce the impact on ELL student performance of limited proficiency in the language in which a test is administered. However, those procedures and the ways in which they are implemented are themselves sources of measurement error. Suppose, for instance, that reading test items aloud for the students in their native language is used as a test accommodation for ELLs. The accommodation may be effective only for those students who are more proficient in L1 in the listening mode than in L2 in the reading mode. In addition, the effectiveness of this accommodation may be shaped by the characteristics of the academic language used in the item. Even some students who could be characterized as being more proficient in L1 than in L2 might be more able to understand the item by reading it in L2 because they are familiar with some of the academic language used in which they have learned at school. In addition, regardless of the effectiveness of the accommodation, the fidelity with which it is implemented may vary tremendously with test administrators, depending on their proficiency in the students' L1. The quality with which test administrators pronounce the students' L1 and their familiarity with the academic language in L1 and the dialect of L1 used by the students, are among many important factors that can influence the fidelity with which they implement this form of testing accommodation.

Language, Score, and Context Variation

A comprehensive view of ELL testing is shown in Figure 3.1, which shows variation in ELL testing as both a process ("Who is given tests in what language by whom, when, and where?") and a system. Three systemic components of ELL testing are identified: population specification, score generalizability, and evidence generalization. Horizontal lines are used to denote the correspondence between ELL testing as a system and as a process. The correspondence between population specification and *Who* is obvious and needs no explanation. Generalizability concerns both the students' knowledge being measured—the object of measurement—and the facets, and classified according to four of the stages in the process of ELL testing: *Tests, Language, By Whom,* and *When* (occasion). Finally, generalization is a matter of *When* (language development and academic language development) and *Where*—the multiple contexts to which findings from research and practice in ELL testing can be reasonably generalized.

Population specification is about language variation and the ability of an assessment system to produce defensible classifications of ELL populations. Traditionally, classifications of ELLs are based on measures of English proficiency. Numerous criticisms have been made about the limitations of current tests of English proficiency in their effectiveness to produce valid information of language proficiency. An additional limitation

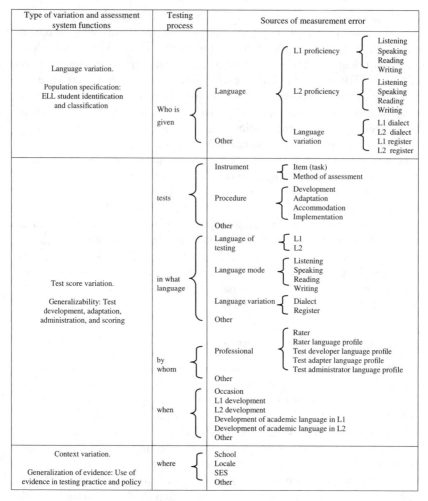

Type of variation and assessment system functions	Testing process	Sources of measurement error			
Language variation. Population specification: ELL student identification and classification	Who is given	Language	L1 proficiency		Listening Speaking Reading Writing
			L2 proficiency		Listening Speaking Reading Writing
		Other	Language variation		L1 dialect L2 dialect L1 register L2 register
Test score variation. Generalizability: Test development, adaptation, administration, and scoring	tests	Instrument	Item (task) Method of assessment		
		Procedure	Development Adaptation Accommodation Implementation		
		Other			
	in what language	Language of testing	L1 L2		
		Language mode	Listening Speaking Reading Writing		
		Language variation	Dialect Register		
		Other			
	by whom	Professional	Rater Rater language profile Test developer language profile Test adapter language profile Test administrator language profile		
		Other			
	when	Occasion L1 development L2 development Development of academic language in L1 Development of academic language in L2 Other			
Context variation. Generalization of evidence: Use of evidence in testing practice and policy	where	School Locale SES Other			

Figure 3.1 Structure of measurement error in the testing of ELLs by assessment system function and ELL testing process component.

arises from the fact that bilingual individuals cannot be characterized properly unless their proficiencies in both L1 and L2 and across language modes in the two languages are examined. In addition, language proficiency varies according to context.

Score generalizability is about test score variation and the extent to which inferences about an individual's or a population's knowledge of a given domain can be made based on a limited number of observations. Facets such as item (task), occasion, and method of assessment (e.g., multiple-choice and constructed response tasks) have been investigated extensively as discussed in chapter 2 by Shavelson and Webb, although in the context of testing monolingual, non-ELL populations. Language and dialect have been investigated recently, as discussed above, as sources of measurement error in the testing of ELLs (e.g., Solano-Flores & Trumbull, 2003). Other language-related sources of measurement error are yet to be investigated. Notice that the number of language related facets outnumber the facets traditionally considered in testing. Notice also that those language related facets have to do with the actions taken by assessment systems.

Evidence generalization is about context variation and the extent to which evidence from research and practice in the testing of ELLs is used to devise effective testing approaches in contexts that are different to the contexts in which the original evidence was generated; it refers to the ability of an assessment system to deal with the fact that the characteristics of ELL populations and their learning contexts vary tremendously. Bilingual populations are heterogeneous, which shapes the effectiveness of bilingual programs and may potentially shape the effectiveness of practices and policies that are not sensitive to this variation. Also, because bilingualism is shaped by multiple factors, it is difficult to determine whether a set of findings obtained from a specific school context (e.g., a specific group of speakers of a given L1, a specific geographical area, a specific set of schools) should be generalized to other school contexts.

ELL Testing as a Stochastic Process

Altogether, population misspecification, measurement error, and evidence overgeneralization may compromise the ability of assessment systems to properly test ELLs. The technical quality of test scores is normally examined exclusively with regards to the second aspect of assessment systems—developing, adapting, administering, and scoring tests. However, from a comprehensive, systemic perspective, good technical properties of scores do not necessarily warrant sound testing practices. For example, even if dependable measures of academic achievement are obtained for a given group of students, the utility of those measures will be compromised if the language proficiency of those students has not been determined accurately. Or, evidence from research on ELL testing will not be properly used to develop testing policies if the contextual factors that may shape the effectiveness of those policies are not taken into account.

The process of ELL testing is operationalized through legal definitions and well established procedures, as is the case of the definition of ELL in the No Child Left Behind Act of 2001, which is mainly based on demographic variables that are associated but do not determine the condition of being an ELL. Also, conventional testing models are silent about assessment system-related sources of measurement error—they appear to be based on the premise that assessment systems are stable, consistent, and fully effective, to the extent that they do not have an effect on the dependability of academic measures for ELLs.

In practice, the process of ELL testing is a stochastic process, a process in which variables behave, to some extent, randomly because of factors that (a) are beyond control (e.g., population heterogeneity, dialect variation), (b) cannot be measured accurately or sufficiently (e.g., linguistic proficiencies of ELLs in the four language modes in both L1 and in L2), (c) have a high level of uncertainty (e.g., linguistic skills in the ELLs' L1 among individuals who implement accommodations, fidelity with which accommodations are implemented), (d) behave inconsistently (e.g., criteria used by states to determine when a student is an ELL), or (e) involve strategies that are ineffective to addressing language proficiency (e.g., testing accommodations that are irrelevant to addressing language). Since "[e]ven the best program in education will fail to have the intended impact if its essential elements are not implemented properly" (Ruiz-Primo, 2006, p. 1), examining the extent to which measurement error builds up along the six components of the process of ELL testing is not unreasonable at all.

A simple stochastic model of the process of ELL testing can be built from six sets of dichotomous questions, which address the capacity of an assessment system to properly test ELL students, as shown below. The questions included in each set are not meant to be exhaustive; they are included with the intent to illustrate each component in the process of ELL testing:

Who: Are ELLs defined and classified based on accurate, valid, recent, and comprehensive measures of proficiency in listening, speaking, reading, and writing proficiency in both L1 and L2 guided by a view of? Is limited English proficiency viewed and defined as a difference rather than a deficiency?

Tests: Are ELLs properly represented as pilot students in the process test development? Are tests properly adapted or translated when they are administered in L1? Are testing accommodations adequate to each ELL student's particular listening, speaking, reading, and writing proficiency in both L1 or in L2?

Language: Is the language used in testing (L1 or L2) the student's dominant language? Is dialect variation (in either L1 or L2) properly addressed in the linguistic features of tests? Are the linguistic features of tests aligned with the register and language usage of the enacted curriculum?

By Whom: Do the individuals who develop, adapt, and translate tests, and the individuals who administer tests and implement testing accommodations for ELLs have adequate linguistic competencies?

When: Does testing in L2 take place at a stage in which ELLs have developed the academic language needed to learn at school and take tests? Is ELL student performance stable across testing occasions?

Where: Are ELL testing research, policy, and practice decisions sensitive to the contextual factors that shape the effectiveness of testing approaches?

Suppose that, according to criteria like those listed above, each stage in the process of ELL testing is rated as successful or unsuccessful, based on surveys, observations, or any other sources of information. Suppose also that success or fail outcomes are represented respectively by the values p and q, being q = 1- p, as Figure 3.2 shows. Although they are part of the same process, we treat these stages as independent trials because the outcome of one does not appear to influence the outcome of the other (e.g., flawed classifications of ELLs do not have any influence on the procedures used to develop tests or adapt them for ELLs).

How successful the process of ELL testing is can be represented as the product of the values of the separate outcomes of its stages:

$$s = p^r q^{n-r} \tag{3.1}$$

where s is success in the entire process of ELL testing, n is the number of stages in the process, and r is the number of stages completed successfully. The equation shows the multiplicative effect of failure in the ELL testing stages and alerts us about the fact that, to produce valid measures of academic achievement and sound testing practices, assessment systems need to address properly all stages in the process of ELL testing.

Final Comments

Legislation, policy, research, and practice reflect an implicit view of ELL testing as a deterministic process. For example, students are classified into a few categories of language proficiency, testing accommodations are provided assuming proper implementation, and the qualifications of individuals who provide testing accommodations are not questioned. However, doubts about the effectiveness with which ELLs are tested arise from inaccurate definitions of ELLs, inconsistent and vague testing policies, poor implementation, and lack of control.

In this chapter, I propose viewing ELL testing as a stochastic process, a process in which the variables involved at each stage may behave randomly because their values or conditions are uncertain or because they are beyond control. Accordingly, the effectiveness with which an

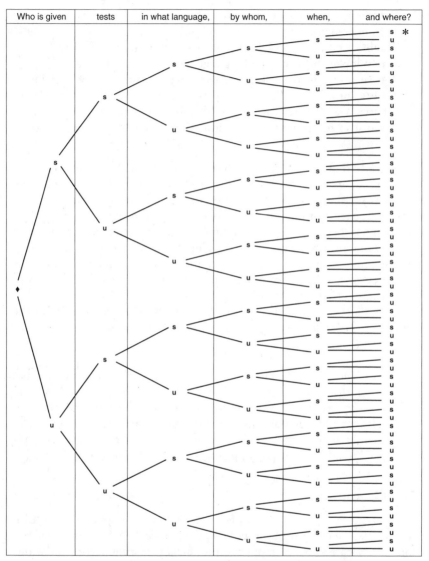

Figure 3.2 Markov chain representing all the combinations of successful (s) and unsuccessful (u) outcomes in the six stages of the process of ELL testing.

assessment system tests ELLs can be examined as to the extent to which testing takes place as a communication process (the linguistic proficiencies of students are identified accurately, the assessment system asks test questions, the students respond to them, the assessment system interprets the responses properly) rather than a stochastic process.

Recognizing the stochastic nature of the process of ELL testing makes the link between assessment and evaluation evident. To be able to judge the quality of the measures of academic achievement for ELLs, it is necessary to have information on the capacity of an assessment system to deal with language variation, score variation, and context variation. Literature on ELL testing tends to focus on the technical properties of test scores. But the dependability of scores is only one part of the story. Minimizing population misspecification, measurement error, and overgeneralization are all equally critical to designing assessment systems (or improving the existing ones) in ways that produce accurate measures of academic achievement and sound testing practices for ELLs.

References

Moschkovich, J. N. (2007). Using two languages when learning mathematics. *Educatonal Studies in Mathematics, 64,* 121–144.

No Child Left Behind Act, 10 U.S.C. 6301 (2002).

Pellegrino, J. W., Chudowsky, N., & Glaser, R. (2001). *Knowing what students know: The science and design of educational assessment.* Washington, DC: National Academy Press.

Ruiz-Primo, M. A. (2006). *A multi-method and multi-source approach for studying fidelity of implementation.* CSE Report 677. National Center for Research on Evaluation, Standards, and Student Testing (CRESST), Center for the Study of Evaluation (CSE), Graduate School of Education & Information Studies, University of California, Los Angeles.

Solano-Flores, G. (Under review). Who is given tests in what language by whom, when, and where? The need for probabilistic views of language in the testing of English language learners.

Solano-Flores, G., & Li, M. (2006). The use of generalizability (G) theory in the testing of linguistic minorities. *Educational Measurement: Issues and Practice, 25,* 13–22.

Solano-Flores, G., & Trumbull, E. (2003). Examining language in context: The need for new research and practice paradigms in the testing of English-language learners. *Educational Researcher, 32*(2), 3–13.

Section I

Highlights

A key component of validity of research interpretations and generalizations is the extent to which the inferences are meaningful for the sample and contexts used in the research as well as beyond these specific research situations to a target set of universe of contexts. Shavelson and Webb present a discussion of generalizability theory (G-theory) in measurement and relate this theory to making generalizations in research. These authors describe how G-theory may help researchers identify sources of limitations in the generalizability of research findings, and how to systematically investigate the extent to which these factors limit research generalization. This discussion of possibilities and limitations of generalizing research findings obtained based on a sample to a population is at the core of discussions throughout this book. Shavelson and Webb address how well can we generalize from the sample of measurements in hand to a broader domain? They identify the focus of G-theory as validity and dependability of measurements, and research generalizability as (a) describing situations, (b) testing conjectures about functional and causal effects, and (c) testing conjectures about mechanisms underlying those effects. These three are possible goals of research, and types of inferences made in research. However, the question of generalizability is more relevant to what extent the description of a situation helps us understand other situations, to what extent functional and causal effects we identify will be similar in other situations and whether these effects will be through similar mechanisms in other contexts.

The generalizability of facets such as raters or item format is related to variability in measurements due to raters or forms. The greater the variability among raters, for example, the greater is the measurement error due to raters. Similarly, the greater the variability due to item format the greater is the error due to format. Higher degrees of variability due to a particular facet indicate that a researcher may obtain different measurement results if a different set of raters were used or if different item formats (e.g., multiple-choice versus performance assessment tasks) were used. Such variability in facets and limitations on generalizability would obviously be expected to have an effect on the degree to which findings from the research can be generalized to contexts, and situations beyond those used in the research. A systematic examination of research generalizability requires the following: Research needs to be explicit about what their construct of interest is, describe student population, and the universe of conditions and situations from which the treatment contexts have been sampled. These requirements make it clear that in education, how the "treatments" such as educational interventions, curriculum implementations are in fact is a sample from a population of treatments (changing curriculum teacher professional development, new resource materials are among many possibilities of educational interventions) and the contexts within which the research is implemented is a sample from a population of contexts (cultural and linguistic context of education, socioeconomic and political contexts are some of the members of the universe of contexts).

Solano-Flores presents an extension of this discussion of measurement generalizability to generalizability of research findings to different linguistic populations and contexts. As Solano-Flores puts it, the chapter provides a "conceptual basis for examining the process of ELL [English Language Learner] testing from a comprehensive, systemic perspective that links the validity of academic achievement measures for ELLs and the capacity of assessment systems to properly test those students." The chapter disentangles the complex interactions among factors when students are tested. First, it clearly demonstrates that simply dividing examinees to ELL versus non-ELL is not sufficient to identify and account for language and cultural effects on validity of test interpretations. Each ELL is described as having unique patterns of bilingualism that is due to a variation in their listening, speaking, reading, and writing language competencies in the first language (L1) and their second language (L2). These unique combinations of L1 and L2 in examinees lead to two key challenges. The first challenge is appropriate identification of these competencies and the second related challenge is development and implementation of appropriate accommodations for examinees.

In addition to language related complexities, ELLs may have very different cultural backgrounds that are expected to affect their performances. In fact, Solano-Flores contends that "bilingualism is not only the condition of an individual who is able to use two languages with varying degrees of proficiency; bilingualism also refers to the behavior of bilingual communities whose use of one or another language (or both) is shaped by multiple contextual factors such as the topic of conversation, the interlocutor, the situation in which communication take place, the motions or affects expressed, and many more factors." To account for all the possible combinations of possible factors that may affect tests, testing conditions, and interpretations, Solano-Flores identifies the following factors:

Who—student socio-linguistic background and the whether the student proficiency in L1 and L2 are accurately identified.

Tests—whether tests are appropriate for ELL students from cultural and linguistic backgrounds.

Language—whether the language of the test (in terms of dialect, whether it's student's L1) appropriate for the student.

By whom—whether the test developers have the necessary linguistic competencies to develop and implement linguistically appropriate tests.

When—whether the timing of the test is appropriate for academic and language preparedness of ELLs.

Where—whether the education system has processes and procedures in place to take into account the contextual factors for ELLs.

Solano-Flores regards answers to these questions as dichotomous. This dichotomization allows him to describe the complexity of the outcome of the ELL testing using stochastic models. However, if we are willing to complicate matters even further, it is easy to see that answers to these questions are "continuous." For example, tests have degrees of cultural and linguistic appropriateness and the appropriateness of the timing of tests is similarly has degrees of appropriateness rather than existence or lack of it.

Section II

Combining and Contrasting Qualitative and Quantitative Evidence

Overview

The chapters in this section articulate possible avenues for combining evidence of different nature (qualitative, quantitative) to support generalizability claims by showing how synthesizing evidence in the form of research findings as well as statistical and other types of arguments. Margaret Eisenhart, an anthropologist by training, strongly disagrees with the generally accepted assumption that qualitative inquiries are not generalizable. In her chapter "Generalization from Qualitative Inquiry," she argues that taking pains to constitute qualitative research as nongeneralizable should not be the norm for qualitative research in education. Eisenhart discusses the kinds of generalizations that are produced by interpretive and practical science studies that rely on qualitative inquiry and argues that generalizations from qualitative research are not only common but also enduring and useful.

Taking their starting point in our own "What Good is Polarizing Research into Qualitative and Quantitative?" Robert J. Mislevy, Pamela Moss, and James J. Gee take a closer look at one important facet of the debate, namely validity, focusing on educational assessment and noting implications for generalization along the way. In their chapter "On Qualitative and Quantitative Reasoning in Validity," the authors focus on the reasoning and the arguments used in validity discussions from psychometric, hermeneutic and anthropological approaches. The authors argue that apparently disparate approaches to validation in qualitative and quantitative work share an underlying commonality, in terms of convergence, coverage, agreement, and details. There are strong connections between the points highlighted in this chapter and those discussed by Solano-Flores. The *Who, Tests, Language, By Whom, When,* and *Where* are all the key dichotomous variables in Solano-Flores' stochastic model. Many of the factors that are the focus of the Solano-Flores chapter are captured in the Mislevy, Moss, and Gee chapter as "context" and "use."

Betsy Becker and Meng-Jia Wu consider the question of generalizability within the practice of meta-analysis, a term that is used to refer to the quantitative synthesis of multiple studies focusing on a common issue. Meta-analysis has been employed in many disciplines including medicine, education, and other social sciences to synthesize knowledge across research studies in an effort to come up with a concise generalization: for example, how is motivation related to learning or "how do gender groups compare on mathematics learning? These two topics are very highly researched areas. For example, when we did a search on Google Scholar, 901,000 citations came up. Similarly, when we searched Google for gender differences and mathematics 82,500 citations came up. In these studies, the findings are not always in the same directions, and even when the direction of the relationship is the same the degree of the relationship varies from one study to another. How does one go about generalizing from 1000s of research studies? In their chapter, Becker and Wu suggest that one of the challenges in synthesizing research is that typically not all studies use the same research design and methodology, even if they purport to examine "the same" problem. This is true when one attempts to synthesize only quantitative studies, or only qualitative studies, but is even more pronounced in syntheses that attempt to bring together studies using quantitative and qualitative approaches. It is rare to see researchers combining qualitative studies and quantitative studies in one synthesis. Becker and Wu write about the challenges of including different types of studies in one synthesis, beginning with an examination of diverse quantitative studies. They discuss even greater challenges of working with both qualitative and quantitative studies, examining both the possibilities and limitations of this idea.

Chapter 4

Generalization from Qualitative Inquiry

Margaret Eisenhart

"Qualitative inquiries normally take pains to make clear that they are not generalizable" (Kilbourn, 2006, p. 534). Although statements like Brent Kilbourn's that disclaim generalizability for qualitative research are commonplace, I disagree that this is or should be the norm for qualitative research. In this chapter, I discuss the arguments about generalization from qualitative inquiry. After briefly reviewing the claims for non-generalizability, I will counter that there are well-established means by which warranted generalizations can be produced from qualitative research and that the most important means, theoretical generalization, is of far greater importance to education research and practice than many educational researchers realize.

Introduction

Researchers, including qualitative researchers, often say that generalization from qualitative inquiry is inappropriate or unwarranted. For example, Yvonna Lincoln and Egon Guba's well-known 1985 book, *Naturalistic Inquiry*, includes a chapter entitled, "The Only Generalization Is: There is No Generalization." Harry Wolcott's in *The Art of Fieldwork* (2005) takes a similar position:

> How do you generalize from a qualitative study? [You] might answer candidly and succinctly, "You don't." That is a safe and accurate answer. It is the basis on which American anthropology was founded under Franz Boas. With an empiricism directed toward rigorous historical particularism, Boas insisted that no generalizations were warranted from the study of any particular society. (p. 163)

Marilyn Lichtman's "user's guide" to qualitative research in education (2006) makes a similar claim, stating on p. 7 that qualitative researchers are "not interested in cause and effect or generalizing, but want people to apply [research findings] to their own situations." And Phil Carspecken

(1996) in his "theoretical and practical guide" to critical ethnography writes: "Generalizing across contexts is dangerous" (p. 25).

Statements such as these appear in books and articles intended for novice and expert researchers alike. They come from authors writing about qualitative research in education from the 1980s to the 2000s. They are made by recognized scholars and relative unknowns. Qualitative research, with its reputation for small-scale, researcher-dependent, and discovery-oriented inquiries, is said to be good for providing detailed descriptions, identifying relevant factors, and generating plausible hypotheses for more systematic study. It is not supposed to be good for developing propositions, models or theories that generalize. Because so many prominent qualitative researchers say so unequivocally that their work is not generalizable, it is probably safe to say that many education researchers believe generalizability is irrelevant or unachievable in qualitative research.

But I think they are wrong. Consistent with Ercikan and Roth's (2006) argument that "generalization is not a feature of mathematization but a descriptor for the tendency of inferences to go beyond the context and participants involved in the research" (p. 22), I make the case that generalizations from qualitative research are both possible and important.

Types of Generalizations

Probabilistic Generalization

Many people who say that qualitative research is not generalizable seem to define the concept in probabilistic terms, i.e., as a procedure for making general claims about a population from a sample, based on statistical probabilities. To generalize in this way, researchers must provide evidence that the study sample was either randomly or representatively selected, according to statistical sampling requirements, from the population to which generalizations will be inferred. If the sampling requirements are met, then generalizations from the sample to the larger population are said to be warranted. Robert Yin (2005) calls this approach "statistical generalization." He writes: "This method of generalizing is commonly recognized because research investigators have ready access to quantitative formulas for determining the confidence with which generalizations can be made, depending mostly on the size and internal variation within the [population] and sample" (p. 32). (See other chapters in this volume for sophisticated discussions of this kind of generalization.)

Wolcott (2005) is one qualitative researcher (of many) who seems to accept this definition. Although he does not explicitly define generalization, he talks about it with reference to averages, frequencies, and distributions. In trying to distinguish his own work from the kind that produces generalizations, he aligns himself with the radical particularism of Franz Boas's style of ethnography, stating that there can be no generalizability from the work of researchers who focus on a site or group chosen by need or convenience, which is often the case with ethnographies.

But despite Wolcott's strong claim that qualitative research does not produce generalizations, he does not necessarily mean it. He subsequently suggests that ethnographic work, even his own, often aspires to a kind of generalization.[1] In cases where ethnographers or other qualitative researchers can provide empirical evidence that a particular study site or group is in some sense typical or representative of a larger population, Wolcott suggests that generalizations beyond the particular study may be warranted. For example, if he shows that a Kwakiutl village he studied is similar in important respects to other Kwakiutl villages, or to villages of other groups living along the northwest coast of North America, or even to villages in other parts of the world, then he believes that findings from his village (despite its being chosen for convenience) can be generalized to the other villages. Borrowing from Margaret Mead, he calls this "approaching generalization" by fitting a particular ethnographic site (however it was selected) into a "larger scheme of things" by which its special characteristics are compared empirically to others. Instead of drawing inferences from a sample to a population based on probabilities, Wolcott draws inferences from a site to others based on observed or reported similarities.

This type of generalization is common in practical reasoning and in education research. Wolcott explains, "I regarded the Kwakiutl village and school of my first fieldwork to be a village and school in certain respects like all other villages and schools, in certain respects like some other villages and their schools, and in certain respects like no other village and its school" (p. 164). To the extent that he can document— usually by reference to previous research—the similarities between his site and others, he makes generalizations from his site to the others. On grounds of similarity, he argues that such generalizations are warranted. Readers may agree or not with his analysis of similarities and thus the appropriateness of his generalizations, but it is disingenuous to suggest that this is not a rational approach to drawing inferences that "go beyond the context and participants involved in the research." Arguably, this is a more sensible approach to generalization in contexts in which interactions among people, regardless of their overt characteristics as measured in random or representative sampling, are multiple and interdependent, as is the case in educational (and most other human) contexts.

Other qualitative researchers use more probabilistic ways of approaching generalizability in qualitative research. Some ethnographers and case study researchers begin with a sample chosen for its convenience or accessibility. Relying on that sample, they explore initial conditions, identify relevant research questions, narrow the focus, and describe initial results. Then they use surveys to determine whether the initial results hold true for a larger random or representative sample. Using this approach, biases inherent in the initial sample but not in larger ones can be identified and eliminated as candidates for generalization.

Consistent with a probabilistic approach to generalization, Joseph Maxwell (2005) makes an important distinction between internal and external generalization in qualitative research. Internal generalization, he argues, is very important, while external generalization often is not:

> [It] is important to distinguish between what I call "internal" and "external" generalizability. Internal generalizability refers to the generalizability of a conclusion *within* the setting or group studied, while external generalizability refers to its generalizability beyond that setting or group. Internal generalizability is clearly a key issue for qualitative … studies…. If you are studying the patterns of interaction between the teacher and students in a single classroom, your account of that classroom as a whole is seriously jeopardized if you have selectively focused on particular students or kinds of interactions and ignored others. (p. 115)

Maxwell's point is well taken. Qualitative researchers in education commonly make internal generalizations of this kind (from a small group of students to the whole class, from one classroom to a school). When they do, they invoke the requirements of probabilistic generalizability and must add methods such as wider sampling and surveys or evidence of close similarities between sampled and non-sampled groups to justify these internal generalizations. For Maxwell, external generalizability is another matter:

> In contrast, external generalizability is often not a crucial issue for qualitative studies. Indeed, the value of a qualitative study may depend on its *lack* of external generalizability in the sense of being representative of a larger population … it may provide an account of a setting or population that is illuminating as an extreme case or "ideal type." (p. 115)

Maxwell's reservations about external generalizations from qualitative research, like Wolcott's, stem from the difficulties qualitative researchers can have in meeting the statistical requirements of probabilistic generalization:

[A] number of features ... lend plausibility to generalizations from case studies or nonrandom samples, including respondents' own assessments of generalizability, the similarity of dynamics and constraints to other situations, the presumed depth or universality of the phenomenon studied, and corroboration from other studies. All of these characteristics can provide credibility to generalizations from qualitative studies, but none permits the kinds of precise extrapolation of results to defined populations that probability sampling allows. (p. 116)

I agree that when generalizations are defined as probabilistic, the people, events, or cases studied must be representative or typical of the larger population for which generalizations are intended or claimed. If qualitative researchers strive for this type of generalization, and they sometimes they do, then the standards of probabilistic generalization—that inferences from a sample to a population be justified by statistical or empirical evidence of the sample's representativeness—apply.

Although these standards can be tricky for qualitative researchers to meet, I do not think they are unmanageable. A number of reasonable approaches are common. Qualitative researchers who wish to make generalizations of this type must give careful attention to sampling decisions in the design of their studies. If the intent is to generalize from a qualitative study to "what usually happens," then the researcher must investigate something that can be documented to be typical or common. This can be done by selecting a typical site or group in advance, demonstrating the site's typicality after the fact, or studying multiple sites and identifying commonalities across them.

I also agree with Maxwell that qualitative researchers need not strive for probabilistic generalizability in order to produce a worthwhile study. As Maxwell says, extreme or ideal cases can reveal what is possible, say when a teacher is particularly successful with normally under-achieving students or when a policy leads to serious unintended consequences in a particular context. Extreme or unusual cases can also illuminate cutting-edge or future-oriented practices, such as teachers who effectively use Web resources in their classrooms. These cases are (presumably) not typical and thus not generalizable (and thus an aside to the main point I am making in this chapter). But their atypicality does not mean they are bad, useless or weak in rigor. Although not generalizable, special cases are critically important for understanding the variations that develop and the possibilities that exist in educational policy and practice.

In summary, probabilistic generalizations—based on statistical probability or near approximations—can be and often are produced from qualitative research. And, this is not the only kind of generalization possible from this type of research.

Nomological Generalization

Lincoln and Guba's (1985) argument that qualitative research does not produce generalizations is based on a nomological definition of the concept. Following Abraham Kaplan (1964), they argue that generalization "must be truly universal, unrestricted as to time and space. It must formulate what is always and everywhere the case, provided only that the appropriate conditions are satisfied" (p. 91). Nomological generalizations are law-like assertions of enduring value that are context-free; any particular phenomenon, sample, data, or example is a special case of such generalizations.

Lincoln and Guba argue, rightly I think, that nomological generalizations are not possible in social science (and perhaps any science), and that qualitative researchers do not accept the reductionist conceit that makes this kind of generalization seem reasonable or helpful. Rejecting nomological generalization and drawing instead on Lee Cronbach's (1975) notion that the results of social science research are never more than "working hypotheses" for subsequent investigation, Lincoln and Guba propose "transferability," or the extent of similarity between two contexts, as an alternative to generalization, an alternative that they believe social scientists, including qualitative researchers, can and should strive for. Transferability of findings or results from one context to another is possible, they argued, if the two contexts are sufficiently similar. The extent of similarity suggests the likelihood of transferability. Thus, arguing from different starting points, Lincoln and Guba arrive at a position virtually identical to Wolcott's and Maxwell's: Generalizations from qualitative studies based on empirical evidence of similarity across sites and people are both possible and warranted.

Providing helpful detail on this point, Lincoln and Guba stress that judgments about transferability depend on detailed knowledge of *both* sending and receiving contexts. Their perspective is echoed by Frederick Erickson (1986): "The search is not for *abstract universals* arrived at by statistical generalizations from a sample to a population, but for *concrete universals* arrived at by studying a specific case in great detail and then comparing it with other cases studied in great detail" (p. 130). (On an expanded discussion of the concept of concrete universal, see Roth, this volume.) Along with Lincoln and Guba and Erickson, I recognize that an individual researcher may not be in a position to have detailed knowledge of more than one case or context, but at least he or she has the responsibility of suggesting the kinds of cases or contexts to which the results might be transferable and providing sufficient detail about the researched context for a person with intimate knowledge of a second context to judge the likelihood of transferability. Sharan Merriam (1998,

p. 211) suggests the term "user generalizability" to refer to another person's recognition that a study's conclusions can be generalized to a context he or she knows well.

Like qualitative researchers who strive for probabilistic generalization, those who strive for transferability must think carefully about the selection of a site or sites to study. Sites in which the context can be investigated and described in detail, in which the site can be shown to be typical of other sites, and in which the contexts of the sites for generalization can be known are good candidates for qualitative research that is transferable. Methods for coming to know these sites and contexts are many and varied—ethnographies, case studies, histories, surveys, censuses, and previous research all might be useful; coming to know and describe the sites and contexts in detail is what matters in making warranted transfers from one site to another.

Grounded Generalization

In their book, *The Discovery of Grounded Theory*, Barney Glaser and Anselm Strauss (1967) propose another kind of generalization from qualitative research. Following their constant comparative method, "grounded generalizations" (or theories) are produced as the researcher moves from local situation to local situation, directly following a phenomenon of interest across time and space, investigating everything the phenomena "touches," describing and interpreting the phenomena in each new situation in terms of the preceding ones, and forming tentative hypotheses that accommodate all previous information and anticipate what new situations will reveal. In this process, the researcher consciously seeks out negative cases, i.e., situations that might force revision or rejection of the emerging hypotheses. The researcher continues this process until new examples of the phenomenon, especially examples that might prove the hypotheses wrong, no longer yield information that is unaccounted for by the hypotheses generated. The final hypotheses become the propositions of a grounded generalization or theory. In this case, the generalization is warranted because it accommodates all the information collected about the phenomenon of interest.

In his early work, Norman Denzin referred to this process of accommodating all the information collected about a phenomenon via the systematic investigation of negative cases as "analytic induction." To illustrate the process, Denzin used a study of opiate addiction conducted by Alfred Lindesmith, whose goal was to develop a theory that could explain all cases of opiate addiction. About this approach to generalization, Denzin (1989) writes,

This strategy not only forces the careful consideration of all available evidence, both quantitative and qualitative, but makes necessary the intensive analysis of individual cases and the comparisons of certain crucial cases. Thus, Lindesmith did not confine his study only to analysis of individual addicts; he also examined statistical reports on opiate addiction. In addition, he explicitly studied nonaddicts who had regularly received drugs in hospitals in order to isolate the causal conditions present in addiction and absent among nonaddicted hospital patients. (p. 194)

To make warranted generalizations of this type, qualitative researchers must give careful attention to the process of the investigation that will lead to a general theory. For this type of generalization, selecting a phenomena or site that is typical or one that is accessible enough to expect its context can be well specified is not of primary importance. The researcher intending to develop a grounded generalization can begin his or her work with any instance of the phenomenon but must commit to following it exhaustively through time and space as its connections to other phenomena and in other sites are revealed. This process of generalization is not complete until a theory has been tested against probable negative instances and thus shown to account for all known and suspected instances of the phenomenon. I will return to this important type of generalization later in this chapter under the heading "Theoretical Generalization."

Syntheses and Meta-analysis as Generalization

Another approach to generalizing from qualitative research is to develop techniques for synthesizing the results of qualitative studies about similar topics or groups. These techniques include case survey method, qualitative comparative method, and multisite analysis; all are strategies for aggregating data across completed qualitative cases. These strategies consist of steps for locating relevant cases, reviewing the cases for examples of specified codes or categories, and then identifying patterns in codes or categories that apply (i.e., generalize) across the cases. Another strategy, called metaethnography, involves the identification and cataloguing of the specific concepts, themes, and metaphors used to report the results of studies of similar topics, e.g., the classroom implementation of a particular mathematics program. Once the catalogue has been compiled, the analyst attempts to "translate" concepts, themes and metaphors from one study into the terms used in another, by asking for example: Are the concepts from the first study of the mathematics program adequate to handle the concepts of the second and vice versa? In this manner, more encompassing (generalizing) concepts can often be identified.

Without belaboring the point, I want to note here that I have just discussed six kinds of generalization that are relevant to and can be obtained from qualitative research: probabilistic generalization, transferability, user generalization, grounded generalization, synthetic generalization, and meta-analytic generalization. There may be others. Let it not be said any longer that qualitative researchers do not "do" generalization. If generalization is a concern for qualitative researchers (and often it is) or for those who evaluate qualitative research, there are a number of established ways it has been and can be addressed. In the next section, I elaborate on one other type, theoretical or analytical generalization, a form that is arguably more important to qualitative researchers and to education research than any discussed so far.

Theoretical Generalization

Although Maxwell (2005) is concerned about probabilistic issues, he is careful to point out, and I agree, that generalizability from qualitative studies is more often based on the development of a theory that can be extended to other cases or refined in light of them. This approach, also referred to as "analytic generalization," has been termed "theoretical inference"—where "the conclusions of [a qualitative study] are seen to be generalizable in the context of a particular theoretical debate rather than being primarily concerned to extend them to a larger collectivity" (Davies, 1999, p. 91). Davies uses the example of Cynthia Cockburn's, *In the Ways of Women: Men's Resistance to Sex Equality in Organizations*, an ethnographic study of the introduction of equal opportunity policies in four British organizations, to illustrate the difference between what she calls "empirical generalizations" (similar to Wolcott's "approaching generalizations") and theoretical inference. Davies writes:

> [Cockburn] offers some empirical generalization in that [her conclusion is] not restricted to the specific four organizations she studied but is meant to be applicable to other similar organizations in British society, and, perhaps with some modifications, to other Western industrial societies. On the other hand, her more significant generalizations [i.e., her theoretical inferences] have to do with the forms of resistance both formal and informal that characterize the introduction of [equal opportunity] policies. Such generalizations are likely to be of much greater explanatory value in quite disparate situations.... This sort of generalization relies upon a case-study method in a very different way than as a representative of a class of cases. (pp. 91–92)

In Cockburn's work, cases (ethnographies, case studies, etc.) are used to develop and then refine emerging theoretical inferences about the nature and process of resistance to equal opportunity policies. Davies continues:

> [This sort of generalization] proceeds by a gradual accumulation and "constant comparison" (Glaser and Strauss, 1967) of cases in which, rather than seeking to show repeated instances of particular conjunctures of occurrences leading to a predictive causal statement, the ethnographer actively seeks the differences and variations whose explanation will refine, strengthen and make more profound the developing explanations that constitute valid generalization in ethnographic research. (p. 91)

In striving for theoretical generalization, the selection of a group or site to study is made based on the likelihood that the case will reveal something new and different, and that once this new phenomenon is theorized, additional cases will expose differences or variations that test its generalizability. The criterion for selecting cases from which one will generalize is not random or representative sampling but the extent to which the cases selected are likely to establish, refine, or refute a theory.

As Davies describes it, the process of theoretical generalization proceeds in a manner similar to the process of grounded generalization outlined by Glaser and Strauss. The difference is that the goal of grounded generalization is to produce new theories or explanations whereas the goal of theoretical generalization is to make existing theories more refined and incisive. It seems to me that particularly strong qualitative research programs would aspire to both generalizing goals—first to develop a grounded theory and then to refine it by extension to other cases.[2]

Howard Becker (1990) describes theoretical generalization as the attempt to develop a refined understanding of a generic process, such as the functioning of Erving Goffman's "total institutions," that have wide applicability in social life. Becker explains that the point of theoretical generalization is not to show that every site with the characteristics of a total institution produces the same results, but rather to show how each new site potentially represents different values of a generic process. In other words, a theoretical generalization can be true although the results in specific cases are different. Becker provides an example from studies of men's prisons (in the 1960s and 70s) and the attempt to generalize their results to a prison for women:

> Students of prisons ... had demonstrated that, in the men's prisons they studied, inmates developed an elaborate culture. They created a

convict government that took over many of the functions of keeping order in the joint; they developed quasi-markets in cigarettes, drugs, tailor-made clothing, and a variety of personal services; they organized sexual activity; they enforced a strict code of convict behavior emphasizing the necessity of never giving information about other prisoners to prison guards and officials.

Analysts of prison culture attributed these inventions to the deprivations of prison life.... The generalization was, prisoners develop a culture that solves the problems created by the deprivations of prison life.

[Other researchers], with this theory in mind, studied a women's prison. They didn't find any of that. Quite the opposite. Even the officials of the prison complained about the lack of a convict code: The women were forever snitching on one another in a way that made a lot of trouble. There was no underground market in much of anything. Sex life was not organized in the predatory style of the men's prison; instead, the women developed pseudo-families, with butches acting as the husbands and fathers of a collection of wives and daughters.

Do these differences invalidate the generalization that the deprivations of prison life lead to the creation of a prison culture?... Not at all.... [T]he theory wasn't wrong, but you had to put in the right values of the variables to see how it was right. You could still say that the deprivations of prison life led to the creation of prison culture, but that this was true only if you understood that prison deprived women of different things than men. Women were not deprived of autonomy because, on their own testimony, they had never had it; they had always lived under the protection of a man—a father, husband, or lover. They were, however, deprived of exactly that kind of protection. So they didn't develop a convict government, but they did develop a system of homosexual relationships in which one woman stood in as the masculine protector...

In short, women are deprived of different things, both because their lives on the outside and, therefore, their needs on the inside differ, and because the prison is run differently for them. Their culture responds to that difference. The generalization is still true, even though the results are quite different. (pp. 240–241)

Note that Becker is not suggesting, and nor am I, that there are no better generalizations, or even that this generalization will endure over time. He is suggesting, however (and so am I), that until a better generalization is proposed and shown to be warranted, this one usefully accounts for multiple, even disparate cases.

Becker's view of theoretical generalization from qualitative research is similar to Clifford Geertz's. In discussing cultural theory, Geertz (1973) writes:

> What generality it contrives to achieve grows out of the delicacy of its distinctions, not the sweep of its abstractions.... Studies do build on other studies, not in the sense that they take up where the others leave off, but in the sense that, better informed and better conceptualized, they plunge more deeply into the same things.... One can, and this in fact is how the field progresses conceptually, take a line of theoretical attack developed in connection with one exercise in ethnographic interpretation and employ it in another, pushing it forward to greater precision and broader relevance. (pp. 25–26)

Geertz continues,

> the theoretical framework in terms of which such an interpretation is made must be capable of continuing to yield defensible interpretations as new phenomena swim into view... If they cease being useful with respect to such [phenomena], they tend to stop being used and are more or less abandoned. If they continue being useful, throwing up new understanding, they are further elaborated and go on being used. (pp. 26–27)

There are many examples of emergent theoretical generalizations in existing qualitative studies in education research, and some of them appear to be strikingly enduring. Janet Schofield's (1989) study of a desegregating school in the United States provides a case in point. About this study, Schofield writes:

> After I observed extensively in varied areas of the school and interviewed a large number of students, it became apparent that the white children perceived blacks as something of a threat to their physical selves. Specifically, they complained about what they perceived as black roughness or aggressiveness.... In contrast, the black students perceived whites as a threat to their social selves. They complained about being ignored, avoided, and being treated as inferior by whites, whom they perceived to be stuck-up and prejudiced.... Such findings appear to me to be linked to the black and white students' situation in the larger society and to powerful historical and economic forces, not to special aspects of the school [she studied]. The consequences of these rather asymmetrical concerns may well play themselves out differently in different kinds of schools, but the existence of these

rather different but deeply held concerns may well be widespread. (p. 221)

Although Schofield's school ethnography was conducted in the 1970s, her conclusion that asymmetrical concerns differentiate the reactions of students from different racial groups in school and thereby maintain social distance between them is almost certainly true in U.S. schools today. Although particular concerns will vary from group to group, school to school and over time, the idea of asymmetry in racial group members' concerns about other groups is likely a pervasive pattern (a generic process?) in contemporary U.S. schooling. Had this idea been systematically pursued (and funded) in subsequent studies of schools, it might have been refined and developed into a theory of inter-group relations in school with broad generalizability to and usefulness in the U.S. context.

Signithia Fordham's (1996) book *Blacked Out* provides another example. She describes in detail how and why Black students in a Washington, D.C., high school struggle with the meaning of school work and achievement. Again, the particular actions and beliefs of the students in her study may not appear elsewhere, but the forms of resistance to schooling that she identified are likely to be widely applicable to minority students in U.S. schools. Norma Gonzalez (2001), in her book *I Am My Language*, describes how Mexican-American students in Tucson make sense of using both English and Spanish in their lives. Here again, the particular characteristics of the students probably do not generalize, but the emotional loading of language use that she identified is likely relevant to multilingual education wherever it takes place. Mary Metz (1990) describes an ideology of schooling that she discovered in a study of several (U.S.) midwestern high schools in the 1980s. At that time she found a common script for a legitimate U.S. school; today, 30 years later, that same script is evident in No Child Left Behind and other current policy initiatives (Metz, 2005). These patterns—of resistance, language loading, and taken-for-granted understandings of what makes a "real school"—are the kinds of (potentially) powerful theoretical generalizations that can and should result from qualitative research in education. They represent in some detail descriptions that capture, and recurring processes that explain (in part), major educational problems, including low achievement, weak second language skills, and sometimes excessive discipline, in the U.S. education context.

A discouraging fact about education research in the United States is that few qualitative researchers pursue investigations designed to test or extend the theoretical generalizability of other qualitative researchers' conclusions. Few even attempt this with their own work. Emergent mid-range theoretical generalizations, such as those exemplified in the research, just discussed would seem to be prime topics for qualitative education researchers who are interested in generalizability to pursue: Each generalization is based on extended and in-depth qualitative research in a particular local context, yet the conclusions from each constitute a plausible explanation for a pervasive phenomenon of U.S. schools and a point of departure for additional case studies and theoretical development. It is surprising to me that studies to extend the theoretical generalizability of qualitative research are so rare, especially when the contribution of such work to the field of education seems so great. Perhaps this lapse is in part a consequence of misguided discourse suggesting that one cannot generalize from qualitative research.[3]

Theoretical generalization from qualitative studies also has been discussed by researchers with critical and postmodern perspectives. Although profoundly skeptical of the way in which generalizations can be used to elide differences and promote essentializing stereotypes, these researchers nonetheless suggest that generalizations can be important. According to some critical researchers, reconstructive analyses of multivoiced texts can illuminate underlying theories (general assumptions) at work in the social and communicative connections that constitute everyday life. According to others, the ways in which some general concepts or theories, for example, environmental protection, global climate change, or academic achievement, become rallying points of convergence for dissimilar people and causes, are important objects for study and deconstruction. These ideas offer new areas of tremendous potential for theoretical generalization from qualitative research.

Conclusion

In 1990, Janet Schofield argued that there was a consensus emerging among qualitative researchers about generalizability:

> First of all, there is broad agreement that generalizability in the sense of producing laws that apply universally is not a useful standard or goal for qualitative research. In fact, most qualitative researchers would join Cronbach (1982) in arguing that this is not a useful or obtainable goal for any kind of research in the social sciences. Second, most researchers writing on generalizability in the qualitative tradition agree that their rejection of generalizability as a search for broadly applicable laws is not a rejection of the idea that studies in one situation can be used to speak to or to help form a judgment about other situations. (p. 208)

If this consensus was emerging in 1990, it seems to have dissipated since then, at least rhetorically in education research. The conventional "wisdom" about qualitative education research now seems to be that it cannot be generalized. In this chapter, I have argued that this view is wrong and misleading. Even those people whose writings have been used to establish this view do not necessarily believe or practice it.

For education researchers, most of whom want to improve education or understandings of education, it hardly seems likely that they would willingly devote their professional time and energy to studies that do not generalize in some way. Who really does not want to apply or infer from what has been learned in a study beyond the particular case? Fortunately, there are numerous, well-established ways of approaching generalization from qualitative research. In my view, theoretical generalization is an especially promising avenue for future qualitative research.

Notes

1. There is a difference between saying that one *cannot* generalize from qualitative studies and saying that one does not *intend to* generalize from them. Some qualitative researchers claim that they never intend to make generalizations. That is, they eschew theory and comparison and focus solely on the unique and contingent aspects of cases.
2. Many education researchers doing qualitative work claim that they are doing "grounded theory research." However, very few follow the methodological steps outlined by Glaser and Strauss and even fewer ever produce a grounded theory.
3. The lapse is also almost certainly due to a lack of funding or other incentives in the United States for this type of research and this type of theoretical development. Arguably, claims that qualitative researchers cannot make generalizations lend credence to those who argue against funding for qualitative research.

References

Becker, H. (1990). Generalizing from case studies. In E. W. Eisner & A. Peshkin (Eds.), *Qualitative inquiry in education* (pp. 233–242). New York: Teachers College Press.

Carspecken, P. (1996). *Critical ethnography in educational research: A theoretical and practical guide.* New York: Routledge.

Cronbach, L. (1975). Beyond the two disciplines of scientific psychology. *American Psychologist, 30,* 116–127.

Davies, C. (1999). *Reflexive ethnography: A guide to researching selves and others.* London: Routledge.

Denzin, N. (1989). *The research act: A theoretical introduction to sociological methods.* New York: McGraw Hill.

Ercikan, K., & Roth, W-M. (2006). What good is polarizing research into qualitative and quantitative? *Educational Researcher, 35*(5), 14–23.

Erickson, F. (1986). Qualitative methods. In M. Wittrock (Ed.), *Handbook of research on teaching* (pp. 119–161). New York: Macmillan.

Fordham, S. (1996). *Blacked out: Dilemmas of race, identity, and success at Capital High.* Chicago: University of Chicago Press.

Geertz, C. (1973). *The interpretation of cultures.* New York: Basic Books.

Glaser, B., & Strauss, A. (1967). *The discovery of grounded theory.* Chicago: Aldine.

Gonzalez, N. (2001). *I am my language: Discourses of women and children in the borderlands.* Tucson: University of Arizona Press.

Kaplan, A. (1964). *The conduct of inquiry.* San Francisco: Chandler.

Kilbourn, B. (2006). The qualitative doctoral dissertation proposal. *Teachers College Record, 108,* 529–576.

Lichtman, M. (2006). *Qualitative research in education: A user's guide.* Thousand Oaks, CA: Sage.

Lincoln, Y., & Guba, E. (1985). *Naturalistic inquiry.* Beverly Hills, CA: Sage.

Lindesmith, A. (1947). *Opiate addiction.* Bloomington, IN: Principia Press.

Maxwell, J. (2005). *Qualitative research design: An interactive approach* (2nd ed.). Thousand Oaks, CA: Sage.

Merriam, S. (1998). *Qualitative research and case study applications in education.* San Francisco: Jossey-Bass.

Metz, M. (1990). Real school: A universal drama amid disparate experience. In D. Mitchell & M. Goertz (Eds.), *Educational politics for the new century* (pp. 75–91). Philadelphia: Falmer Press.

Metz, M. (2005). *NCLB as a tool to build the myth of a single "American" school system.* Paper delivered to the American Sociological Association, August 12, 2005.

Schofield, J. (1989). *Black and white in school: Trust, tension, or tolerance?* New York: Teachers College Press.

Schofield, J. (1990). Increasing the generalizability of qualitative research. In E. Eisner & A. Peshkin (Eds.), *Qualitative inquiry in education: The continuing debate* (pp. 201–232). New York: Teachers College Press.

Wolcott, H. (2005). *The art of fieldwork* (2nd ed.). Walnut Creek, CA: Altamira Press.

Yin, R. (2005). *Case study research: Design and methods* (3rd ed.). Thousand Oaks, CA: Sage.

Chapter 5

On Qualitative and Quantitative Reasoning in Validity

Robert J. Mislevy, Pamela A. Moss, and James P. Gee

Wer fremde Sprachen nicht kennt, weiß nichts von seiner eigenen. (Those who know no foreign language know nothing of their own.)
Johann Wolfgang von Goethe

Prologue

Beginning in the fall of 2001, the Spencer Foundation sponsored an interdisciplinary initiative seeking to expand the foundations of educational assessment. In a series of meetings and essays, the "Idea of Testing" Project (IOT) addressed the theories and methods through which educational assessment is conceptualized, practiced, and evaluated. The project organizers were Pamela Moss (University of Michigan), Diana Pullin (Boston College), James Gee (University of Wisconsin), and Edward Haertel (Stanford University). The working group additionally included King Beach (Florida State University), James Greeno (University of Pittsburgh and Stanford University), Carol Lee (Northwestern University), Hugh (Bud) Mehan (University of California, San Diego), Robert Mislevy (University of Maryland), Fritz Mosher (consultant to the Spencer Foundation), and Lauren Young (Spencer Foundation). The focus of the conversations was the intersection between assessment and opportunity to learn, with particular attention to the implications of a situative/sociocultural perspective on learning for the practice of assessment.

This chapter grows from the authors' sidebar conversations at the Idea of Testing meetings, on the topics of validity and generalization. These are issues of central interest to all three of us, each approaching them from our own personal histories and disciplinary perspectives. Our perspectives invoke the qualitative/quantitative dichotomy on which the present volume intends to shed light. We note, for example, Gee's characterization of validity in discourse analysis, Mislevy's discussion of validity as a psychometric principle, and Moss's contrast between interpretative and statistical approaches in a chapter on validity in educational assessment.

These disciplinary perspectives are "marked by what is attended to and how it is thought about;... by the kinds of problems they address, the solutions they can conceive, and the methods by which they proceed; by the 'generative principles' (Greeno, 1989) through which experts come to reason in a domain. They are also marked by what is not emphasized, indeed what is ignored" (Mislevy, 2006, p. 269). Fulfilling aspirations of IOT, our cross-disciplinary conversations proved particularly helpful in bringing out assumptions that are so deeply ingrained as to remain non-verbalized within disciplinary practice, and thwart understanding across disciplines. We discovered fundamental commonalities under terminologies and techniques that differed on the surface, and thereby brought fundamental differences more sharply into focus.

What follows is cast as dialogue. It reflects bits of real conversations and correspondence in which we proposed and wrestled with assessment issues from our distinctive points of view. However, as we write today, it unavoidably incorporates insights we gained as the conversations proceeded. We offer the reader improved coherence, at the loss of watching us struggle through cross-talk to identify, if not overcome, our disciplinary prejudices—prejudices, that is, in Gadamer's (1994) nonpejorative sense of the word: The concepts and dispositions we bring to any new situation, from which new understandings necessarily begin.

The discussion focuses on one important aspect of the longstanding and generally unproductive debate Ercikan and Roth explored in their article "What Good is Polarizing Research into Qualitative and Quantitative?" We look more closely at one important facet of the debate, namely validity, focusing on assessment and noting implications for generalization along the way. We point out the value of having different methods for different grain sizes of reality, and note how patterns at lower levels of reality (closer to the individual) give meaning to patterns at high levels (groups and institutions). To make our point, we discuss cases from discourse analysis, standardized reading tests, and classroom-level investigations of middle-school mathematics.

While the focus of our conversation is on the validity of assessment-based inferences or interpretations, we note that *generalizations are inferences*. Anytime an interpretation reaches beyond the particular circumstances, situations, or people studied at one point in time to support an interpretation, decision or action involving different circumstances, situations, or people, at different points in time, generalization is involved. Thus, inferences based on standardized forms of assessment (and related validity evidence) always entail generalizations. We note further that the very meaning of the words we use, built of multiple concrete experiences of their use, entails generalizations (e.g., inferences about what different specific situations have in common). (On this point of words as generalizations indexing experiences see also chapters 7 and 11 of this volume.)

Thus, much of what we say about the validity of interpretations or inferences can be extended to the validity of generalizations.

Conversation about Validity

MISLEVY: My research interests nowadays center on the design and analysis of assessments from the perspective of evidentiary arguments—the challenge of making inferences about what students know and can do in what kinds of situations, based on observing what they say, do, or make in a handful of particular situations. This work itself arose from a cross-disciplinary perspective. Familiar test-development and analytic methodologies were falling short for the challenges posed by new forms of assessment, such as computer-based simulations and portfolio assessments. For my colleagues and me, David Schum's (1994) work on evidentiary reasoning cracked the nut. His scholarly approach to evidentiary reasoning integrates insights from philosophy, jurisprudence, statistics, science, and psychology to lay out concepts and language that help workers in any domain understand recurring evidentiary problems and ways of tackling them—adapting them to the kinds of inferences in a particular domain, to be sure, with the forms of evidence, the explanatory principles, and the evidentiary standards of a community.

The structure sketched as Figure 5.1 seemed to us to be a useful way to elucidate the arguments that underlie familiar forms of testing, and to think about new forms as well. Figure 5.1 actually depicts two arguments, the assessment design argument per se in the lower dashed rectangle and an assessment use argument in the upper rectangle (after Bachman, 2003; see also chapter 7). Our attention focuses on the assessment argument, but including the use argument emphasizes that assessment cannot be understood apart from context and use. Assessment claims are shown in the center of the figure, as both the outcome of the assessment argument and data for the use argument. The terms in which they are cast connect our thinking about what is observed in assessment settings and about educational ends such as guiding and evaluating learning. We seek to ground the claim with data. At the bottom of Figure 5.1 is a student's action in a situation: The student says, does, or makes something, possibly extending over time, possibly interacting with others. It is interpretations of the actions that constitute data in an assessment argument. Data include (a) aspects of the situation in which the person is acting, (b) aspects of the person's actions in the situation, and (c) other information about the person's history or relationship to the observational situation that may be important to understand the person's action in the situation.

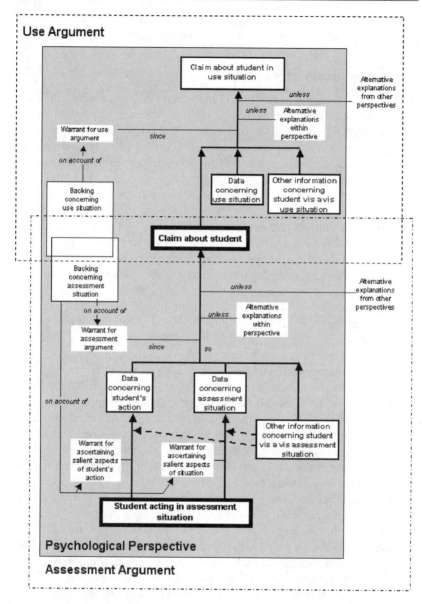

Figure 5.1 Structure for assessment arguments. Lower rectangle shows assessment argument proper; upper rectangle shows assessment use argument. They share psychological perspective, backing, and claim about student based on assessment.

A psychological perspective determines the nature of every element in an assessment argument, and the rationale that orchestrates them: the kinds of things one might say concerning students (claims), what kinds of things one wants to see in what kinds of situations (data), and the larger patterns or generalizations relationships, based on theory or experience, that justify reasoning from one to the other (warrants). Although quantitative models are often laid over this structure to detail strength of evidence about individuals or to critique the fit of these models, the underlying rationale and the substantive arguments that ground it are largely qualitative.

Figure 5.1 does not say anything about the nature of the intended inference about students or data, or about just how one would synthesize evidence from complex performances or multiple observations. What's more, Figure 5.1 is silent about a number of other features of tests in the way we generally think about them, such as whether all or parts of an argument are preconstructed as opposed to custom built; which parts might stay the same in what ways, and which might differ, for assessing different students; the relationships of the rationales and activities to learning; and the way an assessment is, or is not, contextualized in educative and social systems. It doesn't say anything about the use of probability-based reasoning, which lies at the heart of contemporary psychometrics.[1] (I will say more about this later.) We do however have strong preconceptions about these matters from years of experience with the assessment practices we are used to, and the psychological perspectives that underlie them. But I have come to believe the argument structure can be used for assessments cast in different psychological perspectives, leading sometimes to assessments that might look very different on the surface.

I arrived at IOT fresh off the National Research Council's Foundations of Assessment committee, chaired by Jim Pellegrino and Bob Glaser. The National Science Foundation charged that committee with reviewing advances in the cognitive and measurement sciences, as well as early work done in the intersection between the two disciplines, and considering the implications for reshaping educational assessment. Whereas the committee did address developmental, situated, and social aspects of learning, it highlighted the ways that individuals acquire, organize, and use knowledge. There is a common belief about psychometrics by many psychologists with this bent: "Psychometrics might work okay for assessment cast in trait and behavioral perspectives, but it can't address the inferences that are important from a cognitive point of view."

In trait and behavioral psychology, their argument would continue, people are characterized by numbers, and similar behaviors in the same situations justify similar inferences about them in these terms. Such a limitation would miss the key role of knowledge structures for perception, understanding, and planning, for action in situations, and for future learning. An important outcome of the Foundations committee's work was to disentangle the psychological assumptions of standard practices—the surface structures—from the more fundamental principles of evidentiary reasoning, à la Schum, that underlie those practices; then to show how those principles, with new or reinterpreted probability models, could be brought to bear on the inferential problems of assessments created from a cognitive perspective. To my mind, this is the principal contribution of the committee's volume Knowing What Student Know (KWSK; NRC, 2001).

IOT was sparked in part by a desire to go beyond KWSK, to incorporate the nature of knowledge as seen from situative and sociocultural perspectives. The organizers' hope was to

> encourage an even broader multidisciplinary discourse community in the sort of collaborative envisioning [KWSK] illustrates and promotes. By casting a wider disciplinary net—to include sociocultural and situated perspectives from within anthropology, linguistics, sociology, and psychology—we hope to (begin to) problematize a wider range of assumptions about assessment and to imagine a wider range of alternative practices. (Moss, Pullin, Gee, & Haertel, 2005, p. 66)

There is a common belief about psychometrics by many psychologists with this bent: "Psychometrics might work okay for assessment cast in trait, behavioral, and cognitive perspectives, but it can't address the inferences that are important from a situative/sociocultural point of view."

Maybe, maybe not. Finding out requires explicating the core ideas of a situative/sociocultural perspective on learning in such a way as to understand their implications for assessment arguments along the lines of Figure 5.1: Just what the targets of inference might be, the kinds of observations in the kinds of situations that might support them, and the warrants that would connect them. If indeed it would be possible to cast such arguments in this form, could insights and machinery from assessment design and analysis cast under trait, behavioral, and now cognitive perspectives would prove useful?

The first challenge of a cross-disciplinary project is learning how to talk with one another. This can be hard when some of the words we use are different; the words one discipline uses can address concepts or patterns that lie outside the focus of the other disciplines. It can be hard when other words are the same, but they do not mean the same thing—they derive their meanings to workers from different traditions in no small part through their connections to the central concepts and the principles of the different disciplines. We begin with a lack of knowledge all around, filled in by simplifications and misconceptions—cartoon versions of psychometrics or situated cognition. We are all ignorant, as Will Rogers famously said, just about different subjects.

I am hopeful. The IOT meetings, and the forthcoming volume they instigated, ended up focusing on the meaning of "opportunity to learn" from a situative/sociocultural perspective, as a necessary precursor to understanding assessment as it is now and how it might evolve to fit an evolving view of learning. The discussions and the readings they sparked have surely enriched my understanding in ways I discuss in the next paragraph, in my next turn of talk, and my chapter in the IOT volume (Mislevy, 2008). They've helped me see ways that the conception of assessment can be expanded, and ways that insights from the psychometric tradition can be leveraged in doing so. I am further encouraged to recognize what appear to be (from my current understanding, at any rate) some fundamental commonalities hidden beneath disparate practices.

For example, I resonated with Jim's discussion on what constitutes validity in discourse analysis—a situated, non-standardized, qualitative activity about as far from the common notion of testing as we might find. Jim describes 26 questions a researcher might bring to bear in an analysis of, say, a conversation, concerning considerations such as semiotic building, world building, and relationship-building. Validity arises, he maintains, from convergence, agreement, coverage, and linguistic details. "Why does this constitute validity? Because it is highly improbable that a good many answers to twenty-six different questions, the perspectives of different 'inside' and 'outside' observers, additional data sets, and the judgments of 'native speakers' and/or linguists will converge unless there is good reason to trust the analysis" (pp. 113–114). At a higher level, this way of thinking matches exactly the kinds of probability-based reasoning that characterizes the work of the most thoughtful statisticians, as illustrated for example in Mosteller and Wallace's (1964) classic investigation of the authorship of the disputed Federalist papers. Applied thoughtfully to the construction, use, and analysis of educational assessments, in (not necessarily familiar) ways that suit the purposes, contexts, substance, and methods of those assessments, validity of inferences in assessment is fundamentally the same stuff as validity in discourse analysis.

GEE: The IOT project was designed, as Bob says, to cast a wide disciplinary net by including sociocultural and situated perspectives alongside psychological and psychometric ones in a discussion of assessment. Bob points out that it is "a common belief about psychometrics by many psychologists of this [situative/sociocultural] bent that psychometrics might work okay for assessment cast in trait, behavioral, and cognitive perspectives, but it cannot address the inferences that are important from a situative/sociocultural point of view." His view: "Maybe, maybe not," since "[f]inding out requires explicating the core ideas of a situative/sociocultural perspective on learning in such a way as to understand their implications for assessment arguments."

There are problems with meeting Bob's demand that we explicate the core ideas of a situative/sociocultural perspective so as to understand implications for assessment arguments. First, there are a number of different sociocultural and situative perspectives—and, in fact, sociocultural people tend not to be psychologists and situative people often are. Such approaches have rarely if ever been systematically compared.

Second, sociocultural work, in particular, has been cut off enough from psychometric and assessment issues that it has rarely, if ever, been formulated with a focus on "implications for assessment arguments." In fact, some sociocultural people would deny any meaningful form of significance to standard forms of testing based on, at least, trait and behavioral psychological perspectives, and even, in some cases, cognitive ones.

Finally, sociocultural and situative perspectives are often developed at more specific levels (levels of actual practices and activities) than are psychometric perspectives, which tend to be more general and abstract, so that comparison is difficult. It can be hard to tell, at times, whether problems of comparison are just with levels of abstraction or genuine deep-rooted disagreements.

Let me start here, then, with just some of my own reflections (as a sociolinguist and discourse analyst) on a sociocultural-situative perspective, combing the sociocultural and situative in ways that may be more tension-filled for some others than they are for me. I will state some implications for arguments about assessment and uses of assessments, but they will not be, at this juncture, explicit enough to fulfill Bob's demand.

Consider that a girl named Janie has taken a standardized reading test on a given day. The test is the type that gives short passages and asks questions about the passages, some of which are about important topical themes in the passages and others of which are about more minor or backgrounded matters in the passage. So here we have one specific kid, one certain day, one type of test. The way we typically look at such a situation is to conclude that we have learned something about Janie and her "reading skill." A sociocultural-situated perspective looks at the situation somewhat differently.

Many years ago I used to fish for trout in Northern California streams when they were still wilderness sites. I remember fishermen discussing what bait or lure to use on a given day given the water's conditions, the other food available in the river, the time of day, the season, and the weather. Undoubtedly the matter was influenced, as well, by the condition and growth cycle of each fish. So, say, I caught "Herman," a brook trout, with a fly lure on Tuesday, June 4th. I could not fairly conclude that Herman "likes fly lures," let alone that all trout will. I can only conclude that at that point amidst all the complex river, ecological, trout, and Herman conditions, Herman attacked a fly lure. Every fisherman knows that I can release Herman and he will shun a fly lure for a worm the very next week.

Janie is not less complex than Herman. What if we suggest, then, that Janie's case is not that much different from Herman's? What if we see the reading test as just like a piece of bait that caught Janie at that time and place? Why are we so tempted to look at Janie outside her river, but not Herman? What if we conclude that Janie's score on the test is not telling us anything about Janie per se, but about Janie as she swims down a very complex stream? In the case of both Herman and Janie this looks like a council of despair, because it now looks like we cannot conclude anything general at all—just that Herman attacked a fly lure on a given day and Janie failed a reading test on another day. But that is true only if we look at Herman and Janie as single points that at each time and place bear all their essential traits and sit ready to be assessed and understood as is. This is to take what linguists call a synchronic view of Herman and Janie. But there is another possible view.

We also can take what linguists call a diachronic view of Herman and Janie. Rather than viewing them as single points, always "true" to their "nature," we can view them as trajectories through times and spaces, trajectories that bear traits that are products of both the times and space Herman and Janie are in when we "test" them and the times and spaces through which they have moved to get there, traits that may change as they swim on. These times and spaces are, in turn, to be understood in terms of interactions Herman and Janie have had with other fish/people and all aspects of their environments in those times and spaces.

On this view we do not want to—or even believe we can—understand "Janie" or "Herman" in and by themselves. What we can do is seek to understand what the reading test or the fly lure test tells us about Janie's trajectory or Herman's, and for this we will need more samples, with different tests/bait across different times and spaces. We will need, as well, to build up in our minds a model of Janie's or Herman's diachronic interactions across space and time relevant to reading (for Janie) and feeding (for Herman). Any test result must be placed within this model to be truly meaningful (see also chapter 7). If we get really good, we might build up models not of Janie or Herman, but of people "like Janie" and fish "like Herman." But, of course, this is tricky, because, after all, who are people "like Janie" (girls? fourth-grade girls? fourth graders? African Americans? middle class? Etc.) or fish like "Herman" (trout? brook trout? California brook trout? young fish? fish in a crowded river? Etc.). Now we need a model of models.

So on such a diachronic and modeling approach, imagine a given reading test tells us that a first-grade Janie and a first-grade Johnnie are both weak on decoding skills. Nonetheless, when this result is placed within their trajectories, trajectories of children "like them," and model developmental reading trajectories, it may mean quite different things in regard to Janie than it does in regard to Johnnie. For instance, what was Janie's earlier emergent literacy situation at home before starting school, what was Johnnie's? This is to ask about one earlier time and place that affects and renders meaningful in a certain way a later time and place, the one at which we tested. There are quite different predictions we can make about Janie's and Johnnie's future times and places in regard to reading, based on the links (interactions) between these other two (early emergent literacy, later decoding skill on a given type of test). There are many other times and places that need to be considered in our model, as well.

With some of our current reading assessments, built on taking Janie and Johnnie as units storing traits or abilities decontextualized from their streams, we keep getting better scores—Janie and Johnnie keep getting better at passing decoding tests—but the reading gap between black and white children does not close and many children who passed such tests early on turn out not to be able to read to learn school content later on—the phenomenon of the well-known "fourth-grade slump." If children and classes of children were seen as trajectories and classes of trajectories, and we studied these (with lots of lines with different sorts of bait all along the river all through the years) and how they tend to change in response to different kinds of learning experiences, we might have a picture (model) that would lead to gap closing and life-long reading for learning. This is so because we would see reading in a multifaceted way that allowed interventions customized to people, times, places, and situations where they would have the most leverage. It would not be a matter of the same pill for everyone, but different medicine for different people in different situations and stages of life.

So what makes (even true) claims about Herman or Janie "valid"? Any claim about Herman or Janie may be true but pretty meaningless or misleading. The fly lure caught Herman, sure enough, but what if it actually hooked him by accident as he was trying to catch a worm floating by? Janie failed the third-grade reading test, but what if she went home and played Pokemon, a video game that requires sixth-grade reading? So what makes a claim from a test we have given Herman or Janie "valid," something we should trust enough to use, at least for some purposes? In my view, the claim is valid if and only if the model on which it was based and within which it makes sense is valid. Much better to ask what makes models valid.

So what would make a model of Herman's feeding trajectory through spaces and times valid? What would make a model of Brook Trout's trajectories valid? What would make a model of Janie's reading trajectory through spaces and times valid? What would make a model of third graders' trajectories valid? This is a tough question, because a model is by definition a simplification for certain purposes—so it is always possible there are different but better models for the same purposes or different ones (ones which, perhaps, should have been our purposes in the first place).

I clearly am not going to tell you what makes a model valid, since this is, in fact, akin to the whole question of what makes a theory valid and that question takes up much of the philosophy of science. But a model's validity has something to do with the fact that it "works," it leads us to catch fish or do something useful with or for Janie and her reading. But good fishermen are always seeking new and better models, because they want to catch more and bigger fish. We hope good educators are always seeking new and better models because they want to help Janie and other children more and more.

A sociocultural-situated view of Janie—akin to an ecological view of Herman—sees Janie and other human actors as only parts of bigger pictures. The grammar of our language is built on a pattern of ACTOR (Subject) ACTS (VERB) on SOMETHING (Object) as in "Janie failed the reading test" or "I caught Herman." A sociocultural-situated view holds that this grammar is mistaken. Results or outcomes flow from interactions and the history of interactions among actors; situations they are in; activities in which they are engaged; their interpretations of those situations and activities and everything in them; interactions and forms of participation with other actors; mediating devices (objects, tools, technologies) they are using within those situations; and the spaces within which and the times at which interactions take place. Call this mess a "system," some people call it an "activity system" or an "actor-actant network." Thus, the grammar of our educational research and assessment ought to be not ACTOR ACTS on SOMETHING, but something like "RESULT x FLOWED from SYSTEM Y. Janie is out there in the system, totally integrated with it moment-by-moment, just like Herman in his stream. So are all the Janies and all the Hermans. And, no, we cannot just cancel out all the streams and stream conditions, paying attention only to Herman, and successfully bait Herman.

The interpretation part ("their interpretations of those situations and activities and everything in them") here is where Janie most differs from Herman. Interpretations are always social and cultural, that is, flow from people's participation in social and cultural affiliations. In fact, as far as assessments go, interpretation is important at two levels, the level of the researcher and the level of the assessed person. What does "reading" mean to the test maker as far as his or her test is concerned? What does it mean to Janie when she takes the test? There is a problem if the test maker thinks "reading," as far as the test goes, means "being able to draw meaning from print," but the test actually only supports a meaning of being able to decode print and give literal dictionary like meanings to words, meanings far short of the sort of those that would support comprehension. There is a problem, too, if Janie, or lots of Janies, taking the test, thinks reading for this test means "relate the texts to your understanding of the world" and the test has been designed explicitly to make this view of reading fail, but has never told Janie the test is built on a different interpretation of "reading" than hers.

So our models of Janie or Janies for assessment must model complex systems and interpretations within them. A large task indeed, calling for the mixture of several different disciples. Truth in lending would require, I would argue, that every test (and claim) for that matter be always accompanied by the (trajectory) model on which it is based and in terms of which it will be interpreted with a clear indication of how to interpret any score or scores (of any sort) as statements interpreted against the model. I do remember some fishing lure companies that gave you spiffy brochures that spelled out their whole theory of fishing. I have not seen such spiffy brochures with a lot of tests these days. But then, alas, some of the brochures turned out to be pure hype, since Herman almost always got away.

Imagine a system that did not just assign a reading score to Janie, but showed how what Janie did on a given reading test on a given day could be placed as but one dot within a multidimensional space of (a model of) Janie's reading, literacy, and learning trajectory, as well as within a multidimensional space of (models of) such trajectories for children "like Janie" and other sorts of children. Within such a perspective we would have to realize, as well, that the reading test Janie took was itself an event (a literacy event) in her trajectory—it actually cannot rise above the whole trajectory and "judge" it. It can only be seen as itself one moment of Janie's swim down the reading, literacy, and learning stream, a lure we threw in the water at one point of time and space, and now an event for Janie to deal with.

MOSS: Bob has focused our dialogue about validity initially on the kinds of inferences that are valued in psychological and sociocultural domains of discourse. This seems a fruitful place to begin to address his broader questions about whether there are transdomain principles of validity and whether psychometrics and probability based reasoning can play a role in warranting inferences that are valued by those who hold sociocultural perspectives. I should note that I am at least equally interested in the converse of these questions (as I imagine Jim and Bob are too): Whether sociocultural research practices can play a role in warranting (which includes challenging) inferences valued by psychologists and psychometricians and whether there are fundamental differences in approaches to validity from which each perspective can learn. I write as someone who was educated in the discourse of (applied) educational measurement but who has been working for some time within the interpretive social sciences—to learn the discourses of hermeneutics and more recently of sociocultural studies—to see what insights and challenges they hold for educational measurement and to develop a "multi-discourse" practice of educational assessment.

Continuing with our discussion about inferences: In Bob's first turn of talk, he characterizes the target of inferences in his own research agenda on evidentiary arguments as "making inferences about what students know and can do in what kinds of situations, based on observing what they say, do, or make in a handful of particular situations" and he offers Figure 5.1 as a generalized representation of an evidentiary argument that is, arguably, congenial to multiple psychological perspectives. To consider whether sociocultural inferences and arguments might be cast in a similar form, he then asks "what the targets of inference might be, the kinds of observations in the kinds of situations that might support them, and the warrants that would connect them." Jim, after locating his own perspective as only one within set of sometimes competing discourses subsumed by the word "sociocultural," suggests that inferences about "students," per se, are problematic; rather, we need to focus on the relationship between students and their environments. So what does this say about targets of inference? Jim suggests that appropriate targets of inferences might be: (a) models of students' "trajectories" through time and space, recognizing that an inference at one point in time must be interpreted in light of knowledge about students' prior experiences; (b) models of these models, that would let us draw inferences—make generalization or predictions—about students like the ones whose learning we are studying; and ultimately (c) theories of the complex and dynamic activity systems of which students are a part. This suggests to me that Figure 5.1 itself would be a part of the target of inference about an activity system, as assessments and the practices that surround them are integral parts of such systems. Figure 5.1 would then be conceptualized as one of the many "tools" used within an activity system that shapes actors' understandings and actions. What are the implications of this perspective for the practice of assessment and for our understandings of validity?

Two important questions that have not yet been foregrounded in the dialogue about validity—although they are there in the background—are who is making the inferences and why are they making them? So far, the dialogue seems to focus, primarily, on the validity of interpretations, models, and theories that are intended to have some broader relevance in multiple educational contexts or to contribute to the understanding of a field. This is the work of science or other professions of inquirers. A particular validity interest I have is in how those arguably generalizable interpretations, models, theories are taken up in local contexts by the actors who use them to address their own questions and make their own interpretations, decisions, and actions. As Jim's discussion of Herman and Janie illustrates, generalizable interpretations, models and theories (e.g., test scores and their presumptive interpretations, theories of fishing or teaching/learning reading) are always put to work in particular situations with particular people. How they are put to work depends on the sense people can make of them (including whether they attend to them at all), the resources people use to interpret them, the locally relevant questions they provoke or provide evidence for, the other evidence brought to bear, the local supports/constraints for making meaningful interpretations, and so on. A robust theory of validity needs to be able to take situated and dynamic interpretations into account as well as interpretations that are the recorded result of extended inquiry. This is not to argue against our focus on the validity of generalizing interpretations/theories/models (which can and should provide a crucial piece of background against which educators' interpretations are drawn), it is simply to argue that it tells only one important part of the story that theories of validity and generalization need to address.

To provide a more concrete example, consider Magdalene Lampert's (2001) representation of the questions or "problems" she needs address, the kinds of evidence she attends to, and the nature of the interpretations she draws in teaching mathematics to fifth graders. In conceptualizing her problem space, Lampert uses the productive metaphor of a camera lens shifting focus and zooming in and out. This allows her to represent "the problems of practice that a teacher needs to work on in a particular moment … [along with] the problems of practice that are addressed in teaching a lesson or a unit or a year" (pp. 2–3). Throughout her text, we see how she uses evidence to address different sorts of problems on different time scales: to make decisions about what to do next in her interactions with students, to plan lessons, to support them in becoming the kinds of students inclined to collaborate and to reason about mathematical ideas, and to take stock of and inform students and their parents about their accomplishments.

For instance, Lampert describes her questions about students' capacity while preparing for a series of lessons in late September on how and when to use multiplication and division in solving problems. The decision she is facing is about "where to set students down in the mathematical space":

> It would help to know whether any of my students could already multiply large numbers using the conventional procedure. It would help to know if anyone understood that multiplication is about groups of groups of groups, no matter how big the numbers. It would help to know if anyone would be disposed to work independently in ways that were reasonable and if anyone would be likely to focus more on simply producing answers. (p. 108)

In addressing this problem, Lampert draws on a wide range of evidence: Her journaled observations of her students began the first day they entered her classroom. She noted that Enoyat, who was born in Sudan, had "introduced himself in fluent English" and had responded "no" when asked if there was anything in particular he hoped to study. In her journal, she recorded, for the entire class, the names of students who were very active, active, or somewhat active in class discussion that day, listing Enoyat in the "somewhat active" column. She also described what she learned from a review of the standardized test responses of these students from the previous year.

Here, her observations are based not on overall scores but on the ways in which students worked on the problems.

She noted, for instance, that Enoyat, like some other students in the class,

> had not yet made the transition from being able to multiply by a one-digit number to being able to multiply by a two-digit numbers. She noted "a few students produced correct answer to all multiplications by using the conventional procedures, but it was hard to tell from these calculations what they understood about the meaning of the numbers or the procedure. (p. 116)

The mixture of addition and multiplication in the work of these students suggested that the idea of multiplication as "groups of groups" was not guiding their work. Journal entries on subsequent days listed Enoyat as one of the students who did not participate in class discussion but who was "working away in a seriously strategic manner." She explains to her readers that "seriously strategic" on that day meant using patterns and relationship to figure out solutions to the problem, which suggested to her that "they had some disposition to think that mathematics was supposed to make sense and that they were competent to figure things out they had not been told how to do" (p. 112).

A later journal entry listed Enoyat as one of the students who was "not making abstract deduction from the evidence, but who had arranged the information to show a pattern" (p. 112). These observations are based on what students wrote in their notebooks and on what she had observed from her conversations with them and her observations of their conversations with one another. She noted that when Tyrone first joined the class later in September and was seated next to Enoyat, the two were working productively together, and she recorded later in her journal, that Tyrone had picked up the connection between addition and multiplication from Enoyat but had not taken into account the constraints of the numbers in the problem. Thus we see her attend to students' strategies in solving problems— from the previous year's standardized test, from their notebooks, from their talk with her and each others as recorded in her journal; we see her attend to how students interacted with her, with the material, and with one another; and we see her use her daily journal to record observations sometimes by grouping students according to how they approached a problem or interacted with her and the class, sometimes by recording a particularly relevant point about a particular child. This sort of information—along with what she knew from coursework, reading, her own work with the problems, and previous experience with fifth graders—helped her make decisions about what problems to select and how to support students' dispositions to reason and collaborate. Her attention to evidence in solving a teaching "problem" was routinely situated in the ongoing interaction of which it was a part, cumulative in the sense of drawing on other available evidence (fitting this piece of evidence into her evolving understanding of students' learning), and anticipatory in the sense of considering how her next move was likely to affect students' learning. Her interpretations and actions were also, of course, informed by a robust theory about a productive activity system for teaching mathematics to children.

Lampert depicts her problem space in a series of figures, one set of which are depicted in Figure 5.2, which illustrate the ways in which the inferences she needs to draw vary by grain size and time scale.

She depicts a primary relationship among a teacher, some content, a student, and the student's relationship with the content ("studying") (Figure 5.2a), expanded to include relationships with and among multiple students in small and whole groups (Figure 5.2b), which change over time (Figure 5.2c), and across different classes of students (Figure 5.2d). The figures in her text become even more complicated as she unpacks "content" and its relationship with different students and depicts the various influences from outside the classroom on teacher, students, and content. Vis-à-vis Bob's Figure 5.1, we might interpret these figures as representing targets of inference, or the contexts within which particular inferences are made, or the aspects of the system about which evidence is needed to support an interpretation.

Whereas the focus of this example has been on the teacher as interpreter, an analogy may be easily drawn to the problems or issues facing professionals in other contexts. Many of the problems are of the "what do I/we do next?" variety, albeit at quite different levels of scale. What does this suggest about what a theory of validity needs to accomplish? My colleagues and I tried our hand at sketching an answer informed by the discourses of hermeneutics[2] and sociocultural studies (Moss, Girard, & Haniford, 2006):

> What's needed is a flexible approach to validity that begins with the questions that are being asked; that can develop, analyze, and integrate multiple types of evidence at different levels of scale; that is dynamic in the sense that questions, available evidence, and interpretations can evolve dialectically as inquirers learn from their inquiry *and* that allows attention to the antecedents and anticipated and actual consequents of their interpretations, decisions and actions....

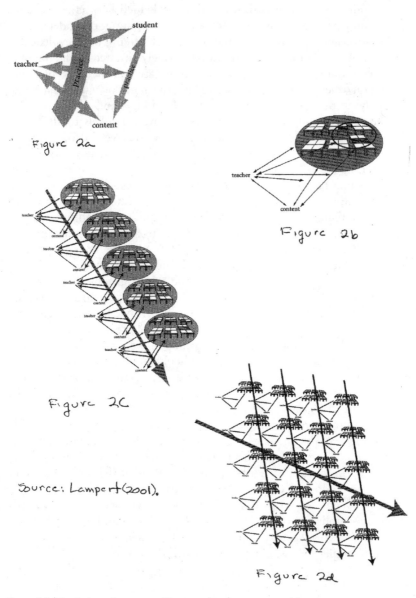

Figure 5.2 Depiction of aspects of Lampert's assessment problem space.

We also need to recognize that not all [interpretations, decisions, or action] should or can be subjected to an explicit reflection on or documentation of their validity—in fact most ... are of this variety. Much that might be called assessment is simply a routine part of social interaction in a learning environment. Given this, we need a set of conceptual tools that can be applied, explicitly when needed, but that can also provide actors with adequate information and rules of thumb to shape their daily practice. Validity theory should also speak to the meta-issue of how learning environments are resourced—with knowledgeable people, material and conceptual tools, norms and routines, and evolving information about learning—to support sound evidence-based [interpretations, decisions and actions] when explicit inquiry is not possible. It should speak to the issues of how assessment is supporting the professionals' learning to support students' learning and one another's learning.

Finally, we need to recognize that assessment practices do far more than provide information, they shape people's understanding about what is important to learn, what learning is, and who learners are. Thus any validity theory needs to take into account the way in which assessment functions as part of—shaping and shaped by—the local learning environment and its learners. (p. 111)

Pulling together ideas from across our turns of talk, I see a potentially productive synergy in how we might think about theories of validity. We need to be able to address the validity of inferences at various levels of scale: This includes theories of activity systems, especially those that "work" in enhancing students' learning. It also includes understandings of how their actors develop well-warranted interpretations, decisions and actions as a routine part of their work. And this in turn includes the meanings actors' give to existing artifacts that have been the focus of validity inquiry, like test scores, or the interpretive process depicted in Figure 5.1, or models of learning and theories of activity systems to which they have access.

MISLEVY: Pamela describes "Magdalene Lampert's (2001) ... use [of] the productive metaphor of a camera lens shifting focus and zooming in and out." The metaphor is consistent with her conception of "a flexible approach to validity that begins with the questions that are being asked; that can develop, analyze, and integrate multiple types of evidence at different levels of scale; that is dynamic in the sense that questions, available evidence, and interpretations can evolve dialectically as inquirers learn from their inquiry and that allows attention to the antecedents and anticipated and actual consequences of their interpretations, decisions and actions..."

I would suggest that the metaphor is also consistent with an idealized or best case view of statistical modeling, of which psychometric methods and models are a special case. The models we use in large- and medium-scale assessment are focused at a scale that is coarser than discourse analysis or cognitive task analysis—less contextual-ized, less sensitive to patterns and explanations of actions of indi-viduals within situations. They are correspondingly better suited to exploring patterns and explanations of selected aspects of phenom-ena across many individuals and many situations. "Variables" are the boundary objects: aspects of actions, situations, and individuals' propensities toward actions in kinds of situations that are what gets identified and transported from each of many unique individual's actions within situations. "Boundary object" is one way in which to manage the tension in scientific research between diverse viewpoints of those involved (including those using and providing the informa-tion) and the need for generalizable findings. As Star and Griesemer (1989) note, participants from different social worlds each "answers to a different set of audiences and pursues a different set of tasks" (p. 388) and "because ... objects and methods mean different things in different worlds, actors are faced with the task of reconciling these meanings if they wish to cooperate" (p. 388). Further, "unless they use coercion, each translator must maintain the integrity of the interests of the other audiences in order to retain them as allies" (p. 389). A boundary object is thus an object (conceptual or mate-rial) that inhabits multiple heterogeneous social worlds [or activity systems] and that enables communication and cooperation across boundaries, but without coercion. Thus different kinds of phenom-ena can be conceived of, become manifest, and explored at different levels of analysis, with different methods that suit their respective levels, as when biologists study transmission genetics at the levels of molecules, cells, individuals, and species.

Rather than looking for a winner (one source of spurious argu-ments over the superiority of qualitative and quantitative methods), the trick is making use of connections across levels to enrich under-standing within each. For the ethnographer (or the fisherman trying to catch Herman today), for example, this means appreciating that studying patterns across many individuals and situations provides modeling frameworks, or starting points, within which to recognize, frame, elaborate, and flesh out analyses of finer-grained situated phe-nomena. For the statistician (or the ichthyologist studying the behav-ior of brook trout under varying situations), this means appreciating that the meanings of variables are situated in the circumstances in which they are defined and the values are ascertained—picking up selected information regarding aspects that experience suggests can be useful, but disregarding other information as the cost of moving to a different level. For both the ethnographer and the statistician, it means appreciating not only the kinds of inquiry that their perspectives are best suited to, but the complementarity across perspectives. I suspect that the best practitioners of applied work from a given perspective are aware of this, at least implicitly, and use insights from outside their discipline to carry out good work within their discipline.

Having been trained initially in statistics, I can say more about this as it applies to "great" applied statisticians such as John Tukey and Edwards Deming. Let's compare the approaches that a hypothetical "bad" statistician, "good" statistician, and "great" statistician would bring to the question of the relationship of class size to learning. This topic has inspired a great many studies at the level of achievement variables and counts of students in many classrooms. Discussion is also informed by ethnographic studies of the dynamics of interactions in classrooms of any size, indeed differing dynamics from teacher to teacher, student to student, and moment to moment within any classroom. There are too many classrooms, teachers, students, and moments in this problem to study all of them in depth in an ethnographic manner, although we can do some selective investigations, and we can obtain values of summary variables from many classrooms.

A "great" statistician would probably work on this problem by trying to understand the interplay among four distinct levels:

1. Unique interactions happening in all of the classes in the study and all of the times.
2. Patterns or regularities within those locations we could discern and characterize, either qualitatively, quantitatively, or some mix.
3. Data sets containing the summaries from Level 2.
4. Probability models that characterize patterns in the Level 3 data.

A "bad" statistician fits models to Level 3 data, with the data taken as is, models plunked onto them, and interpretations taken mechanically from the model and summary descriptions of the variables. We do not have to look hard to see lots of research like this in journals, in textbooks, and in policy deliberations.

A "good" statistician carries out what amount to a hermeneutic analysis of Level 3 data with Level 4 techniques, using probability to help discover and characterize patterns based on what s/he knows about the substantive situation, and uses probability to highlight residuals and patterns among them that suggest new substantively meaningful patterns to enrich understanding. There are cycles of fitting models, examining residuals, gaining insights, fitting revised or wholly new models. There is a saying in exploratory data analysis that "you need structure to detect structure," a case of creating new meanings by starting with the "prejudices" we arrive with, à la Gadamer.

Here the "good "statistician examines the relationship of class size and achievement (however measured) in light of other variables we may have available, such as teacher practices, country (high achievement in large classes in South Korea), homogeneity or heterogeneity of students in the class, and so on. There is no assignment of a probability to a claim such as "small classes lead to higher achievement." Rather, patterns that might relate class size and achievement, in light of other variables, are explored and characterized, through regression models, latent class models that identify groupings, mixture models that highlight qualitative different patterns, and so on. Of particular importance are variables associated with residuals from larger trends, as attempts are made, from data and from theory, to better understand the relationship. Sometimes it turns out that an apparent relationship disappears when other factors are taken into account. Sometimes there are relationships when enough other variables are taken into account, but the result isn't useful because the impact of the other factors is overwhelmingly more important. Sometimes characterizing the pattern or following up residuals leads to alternative understandings, or different directions to pursue.

A "great" statistician knows that all of the numbers in Level 3 are filtered summaries of unique events, through the "prejudices" that enable the move from Level 1 to Level 2. This statistician extends analysis down to Level 2 and to Level 1 as resources allow and usefulness suggests. Level 4 analyses can cause reverberations down to Levels 1 and 2, to examine well-chosen sites and events to understand what is happening in both typical and unusual situations. The "great" statistician does not take Level 3 data as given and with fixed meaning, but as provisional understandings with situated meanings, based on previous experience. The thinking that led to them can be revisited or improved in the future. We can discover better ways to carry out observation (Level 1) or more useful ways to see and characterize what's important (Level 2). The "great" statistician uses mathematical tools in Levels 3 and 4, but interacts with unique situations at Levels 1 and 2. Moreover, this statistician often works with people who are living the specifics such as teachers or workers on the factory floor, and with experts like ethnographers with disciplinary tools for thinking at those levels.

This interplay situates and improves statistical modeling, but at the same time provides one juncture where probability-based modeling such as used in psychometrics "can play a role in warranting inferences that are valued by those who hold sociocultural perspectives," a point Pamela raises in her previous turn of talk. In his work on work on quality control, Deming (1975) uses statistical reasoning to model variation and patterns in very large systems. Working back and forth between larger patterns and outliers helped call attention to "special" causes—atypical incidents, which in the business setting require special solutions, as opposed issues within the range of "systemic variation" which only get resolved by changing the system. Myford and Mislevy (1995) study the dance between qualitative and quantitative methods, the precise analyses of special cases and broad analyses of summary data, in the context of the Advanced Placement Studio Art portfolio assessment, an assessment grounded solidly in a sociocultural perspective on learning. Different tools, backing, warrants, and evidence at different levels, but ideally compatible (if not fully consistent, coherent, and complete) models. (Full consistency, coherency, and completeness are pretty hard to come by, even in physics, as witness nearly a century now of efforts to unify models of quantum effects and gravity.)

What does this imply for making sense of reading test scores? It affirms Pam's and Jim's contention that "inferences about 'students,' per se, are problematic; rather, we need to focus on the relationship between students and their environments." First we use understandings of how students become proficient at various aspects of reading, in various ways, for various purposes, for various situations. Researchers in language testing call this an interactionalist (or interactionist) perspective in language testing, and they have started to use it to guide the design and use of language tests in light of constraints and purposes for given assessments. The same perspective applies in practically any area we might want to do assessment, but it has become the most important front in language assessment research because the situated, culturally-embedded, and purposive use of language cannot be ignored—a common conclusion from many directions, including psychometric test validity studies.

Theories, based on psycholinguistic and sociolinguistic research which includes both qualitative and quantitative work, inform the construction of language assessment tasks for inferences for target situations. They help assessment designers define important variables to characterize selected aspects of persons' performances, selected aspects of the situations in light of matches and mismatches with the target situations, and identify background information about examinees that may be important to take into account in inferences about them as individuals when considering target situations (e.g., using English as an emergency room nurse). Sometimes the resulting tests look like familiar reading tests, but often they don't; "reading comprehension" is not viewed as a simple and single skill or a unitary trait, but a myriad of capabilities, accumulated through experience, that a student might be able or might be inclined to bring to bear to work with various kinds of information in various kinds of printed forms in various situations. There is a stronger connection between the argument for test design and the argument for test use, based on a perspective that encompasses both. Knowing What Students Know provides examples of theory-based ways of designing assessments and grounding scores, such as James Minstrell's "facets" analyses of learning physics (NRC, 2001) and the Australian Council on Educational Research's "progress maps" in number sense and building arguments.

An important front in probability-based reasoning is the development of models for analyzing data like these in terms of development over time and in light of background factors—one way of operationalizing the idea of trajectories Jim mentions. Knowing What Students Know looks ahead toward this work. For example, mixture model for latent growth curves play between archetypical trajectories and the particulars of individuals like Janie and Johnnie, in terms of their test performances and background variables. Multivariate versions of these models can address patterns like the ones Jim mentioned, where the same decoding score at a given point in time might carry different meanings for Janie and Johnnie, when viewed (modeled) in conjunction with observations over time on, say, "academic" words and sentence structures when they tell stories orally. Viewed at the level of a statistical model, through the lens of a multivariate mixture latent growth curve model for kinds of variables and in terms of patterns provisionally warranted by previous qualitative and quantitative studies, we iteratively discover patterns from individual scores and understand individual scores in light of broader patterns. Validity arises from coherence of the multiple strands of the argument, across levels and perspectives; the strength of the backing for the many warrants involved; robustness against alternatives; and the compatibility of data, models, theory, and experience.

I have talked here at some length about ways of thinking about assessment that build on resonances of methods and concepts across probability-based modeling and of varieties of situative and sociocultural perspectives, and take advantage of insights and tools that are tuned to particular levels and patterns. Current work in domains such as language testing and simulation-based assessment in computer networking convinces me that this is not only possible, but natural and productive.

GEE: I find myself quite in agreement with Bob's remarks in his response to myself and Pam. Bob is arguing for different methods for different grain sizes of reality and a focus on how patterns at lower levels of reality (closer to the individual) give meaning to patterns at high levels (groups and institutions). I agree that for the "'good' statistician": "There is no assignment of a probability to a claim such as 'small classes lead to higher achievement.' Rather, patterns that might relate class size and achievement, in light of other variables, are explored and characterized." A probability for a generalization like "small classes lead to high achievement" is pretty meaningless unless we know what patterns and sub-patterns on the ground of practices inside specific classrooms are contributing (tending) to the "truth" of this claim and which are contributing (tending) to its "falsity." But what exactly is that "ground"—the "ground of practices" that anchors the significance of our generalizations all the way up?

Reading both Pam and Bob's remarks I was struck with the phrase (and book title): "what students know" (NRC, 2001). Assessment in education is largely about finding out what people know—students or teachers or someone. People working on sociocultural approaches to language and learning, and, more particularly, people working with discourse analysis, don't usually ask this question, rather, they ask the related question: What do people mean? When any person gives any response on any sort of assessment, assessment psychologists might ask what the response means, but we sociocultural language people want to know, first and foremost, what did the person mean by the response? We want to know, as well, what did the assessment itself (the question or the task) mean to the person?

So, let's say, that Janie gets a reading passage of some sort on a reading test. What does the passage mean to her here and now on this test, in this situation? When she responds by answering questions about the passage, what do her responses mean to her, what does she mean by them? In a classroom with 15 kids (a "small class"), what does the class and the class size mean to a particular kid? To the teacher? What does the teacher mean to the kid and the kid to the teacher?

If the reading passage on the reading test means very different things to different children (or different sorts of children) or if the children mean quite different things by their responses on the test questions, then they have not, in a sense, taken the same test. If the "small class" means different things to different kids or different teachers, then the class is "small" in different ways, ways that can count in terms of the patterns below that make patterns above meaningful.

An example: Some people (they tend to be people less affiliated with school and schooling) tend to bring their real world experience strongly to bear in answering questions on standardized reading tests, drawing inferences that go beyond the text, inferences based on those experiences. They do this on other sorts of tests, as well, including, for instance, math word questions. Other people do not do this on such tests, though they will readily do it in other reading contexts in other parts of their lives. The strategy of making such experience-based inferences often leads to "incorrect" answers on such tests, which, in fact, even sometimes have distracters to tempt such people. Such tests want inferences to be based closely on the text or to stay very close to it. When we find this out, this difference about people, we realize that reading in this context meant different things to different people (and, in fact, in other contexts, the same people might agree on what reading means and both use their experience to draw inferences). These people, in a sense, took different tests. The failed scores of some means that some of the test-takers have a different "theory of reading" (while taking the test) from others who took the test, and, indeed, from the test makers. It does not necessarily mean that they "read poorly" in comparison to others who "read well" relative to the same theory of reading.

There is nothing here, I think, that Bob or Pam would disagree with—the level at which things take on certain meanings to individual people is just the foundational level at which patterns at high levels (e.g., groups and institutions) ultimately "cash out" (make sense). Since such meanings are discovered as the result of so-called "qualitative analysis" (actually in these examples, specific versions of discourse analysis), such analysis is the foundation of the "meanings" that quantitative research has.

Faced with any assessment, we can always treat such differences in meaning as a "variable" "in light of which" our larger generalization or pattern is qualified. Fair enough, as long as we actually search for such variables from the ground up and not just by assuming them from numerical clumps in the data. And, goodness knows, many widespread assessments have done no such thing.

However, there is a somewhat deeper issue here. Meaning is not really "personal" or "individual" or just "in the head." In reality, when actual groups of people, engaged in tasks in the world, want to know what people in their group "know" or "can do," they ask this question against the background of lots of work that has gone into "norming" people so that they share similar sorts of values and meanings and "theories." If one wants to know if someone is a "good gamer" (video gamer)—in the sense of being a member in good standing of the gamer community—or a good "bird watcher"—

in the sense of being a member in good standing of the local bird watcher group—they "assess" this against (a) knowledge they have of where the person stands in the community, (b) knowledge about what opportunities the person has had to be normed by the group in such a way that he or she shares meanings and values with it, and (c) knowledge about what "stages" or "places" there are in terms of relatively normal trajectories toward mastery or full participation (should the person want it) in the community.

Assessments in this sense are made relative to communities, opportunities, and trajectories (personally I don't like the word "community" much here—in other work I use the term "affinity groups" or "spaces"). In part this is a matter of ethics. But it is always a matter of rationality: It is an attempt to ensure that the "assessment" and a person's responses to it mean the same thing as they do to other people and that they mean what they should in the context (and that the person knows what they mean and what meaning is intended).

Assessing people who are not in the same "discourse community" (for the purposes of the assessment)—in the same "discourse community" in the sense that they share meanings—is meaningless and sometimes unethical. Worse yet is the situation where we fail to ensure that kids in a classroom are in the same discourse community and assess them as if they were any way. This is for me the bite of Lampert's (2001) work, to which Pam refers: She ties her sense of assessment to creating a shared mathematics discourse community.

So we need to know when we assess people in reading or mathematics, for instance, whether the people we are assessing are in the same discourse community in any relevant sense. We then need to interpret our assessment in terms of where the people stand in the discourse community, what opportunities they did or did not have to be normed towards shared meanings and values for that community, and where they are in relation to stages or places of development toward mastery or full participation (should they want it) in that community.

It is, however, often a vexed matter to determine in, say, a science or math class in our schools today what the requisite "discourse community" is, what its norms are, what practices exist to see that meanings and values are shared, and what possible trajectories exist and are facilitated. I am suggesting that if these questions are not answered or answerable (and in a relatively uniform way for all the learners in the class), then assessment is, in a sense, "meaningless" and, quite possibly, unfair and unethical.

MOSS: Viewed from the frame with which Bob began our dialogue— regarding inferences about students' learning and validity inquiry to support them—there is much that we agree on. We agree:

- that valuable inferences about students' learning occur at various levels of scale (or grain sizes of reality) and take into account the relationship between learners and their environments,
- that, as Bob says, "different kinds of phenomena can be conceived of, become manifest, and explored at different levels of analysis, with different methodologies that suit their respective levels,"
- that the validity of inferences at any particular level of scale can (and should) be supported and challenged by inferences at other levels of scale,
- that generalizations are inferences and that most useful inferences in educational assessment entail generalizations to circumstances, situations, people, and times beyond those studied, and
- that validity inquiry is best treated as a dynamic process that seeks corroboration and challenge for evolving inferences or models from multiple perspectives and sources of evidence.

Jim calls particular attention to the always crucial question about the meanings that different actors (e.g., students, assessment developers) bring to the assessment and to the socially situated nature of those meanings, arguing that the validity of any assessment based inference depends on an understanding of those meanings, from the ground up. (Actually, Jim said something a bit stronger, that I'll return to shortly: He said "that if these questions [about shared meanings] are not answered or answerable [and in a relatively uniform way for all learners in the class], then assessment is, in a sense, 'meaningless' and, quite possibly, unfair and unethical.") Bob's great statisticians complement this perspective, in part, by grounding their models in an understanding of the variety of always partially unique local interactions whose patterns their models characterize and anticipate. Of course, the relevance of the developed model to any particular situation in which it is later applied must rest on local interpreters who are familiar with particular local evidence (including evidence about meaning) that might support or overturn it.

These agreements and complementarities have, it seems, a number of implications for the practice of assessment in classrooms, schools, districts, and so on. If you look across the examples of (arguably good) assessment we have provided, they range from the sorts of situated judgments that accomplished teachers (or fishermen) make about next steps in light of the always partially unique evidence available in their environments to sophisticated large-scale assessments that support inferences about "development over time and in light of background factors." They include endogenous forms of assessment that develop naturally within communities (or affinity groups or spaces as among bird watchers or gamers) to the more exogenous forms of assessment that cross the boundaries of activity systems to serve administrators' or policy makers' purposes. Conceived of in this way, assessment would include those discrete events that we recognize as an assessment, and it would also include those on-going aspects of interaction in an activity system in which actors make evidence based interpretations and decisions and take actions. A characterization of "assessment" by anthropologists Jordan and Putz (2004), who have studied assessment practice in various workplace contexts, includes "inherent assessment," which involve the tacit judgments we make about what to do next in any interaction, "discursive assessment" when judgments about progress are brought explicitly into the dialogue, to documentary assessments where records of the assessment are produced and therefore available for interpretation, comparison, and aggregation by those not present in the immediate context. The generalizations entailed in assessments that cross boundaries require more skepticism, closer scrutiny, and stronger empirical verification of their meaning and consequences. And, to the extent they are taken up in local contexts, they require local verification.

Our agreements imply that all practices of assessment, including those standardized assessments which result in (patterns of) scores for which a common interpretation and validity argument has been built, need to be interpreted in light of other relevant evidence about the particular individual or group and their situation. The results from a standardized assessment form, at best, a good hypothesis about a particular case that must then be evaluated from the ground up by local interpreters who are using it in their own contexts of work. This means that any practice of assessment depends, in large part, on the capacity of local interpreters (e.g., teachers making instructional decisions; school and district leaders making decisions about allocating resources; students whose understandings of themselves may well be shaped by the assessment) to interpret it in light of other relevant evidence and in light of the questions or problems they are using it to address. And it puts a heavy premium on professional development and on a professional environment that supports this sort of inquiry into students' learning. Further, it calls into serious question prominent practices of large-scale assessment that enforce particular decisions or actions based solely upon the (patterns of) scores a particular individual or organization has received. Strong generalization across social boundaries requires strong local verification.

Our agreements point further to the importance of understanding assessment(s), especially those that learners routinely experience, as aspects of the learning environment with which learners are interacting and that is shaping their learning. The design of an assessment system provides opportunities for participation in a social practice. In the case of conventional large-scale assessments, for instance, the practice includes concepts that represent what is important to learn and what counts as evidence of that learning; rules and norms like standardized administration formats, independent work, and so on; and an implied division of labor (different roles for test developers, teachers, students, parents, administrators, policy makers, and others) in the construction and use of the information. Thus, understanding the learning trajectory explicit (or implicit) in any assessment requires addressing questions not just about what it intends about what students know, or even what they mean, but how they are positioned (with respect to the subject matter and other people) and what identities they are afforded (issues that are prominently addressed, for instance, in Lampert's practice). In fact, Jim's 26 questions guiding discourse analysis to which Bob refers in his first turn include, prominently, questions about identities, relationships, and the distribution of social goods that are enacted through discourse, as well as questions about meaning and significance. The generalization that should be of interest to us as educators (but is not typically studied in measurement validity research) is, as Jim suggests, to other social practices that prepare students for future learning and to participate in valued practices in the world. This again points us to the need for evidence—both locally developed and based on large-scale studies—beyond the particular assessment including evidence about the effects of the assessment on students' learning.

We've all three affirmed the value of evidence based inferences at various levels of scale, including those that large scale assessments allow. As Bob notes, while "large and medium scale assessment ... are less contextualized, less sensitive to patterns and explanations of actions of individuals within situations, they are correspondingly better suited to exploring patterns and explanations of selected aspects of phenomena across many individuals and many situations." And yet, Jim's concern about shared meanings being "answerable ... and in a relatively uniform way for all learners"— another issue of generalization—may seem to call into question the meaningfulness of such patterns and explanations across many local contexts. It does, as I note above, call into serious question the use of large-scale assessment for consequential decisions about individual cases without capable local inquiry and authority to challenge the presumptive interpretation. And we would agree that all students are entitled to experience generative learning trajectories that prepare them for future learning and for participation in valued social practices. That said, I believe we would also agree that we cannot (and that it would be counterproductive to try to) create uniformity in shared meanings across diverse local contexts. While meanings always draw on shared resources and common experiences, and thus entail "generalizations," they are also always locally situated and partially unique.

So what does that imply for large-scale assessment? Bob's reference to variables as "boundary objects" points us in a fruitful direction for conceptualizing the role of large-scale assessment. A large-scale assessment would function as a boundary object when actors in the local context are able to cooperate in providing necessary information to outsiders while maintaining a productive level of authority and agency over their own practice. Returning to Jordan and Putz's (2004) characterization of large-scale ("documentary") assessment, "the question that remains to be answered is: how can we negotiate the trade-off between the requirements of institutions that need comparable numbers ... for their purposes and the learners and teachers in schools and workplaces who need endogenous assessment derived from the activity to be mastered" (p. 356)? Drawing on their own research in multiple work place contexts, they argue for the importance of research that (a) illuminates how documentary assessment actually functions in both the local context where the information is produced and the external contexts where it is used and, equally important, (b) how endogenous forms of (inherent and discursive assessment) assessment function in the local context and how the design of the environment might further enhance their use. They see these questions as crucial for leaders in local contexts to address. And, I should note, while district and state educational systems cannot have access to such evidence for every school and classroom, it is equally important for those who develop assessments to have access to cases that illustrate a range of different responses (as Bob has argued great statisticians do). Such multilevel research could, as Jordan and Putz note, "be a step toward collaborative codesign of new organizational structures within which endogenous as well as exogenous informal and well as formal, evaluation criteria can flourish" (p. 356).

The agreements about validity that Bob, Jim, and I have accomplished across our years of dialogue together illuminate, ultimately, a fundamental question about the balance among expert knowledge, administrative authority, and professional autonomy in the development of assessment policies and practices. What elements of local practice can be productively designed from afar, and what elements left to local agency? How do different answers to this question shape the collective capacities, commitments, and cultures of educators, students, and the organizations in which they work? How do they enhance or impede equity in students' learning and opportunities to learn?

Epilogue

Our discussions thus far have led to the broad areas of agreement about issues in validity from assessments that Pamela discussed in her last turn. Differences in perspectives remain, some we are aware of, prompted by previous turns, and others we know we don't yet recognize. Were it not for page limits, we could happily and productively continue this process for quite some time. We can add to the list of agreements the belief that the exercise has enriched our thinking about assessment. Our conversations, the readings, the examples, and the issues they provoke, help us each see assessment in ways we may have not considered or appreciated previously.

Will it do any good? There is a big world out there, with millions of people involved in educational assessments in some way and at some scale: teachers, students, parents, researchers, policy makers, members of the public interested in the quality of education—actually, just about everyone. Their activities are enmeshed, for the most part, in familiar practices in established systems, not the esoterica of Messick, Vygotsky, and Gadamer with which we have amused ourselves.

Yet it is important to ask what the work of assessment is, what purposes it is meant to serve, and what purposes it may unintentionally serve as well. Assessment often serves learners themselves as they make judgments about their own learning. It often serves people who want to help other people to learn, and to learn better and more deeply. However, it often serves the needs of institutions more directly than it serves the needs of learners and their teachers, sometimes for good, but often for bad. As we have discussed, errors of inference and generalization can result when they are based on test scores alone, losing their connection with the more detailed processes and patterns that become apparent only from a closer perspective. Because the full picture of desired learning and the practices that support it cannot be fully seen in score summaries from large-scale testing, for example, mismatches between learning activities and assessment systems can result in misinterpretations and in unintended and unfair consequences for individuals and institutions.

Furthermore, as can happen with any social policy or research in the social sciences, people can be directly or indirectly influenced by these institutional policies, practices, and beliefs, internalize them, and use them to judge themselves, others, and the society around them. Thus, a whole society can come to adopt cultural models of what learning, competence, intelligence, and worth are from institutional realities. And people "on the ground" can have their lives deeply influenced by assessment professionals, and the tests they develop, thanks to the way institutional realities mediate these professionals' influence on society. It is precisely because those who support Janie's learning do not have time to pursue what insights Messick, Vygotsky, and Gadamer might hold for assessment, that it becomes an ethical imperative that we do—and that we act accordingly.

We thus seek in our own work to improve practice in ways large or small that embody insights that come from the interplay among levels, methods, disciplines, and traditions. Interdisciplinary conversations among researchers can be useful, but the conversations are not enough. Synthesizing ideas and contributing to the research literature can be useful as well, but it too is not enough to change practice. Making a difference requires, in part, models of visibly better practices that arise from the new ways of thinking and approaches that help others put them to work widely. It also requires the political will and resources to pursue forthright empirical questions about the effects of institutional polices and practices—and to put those learning outcomes into action. Of course, there is more to say, but even more to be done. So we shall stop here and let our readers take the next turn of talk.

Notes

1. At the Fiftieth Anniversary Meeting of the Psychometric Society, Charlie Lewis observed that "much of the recent progress in test theory has been made by treating the study of the relationship between responses to a set of test items and a hypothesized trait (or traits) of an individual as a problem of statistical inference" (Lewis, 1986, p. 11).

2. At the most general level, hermeneutics characterizes an integrative approach to combining sources of evidence in developing an interpretation. In this approach, inquirers seek to understand the "whole" body of evidence in light of its parts and the parts in light of the whole. Interpretations are repeatedly tested against the available evidence, until each of the parts can be accounted for in a coherent interpretation of the whole. This iterative process is referred to as the *hermeneutic circle*. The approach to hermeneutics on which I draw most heavily is based in the hermeneutic philosophy of Gadamer (2004). Here the hermeneutic circle can be characterized as also representing an iterative process involving the available evidence and the interpreter's preconceptions or foreknowledge. Thus interpretations evolve as new evidence and new understandings are

brought to bear. This conception of "validity" can be seen to share elements in common with Bob's characterization of validity in psychometrics and Jim's of validity in discourse analysis. On hermeneutics in policymaking see Luke, this volume (chapter 9).

References

Bachman, L. F. (2003). Building and supporting a case for test use. *Language Assessment Quarterly, 2*, 1–34.
Deming. W. E. (1975). On some statistical aids toward economic production. *Interfaces, 5*, 1–15.
Gadamer, G. H. (1994). *Truth and method* (G. Barden & J. Cumming, Trans.). New York: Seabury. (Original work published in 1975)
Jordan, B., & Putz, P. (2004). Assessment as practice: Notes on measures, tests, and targets. *Human Organization, 63*, 346-358.
Lampert, M. (2001). *Teaching problems and the problems of teaching*. New Haven, CT: Yale University Press.
Mislevy, R. J. (2006). Cognitive psychology and educational assessment. In R. L. Brennan (Ed.), *Educational measurement* (4th ed., pp. 257–305). Westport, CT: American Council on Education/Praeger Publishers.
Mislevy, R. J. (2008). Issues of structure and issues of scale in assessment from a situative/sociocultural perspective. In P. A. Moss, D. Pullin, E. H. Haertel, J. P. Gee, & L. J. Young (Eds.), *Assessment, equity, and opportunity to learn*. New York: Cambridge University Press.
Moss, P. A., Girard, B. J., & Haniford, L.C. (2006). Validity in educational assessment. *Review of Research in Education, 30*, 109–162.
Moss, P. A., Pullin, D., Gee, J. P., &. Haertel, E. H. (2005). The idea of testing: Psychometric and sociocultural perspectives. *Measurement, 3*, 63–83.
Mosteller, F., & Wallace, D. L. (1964). *Inference and disputed authorship: The Federalist*. Boston: Addison-Wesley.
Myford, C. M., & Mislevy, R .J. (1995). Monitoring and improving a portfolio assessment system. *CSE Technical Report 402*. Los Angeles: National Center for Research on Evaluation, Standards, and Student Testing (CRESST). Retrieved August 3, 2008, from http://www.cse.ucla.edu/products/Reports/TECH402.pdf
National Research Council (2001). *Knowing what students know: The science and design of educational assessment*. Committee on the Foundations of Assessment, J. Pellegrino, R. Glaser, & N. Chudowsky (Eds.). Washington DC: National Academy Press.
Schum, D. A. (1994). *The evidential foundations of probabilistic reasoning*. New York: Wiley.
Star, S. L., & Griesemer, J. R. (1989). Institutional ecology, 'translations' and boundary objects: Amateurs and professionals in Berkeley's Museum of Vertebrate Zoology, 1907–1939. *Social Studies of Science, 19*, 387–420.

Chapter 6

Generalizability and Research Synthesis

Betsy J. Becker and Meng-Jia Wu

Many authors have written about the generalizability—or external validity—of single studies. Generalizability, along with internal validity, is a key factor in what we can learn from a study. Obviously, generalizability relates most closely to external validity—or the question of whether the results of a study apply beyond the exact situations (subjects, conditions, etc.) that are examined in the study (or in our case, the studies) at hand. In this chapter, we are concerned with the issue of generalizability in meta-analysis or quantitative research synthesis, which has not been discussed much by meta-analysts or methodologists who study meta-analysis.

What is Meta-Analysis?

Meta-analysis is a set of quantitative methods for combining and comparing the results from studies that focus on the same research topic. The term "meta-analysis" was coined by Gene Glass (1976) to mean "analysis of analyses." Glass noted that the proliferation of empirical investigations in psychology and education had made it difficult (if not impossible) to draw systematic conclusions from narrative reviews of the literature, and proposed the use of statistical analyses of the results of studies as a way of drawing conclusions from sets of related studies.

The general process of conducting a meta-analysis involves gathering a set of related studies, extracting comparable *effect sizes* from those studies, and analyzing them systematically. Effect sizes are the "data" for meta-analysis, which show the magnitudes of effect from different studies in a common metric. Putting the effects on a common metric makes it possible to combine the results originally measured using different scales in the studies included in the meta-analysis. An average effect is often calculated as an indicator of the size of effect for the research question asked in the meta-analysis. Variation among the effects across studies and potential sources of that variation are described and studied in order to understand the reasons that the effects differ. Meta-analysis allows the accumulated evidence on a research question to be examined across different samples, different versions of measures, and sometimes different treatment variations in a variety of research settings. The extent to which the primary studies in the synthesis vary along these dimensions is a key determinant of whether and how far the results of the synthesis can be generalized.

Whereas there are clearly parallels with generalizability and external validity concerns in primary-study research, some issues are unique to meta-analysis. In this chapter we focus on those concerns unique to generalization in meta-analysis. We begin by examining what might be called a "traditional meta-analysis"—a systematic quantitative review of studies on a particular topic. Issues of generalizability arise even there, due to variations in measures used, samples studied, treatment variations, and the like. We focus on how one decides whether studies are indeed asking "the same question," when all use very similar data collection designs and analyses, and more critically when study designs are diverse. We then move to the issue of how to incorporate quantitative and qualitative studies together in research synthesis. Whereas this is a rather new part of research synthesis activities, more and more reviews are seeking to bring all kinds of evidence to bear on questions of interest. We examine some efforts to incorporate both quantitative and qualitative evidence in research reviews, and discuss the implications for the generalizability of review findings when this is (or is not) attempted.

Generalizability of Conventional Meta-Analysis (Quantitative Synthesis)

By examining multiple studies together, a well-conducted meta-analysis provides the potential to increase the external validity of a finding and to reveal whether one can generalize the finding to a more broadly defined population than would typically be examined in one study. However, when a meta-analysis is conducted improperly, such as by synthesizing studies that are asking different research questions or including effect sizes that are not comparable, the results can be invalid and misleading.

Cooper (1998) described the validity issues that arise at the five stages that every meta-analyst must encounter: problem formulation, data collection, data evaluation, data analysis, and interpretation and presentation. In the following sections, we discuss how choices made at each stage can impact generalizability of the results of the meta-analysis.

Problem Formulation

The problem formulation stage of a meta-analysis is the stage at which the reviewer defines the problem of interest—conceptualizing predictors and outcomes (and operationalizing them as well), and choosing the population(s) of interest. Here is the first point at which the reviewer can start to determine the extent to which the results of a review will be generalizable.

Problem formulation can limit generalizability by focusing on a very narrow problem, or by focusing on specific outcomes, types of treatments, or particular study designs. Some have argued that the work of the National Reading Panel (National Institute of Child Health and Human Development, 2000) suffers from a narrowness of definition that has limited the potential generalizability of its findings. The goal of the National Reading Panel (NRP) was to consider instructional approaches and interventions aimed at increasing reading ability. However, the panel did not actually ever develop a definition of reading ability. They instead opted to select seven skill areas, including alphabetics (phonics and phonemics) and fluency, that were viewed as components of reading comprehension (p. 2). In particular, Yatvin (2002) noted that by limiting the model of reading to one based on decoding, versus a "holistic constructivist view," the panel necessarily eliminated from consideration such factors as parental involvement or reading/writing activities. Yatvin, herself a panel member, described the panel's review as "incomplete, flawed, and narrowly focused" (p. 367).

Problem formulation that takes a broad view can also set the stage for wider generalizations by setting more inclusive criteria for the studies that will be considered legitimate candidates to inform about the problem of interest. An excellent early example of a broadly inclusive meta-analysis was the early synthesis on psychotherapy by Smith and Glass (1977). In this study, the authors tried to sort out the effects of psychotherapy. They used the definition of psychotherapy presented by Meltzoff and Kornreich (1970) and selected the studies using

> informed and planful application of techniques derived from established psychological principles, by persons qualified through training and experience to understand these principles and to apply these techniques with the intention of assisting individuals to modify such personal characteristics as feelings, values, attitudes, and behaviors which are judged by the therapist to be maladaptive or maladjustive. (p. 6)

They included outcomes that were related to "well-being" to represent outcomes of the different kinds of psychotherapy. In the studies they included, the participants ranged from students seeking therapy at college counseling centers to inpatients hospitalized for debilitating mental illness. Though Smith and Glass were severely critiqued by others who thought their synthesis had been overly inclusive, by examining this diverse collection of research settings, designs, and results, they were able to comment both on the overall effectiveness of psychotherapy and on its differential effectiveness for different recipients, on different outcomes, as well as to compare the effects of different types of psychotherapy. Only by including this diversity of studies could these meta-analysts ask whether the results generalized across participants, settings, treatment modalities and outcomes.

Whereas it is beneficial to take a broad view and include diverse studies in meta-analysis, synthesis should be done only when the construct underlying the research question asked in each study fits the broad view that the meta-analyst takes. In the Smith and Glass example, each of the 375 studies included in the meta-analysis studied the effectiveness of specific type(s) of psychological treatment (the construct). All of the studies examined the effectiveness of psychotherapy (the broad view), though there was much variation in the kinds of psychotherapy interventions that were studied. Therefore, in their major finding Smith and Glass concluded that the clients who received psychotherapy had better outcomes than those who did not receive the treatment. They could make this conclusion only because the multiple constructs from studies could be argued to represent the broad view of psychotherapy they wanted to consider. If the constructs examined in studies included in the meta-analysis do not fit or link to the broad view of meta-analysis, the results from the synthesis may be critiqued as representing "apples and oranges," which is one of the most common criticisms applied to meta-analyses. This potential problem can be reduced if the meta-analyst states a clear and specific definition of the research question. Furthermore the issue of whether overly disparate studies have been combined can be addressed empirically (at least in part) by examining differences among studies (e.g., according to type of psychotherapy used) in the data analysis.

Shadish, Cook, and Campbell (2002) describe two principles that are relevant here—"surface similarity" of the studies in a synthesis and the principle of making discriminations. They argue that reviews have studies that represent more constructs (and operationalizations of those constructs) than any single study would ever examine. This is where surface similarity (the match between operations and the "targets of generalization") is relevant. By representing more constructs and their operationalizations, reviews allow for generalizations to more situations than possible in a single review. Also this variety in study implementation allows the reviewer to discriminate between effects for different operations (different measures of outcome, different treatment variations, etc.). Decisions about how broad the set of constructs and operations in a review should be are made in the problem formulation stage.

Data Collection

Problem formulation is iterative, and often alternates with data collection (the literature search stage). Say that a problem is defined in a particular way, but the literature search with that focus identifies a rather limited selection of studies. A reviewer then may choose to broaden the set of outcomes, the set of treatments, or the populations of interest so as to gather a larger set of studies. Conversely, if a broadly stated problem leads to a vast collection of studies, a reviewer may narrow the problem definition.

Often during this process decisions are made that impact generalizability. A simple example would be that a reviewer may limit the time frame covered by a review. In education, some have argued that most findings are time-bound. Berliner (2002) wrote about "decade by finding interactions" (p. 20)—the result of the fact that schools and society (at least in the United States) have changed so dramatically over time that results from, say, 1980, might not apply today. So a reviewer must consider whether the scientific findings of times past are still applicable today. However, to even *ask* whether an effect has changed over time, a meta-analysis must include studies over the time frame of interest.

It is possible that hard-to-retrieve studies have different findings than those that are more easily obtained. For example, some people believe that excluding unpublished studies, such as dissertations and reports, and including only journal studies may over-represent the statistically significant findings on a research question, because studies with statistically significant findings are more likely to be published than those studies with non-significant results. This is called *publication bias*. Publication bias may not only reflect stronger results, but it also can limit generalizability to the populations that were depicted in published studies. Therefore, meta-analysts are encouraged to include both published and unpublished studies in their reviews.

A thorough search for the potential studies to be included in a meta-analysis is one important key to having results that can be generalized to a wider context. A search that is considered thorough not only uses online databases that pertain to the research field, but also includes manual searches of related journals and references of the candidate studies. Moreover, making personal contact with experts in the field and asking them to identify other studies is an important method of finding appropriate studies. With more appropriate studies included, the research question can be studied from more angles, based on more samples, leading to increased potential generalizability of the results from the meta-analysis.

Data Evaluation

At this stage meta-analysts evaluate the adequacy of the data points to be included in the synthesis. This is often the first stage where design issues begin to mediate generalization in meta-analysis, because reviewers often limit the sets of studies they will include in a review by selecting only particular kinds of study designs. A current theme in educational research concerns the use of randomized controlled trials (RCTs), often called the *gold standard* for inference about treatment effectiveness. Whereas there are strong benefits from the use of RCTs for the strength of internal validity inferences, by limiting a meta-analysis to include only RCTs the reviewer will necessarily exclude studies that may help to broaden the inferences that can be made from the review. The RCT's strength is to enhance the researcher's ability to answer the question "Did the treatment really cause the effects that are observed?" However, this question is independent of how generalizable those observed effects may be. This is another feature on which the National Institute of Child Health and Human Development (2000) narrowed the domain of their review. Their studies were limited to experiments and quasi-experimental studies published in peer-reviewed journals.

In some areas where treatments have been of primary concern, there has been a move to limit meta-analyses to include only RCTs. Initially the Cochrane and Campbell Collaborations, two international groups of researchers committed to the growth and development of evidence-based medicine and social sciences (respectively), were reluctant to endorse meta-analyses that included studies other than RCTs. However, Cochrane has a Non-randomised Studies Methods Group that is working to outline considerations needed when non-experimental studies are to be included in a review, as it has become recognized that inclusion of observational and other non-experimental studies can benefit evidence based medicine. Current Cochrane policy allows reviews that include non-experimental studies to become approved Cochrane reviews. The Campbell Collaboration includes a Quasi-experimental Design Group, and also allows reviews to include non-experimental and even qualitative studies.

Even in medical treatment research, there are areas where it is not possible to use random assignment. Kahn et al. (2000) examined studies of medical abortion-termination of pregnancy via the administration of a variety of drugs regimens. In the primary studies, it was not possible to randomly assign women to receive a placebo or another type of abortion (e.g., surgical), so all of the studies had simply examined the outcomes of different drug regimens (treatment vs. treatment comparisons).

Including studies with different designs should improve generalizability to more complex situations. With the development of new analytical techniques and related statistical software, researchers are more willing to use cutting-edge statistical methods to analyze their primary-study data, which brings new issues to meta-analysis. When meta-analysts include studies using complex designs or methods, it increases generalizability but also increases the difficulty of the next steps: effect-size computation and data analysis. One issue that has arisen as the primary quantitative research has increased in complexity concerns what might be called "methodology bias." When a meta-analysis is conducted it is typical for researchers to limit their studies to those for which some measure of effect size can be computed or recorded. Unfortunately, the existing measures of effect, and the ones for which quantitative-synthesis methods exist, are generally simple, "zero order" indices. For instance, two commonly used effect sizes, the standardized mean difference d and Pearson's correlation coefficient r, show the relation between just two variables and ignore the influence of other variables. Consider d, defined as

$$d = \frac{(\bar{Y}^T - \bar{Y}^C)}{S}, \qquad (6.1)$$

the difference between the means of the treatment and control groups, divided by the pooled standard deviation. This index represents the relationship between a treatment or grouping variable and the measure of some outcome of interest. In the case of r, the index shows the strength of the linear relation between two variables. In both cases no third (or fourth or other) variable is controlled for, and in many cases such lack of control would raise questions about the validity of conclusions.

One example from an ongoing project to study teacher qualifications arose in examining the impact of different routes to certification for prospective teachers. Teachers in the United States traditionally become certified by pursing a four-year college degree in education, or by completing a master's degree following a four-year program of study in some specific subject area such as math, science, or history. As an alternative to this approach, some school districts and universities have created shorter "alternative certification" programs—some only a year or two in length. Potential teachers who already have completed a college degree can avoid doing a second college degree or extended advanced study to become a teacher. Also in times of severe teacher shortages, school systems have granted emergency certificates to individuals with essentially no study of pedagogy or teaching methods.

The issue for meta-analysts comparing teachers with alternative or emergency certificates to traditionally certified teachers is that often the alternate-route teachers are older than traditionally certified teachers. These may be career changers who have already worked in other fields for years. It is a question whether this life experience may make up for the lack of training or coursework that traditionally certified teachers would have experienced. So a key variable in any investigation of the effectiveness of such nontraditional routes to certification is whether the studies in the review have controlled for the ages of the teachers being compared.

Data Analysis

At this stage of the meta-analysis, the results from the primary studies are analyzed using quantitative methods. One task at the beginning of the data-analysis stage is to decide whether all the samples from studies are expected to be from the same population (fixed effects across studies) or multiple populations (random effects across studies) and to select an appropriate model to quantify the effects of interest. Cook and Campbell (1979) used the terms "generalize to" and "generalize across" to distinguish between situations in which the findings based on a random sample are generalized to a specific population represented by the sample, and ones in which findings are applied to populations that the sample did not represent. In the meta-analysis context, Cook and Campbell's thoughts about generalizability can be linked to the adoption of fixed and random effects models for analyzing the effects. Under the fixed-effects model, all the effect sizes are assumed to be from "a single population." Therefore, the differences we observe among effect sizes are simply attributed to sampling error. In other words, when applying the fixed-effects model to describe the effects, the findings in the meta-analysis can be generalized to a specific population that is defined by the primary studies. Under the random-effects model, the effect sizes differ not only due to the sampling errors but also because they are "from different populations." The variation in effects among those populations is taken into account when calculating the average magnitude of the effect. Therefore, the findings can safely be generalized to the populations that were not represented by the specific samples included in the synthesis.

One somewhat contentious issue relevant here concerns the fact that studies in meta-analyses typically are not actually sampled from any well defined population, even though the meta-analyst may want to generalize to that population of studies.

If analyses suggest that the simple fixed-effects model of a common effect across studies is appropriate for our data, this means we can assume that all effects are basically identical. However, we should still ask, what is the one population from which our results have arisen or been derived? Whereas the adoption of a fixed-effects model implies that the effect of interest is common to all populations studied (or equivalently that there is only one population), what is not implied is that those populations are identical in all other ways as well. In fact, to the extent that empirically consistent effects are found in the context of diversity of other features, the reviewer can argue that the results can be generalized to more settings, varieties of treatments, and different participants than if they arose from a set of studies that are homogeneous in terms of measures, settings, treatment implementations and the like.

Cook (1993) has labeled these varying auxiliary study features "heterogeneous irrelevancies," and he argues that finding heterogeneous irrelevancies strengthens the reviewer's ability to generalize or apply findings more broadly. Consider an example. Suppose we are examining a set of studies of the usefulness of a teacher interview for selecting qualified teachers. Metzger and Wu (in press) have conducted such a review of studies of the Teacher Perceiver Interview (TPI). The TPI has been empirically linked to a variety of ratings of teacher performance, including student, administrator, and outside observer. One question is, does the TPI relate to each of these indicators of teacher quality in a similar or identical way? The results show the TPI associated highest with administrator rating and lowest with the observer ratings.

Conversely very few studies have examined how the TPI relates to academic outcomes. Indeed only one study was located that looked at whether the TPI predicted student achievement and it is statistically non-significant. Would similar results be found for other achievement measures? Or for the same measure if it were given at a broader range of grade levels or to a more diverse set of students? Without a set of studies that vary, and in this case with the slimmest amount of existing data—one study—we cannot even guess as to whether the effect found for this one sample would hold elsewhere.

Interpretation and Presentation

Like in any single study, the information that can be reported in a meta-analysis is limited due to the constraints of time and space available for presenting the findings. The omission of information reported can either limit or exaggerate the generalizability of the findings from the meta-analysis, if the characteristics of the primary studies or the steps of conducting the meta-analysis are not well described.

Meta-analysis has the potential to strengthen the generalizability of the findings by including a wide range of "representative" samples. This is something that a single study cannot achieve. Again here the initial source of information on what would be representative comes from the problem formulation stage of the review. This is not to say that every review must include the broadest possible set of angles, but that the reviewer should decide "up front" about how broad they want the set to be. A rather broad population was defined for our ongoing synthesis of studies of teacher qualifications. We chose to examine studies done since 1960, of U.S. K–12 teachers. Even so, this definition excludes some studies of pre-service teachers, pre-kindergarten and post secondary teachers, and studies of international samples. For the most part in the problem formulation stage, the issues are substantive—limiting the set of target studies in terms of sample features, time frame, constructs measured and treatment definitions (if treatments are being studied).

We may use meta-analysis to generalize beyond the studies at hand. This idea was proposed by Rubin (1990) in the form of response surface modeling. Rubin argued that the meta-analyst could project out from the data at hand to model the potential effects for a study that had not yet been conducted. This of course may involve extrapolation beyond the range of situations studied, and merits caution in such cases. Yet the idea of predicting the results of a "perfect study" is tantalizing.

One of the most vexing aspects of meta-analysis that has a clear impact on generalization concerns the treatment of variations in study design. Including studies with different designs should improve the potential for generalizability of results to more varied situations. However, it increases the difficulty in meta-analysis at the data evaluation stage. Most methods for quantitative synthesis of study results are geared for simple effect measures such as correlations, mean differences, and proportions or simple odds ratios. Until recently this has not been a great problem for reviewers, because the bulk of studies did not use complex analyses, and those that did often also reported simple forms of their results. However, in some fields, such as the one we have recently been trying to review, more complex designs and analyses have become commonplace and now the simpler studies are no longer believable. To be able to generalize the results to a broader defined context, new methods that can incorporate the results from complex designs are needed.

The Inclusion of Qualitative Studies into the Conventional Meta-Analysis

Because the conventional meta-analysis focuses on synthesizing the results from quantitative studies, qualitative studies have been little used in such syntheses. Popay and Williams (1998) have argued however that qualitative research should have a role in systematic review. Unfortunately, few specific guidelines have been created thus far for how to incorporate qualitative studies along with quantitative studies in a review.

The Campbell Collaboration's Web site argues for the inclusion of qualitative studies in its systematic reviews, and makes these suggestions:

Treatment of qualitative research. In the context of a Campbell review, qualitative studies in the relevant field can (a) contribute to the development of a more robust intervention by helping to define an intervention more precisely, (b) assist in the choice of outcome measures and assist in the development of valid research questions, and (c) help to understand heterogeneous results from studies of effect. (http://www.campbellcollaboration.org/guide-lines.asp, retrieved August 3, 2008)

Intuitively, it seems impossible to merge quantitative and qualitative studies due to the fundamentally different natures of two kinds of studies. Qualitative research has been described as more contextual and inductive, and researchers using this type of study are often most interested in process in micro-level events, and in detailed descriptions of events, individuals, and their interactions. Quantitative research by contrast is often experimental and deductive, and quantitative researchers are interested in the experimental relationships among variables. It goes without saying that numerical effect sizes are not reported in qualitative studies, even though numbers and counts are sometimes presented. Thus current available methods for meta-analysis are not workable.

Popay and Roen (2003) reviewed the methodological work on the synthesis of qualitative and quantitative evidence drawing on their existing knowledge in their field and contact with experts. They identified six groups who have attempted to incorporate quantitative and qualitative research results in certain ways. The groups and their significant contributions are shown in Table 6.1.

Several of these groups involve researchers in health-related field who have tried to utilize evidence from both qualitative and quantitative studies. In the following section we describe two different applications where attempts have been made to combine these two types of studies in a meta-analysis.

Example 1: Merging Qualitative Studies into Quantitative Studies—Bayesian Perspectives

Roberts, Dixon-Woods, Fitzpatrick, Abrams, and Jones (2002) synthesized 11 qualitative studies and 32 quantitative studies published from 1990 to 1999 to evaluate the importance potential factors that affect uptake of childhood immunization. They adopted a Bayesian perspective which combines objective evidence from studies included in the meta-analysis and subjective opinions from the experts in the field, to document the likelihood (probability distribution) of the effect size of interest. In this study, the researchers asked five experts in the field about their subjective judgments and pre-existing beliefs regarding the importance of potential factors. Those beliefs were used to assign the probabilities for each of the identified factors and form the prior distribution

Table 6.1 The Groups and Their Contributions on Incorporating Quantitative and Qualitative Research in Syntheses

Researchers	Significant Contribution
The Evidence for Policy and Practice Information (EPPI) Centre	Developing a "mapping" approach to include varying study designs and types of data in health promotion and education. More details can be found in Harden (2003).
Dixon-Woods (Leicester University) and colleagues	Applying Bayesian techniques to synthesizing quantitative and qualitative evidence mainly in health-related field. An example can be seen in the following section.
Banning and colleagues (Colorado State University)	Conducting the review of "what works for young people with disabilities" that includes any studies that seek to evaluate a relevant intervention regardless of methods/design.
The UK Centre of Evidence-based Policy	Using-theory-led approach to incorporate non-research based evidence alongside research findings. The work has been undertaken by Ray Pawson from Leeds University.
The UK Evidence-based Policy Network	Funded by Economic and Social Research Council (ESRC) to develop methods for synthesizing quantitative and qualitative evidence. More details can be found at http://www.evidencenetwork.org.
Popay, Roberts and colleagues	Also funded by ESRC to focus on the development of narrative synthesis of quantitative and qualitative findings in the context of systematic reviews.

to represent the importance of these factors. The factors are shown in column 1 in Table 6.2. The reviewers then read the 11 qualitative studies, extracted the factors examined in the studies, and revised their list of the importance of factors. As shown in Table 6.2, information based on the reviewers' thinking, knowledge, experience, as well as the evidence of qualitative studies was used to elicit the prior distributions of the potential factors that impact on whether parents choose to have their children immunized. The prior probability for each factor was combined with the evidence from the 32 quantitative studies to form a posterior probability for each identified factor. Therefore, the posterior probabilities contain evidence from both qualitative and quantitative studies and the importance of each factor is designated by these values.

In this synthesis, the researchers compared the results from qualitative studies only, quantitative studies only, and mixed studies. Table 6.3 summarizes the findings based on different types of studies. The results based on different data sources reached different conclusions, which is a major issue when using this method. Apparently, the results from

Table 6.2 Prior Probabilities of Factors Affecting Uptake of Immunization and
Posterior Probabilities for the Four Factors with Highest Prior Probabilities

Factors	Prior probability	Posterior probability
Lay beliefs about immunization	0.177	0.219
Advice received from health professional against immunization	0.145	0.063
Child's health history and on day of immunization	0.145	0.355
Structural issues (including access and appointment times)	0.138	0.089
Social position (including socioeconomic status)	0.088	—
Forgetting that an immunization was due	0.072	—
Religious or moral beliefs against immunization	0.070	—
Role of parent (not to expose child to potential risk such as side-effects)	0.059	—
Features of the post-partum period	0.048	—
Media representation of immunization and potential side-effects	0.039	—
None of the above factors	0.018	—

this method can be impacted greatly by the prior probabilities, which were based on the reviewers' subjective evaluations and beliefs about the factors. However, the qualitative studies included in this meta-analysis identified some potentially important factors that had not been examined in the quantitative studies. That kind of evidence would have been missed if only a conventional meta-analysis had been conducted. In this example, by incorporating qualitative studies, the result of the synthesis extends the territory of possible factors that have influence on the uptake of childhood immunization. The extent to which these results can be generalized is broader than the results that would have arisen from a conventional meta-analysis. One limitation is that this particular mixed method may apply best to specific research questions in which the probabilities of the elements that pertain to the research can be objectively estimated.

Example 2: Using Qualitative Studies to Complement Meta-analysis

Another example of a review including both quantitative and qualitative studies is a synthesis focusing on the healthy eating behavior of young people between 11 and 16 years old (Shepherd et al., 2006). In this study, the researchers studied the barriers to and facilitators of healthy eating

Table 6.3 The Important Factors Identified by Each Type of Data Source

Qualitative only	Quantitative only	Mixed
Forgetting that an immunization was due	Type of health-care service used	Lay beliefs about immunization
Religious or moral beliefs against immunization	Pattern or frequency of use of health-care service	Advice received from health professional against immunization
Features of the post-partum period		Child's health history and health on day of immunization
Media representation of immunization and potential side-effects		Structural issues (including access and appointment times)
		Role of parent (not to expose child to potential risk such as side-effects)

among socially excluded young people. They tried to answer a broad question: "To what extent do interventions address the barriers identified by young people and build upon the facilitators for healthy eating?" (p. 243).

Three types of analyses were conducted in this synthesis: a narrative synthesis of 22 quantitative intervention studies; narrative synthesis of eight qualitative non-intervention studies; and the combination of the two. Seven out of 22 methodologically sound intervention studies were summarized systematically in a table, recording the population, the setting, the objectives of the intervention, providers, and program content of each study. For the eight qualitative studies, young people's perceptions of or attitudes towards healthy eating were recorded, as well as the aims of each study and the sample characteristics. In the end, the researchers created a matrix that juxtaposed the barriers and facilitators identified in the qualitative studies alongside results of the quantitative studies. The answer to the question asked in the quantitative part of the review "what are the effects of interventions to promote young people's healthy eating" was elaborated and further explained by answering the question asked in the qualitative part, which was "what are young people's views on the barriers to, and facilitators of, their healthy eating?"

In this example, the qualitative studies were used to interpret the meaning and the magnitude of the effects found in the quantitative studies. They were used as "complements" to understand in more depth the suggestions of the quantitative studies. This method is less subjective than the one used in the previous example in the way that the results from quantitative studies were not impacted directly by the reviewers' judgments and the interpretations of the qualitative results. However, the generalizability of the results from this method would be limited to the contexts described in the included qualitative studies.

Conclusions

In this chapter, we discuss how generalizability can be limited or enhanced in each of the steps of a meta-analysis. Increasing the number and variety of appropriate studies included in meta-analysis usually increases the generalizability of the review. However, incorporating evidence from qualitative studies can increase or decrease the generalizability, depending on the nature of those studies and then methods used to combine the results. As in the first example, when the qualitative studies included in the meta-analysis identified the factors that were not examined in the quantitative studies and when the information of these two types of studies combined, the results are extended to a broader horizon. On the contrary, if the researchers decide to include both types of studies and some of the quantitative studies are excluded because they do not have the information examined in the qualitative studies or vice versa, then the generalizability can be limited. The current methods for performing a mixed-method synthesis may not be applied to all kinds of research questions that interest reviewers and further investigation of the quality of the methods is needed.

References

Berliner, D. C. (2002). Educational research: The hardest science of all. *Educational Researcher, 31*(8), 18–20.

Cook, T. D. (1993). A quasi-sampling-theory of the generalization of causal relationships. In L. Sechrest & A. G. Scott (Eds.), *New directions for program evaluation: Understanding causes and generalizing about them* (Vol. 57, pp. 39–82). San Francisco: Jossey-Bass.

Cook, T. D., & Campbell, D. T. (1979). *Quasi-experimental experimentation: Designs and analysis for field settings.* Boston: Houghton Mifflin.

Cooper, H. (1998). *Synthesizing research* (3rd ed.). Thousand Oaks, CA: Sage.

Glass, G. V. (1976). Primary, secondary, and meta-analysis of research. *Educational Researcher, 5*(10), 3–8.

Kahn, J. G., Becker, B. J., MacIsaac, L., Amory, J. K., Olkin, I., Stewart, F., et al. (2000). The efficacy of medical abortion: A meta-analysis. *Contraception, 61*, 29–40.

Meltzoff, J., & Kornreich, M. (1970). *Research in psychotherapy.* New York: Atherton Press.

Metzger, S. A., & Wu, M. (in press). Commercial teacher selection instruments: The validity of selecting teachers through beliefs, attitudes, and values. *Review of Educational Research.*

National Institute of Child Health and Human Development. (2000). *Report of the National Reading Panel. Teaching children to read: An evidence-*

based assessment of the scientific research literature on reading and its implications for reading instruction (NIH Publication No. 00-4769). Washington, DC: U.S. Government Printing Office.

Popay J., & Williams, G. (1998). Qualitative research and evidence-based health care. *Journal of the Royal Society of Medicine, 91*(Suppl. 35), 32–37.

Popay, J., & Roen, K. (2003). *Using evidence from diverse research designs* (Report No. 3). London: Social Care Institute for Excellence (SCIE).

Roberts, K., Dixon-Woods, M., Fitzpatrick, R., Abrams, K. R., & Jones, D. R. (2002). Factors affecting uptake of childhood immunisation: A Bayesian synthesis of qualitative and quantitative evidence. *The Lancet, 360,* 1596–1599.

Rubin, D. B. (1990). A new perspective. In K. W. Wachter & M. L. Straf (Eds.), *The future of meta-analysis* (pp. 155–166). New York: Russell Sage Foundation.

Shadish, W. R., Cook, T. D., & Campbell, D. T. (2002). *Experimental and quasi-experimental designs for generalized causal inference.* Boston: Houghton Mifflin.

Shepherd, J, Harden, A., Rees, R., Brunton, G., Garcia, J., Oliver, S., & Oakley, A. (2006). Young people and healthy eating: A systematic review of research on barriers and facilitators. *Health Education Research, 21,* 239–257.

Smith, M. L., & Glass, G. V. (1977). Meta-analysis of psychotherapy outcome studies. *American Psychologist, 32,* 752–760.

Yatvin, J. (2002). Babes in the woods: The wanderings of the National Reading Panel. *Phi Delta Kappan, 83*(5), 364–369.

Section II

Highlights

The chapters in this section deal with three key issues in generalizing: (a) generalizing in qualitative research; (b) generalizing from quantitative research; and (c) generalizing using "qualitative" and "quantitative" evidence. In "Generalizing from Qualitative Inquiry" (chapter 4), Margaret Eisenhart challenges the common beliefs that qualitative inquiries do not lend themselves for generalizing. She makes strong arguments for the case that generalizations from qualitative research are both possible and important. Eisenhart describes and discusses four types of generalizing: (a) probabilistic (statistical) generalizing; (b) nomological generalizing; (c) grounded generalizing; (d) syntheses and meta analyses; and (e) theoretical generalization. These five forms of generalizing are linked to specific forms of argument, as available from the following list.

a. *Probabilistic generalizing (from sample to population)*: The sample is representative of the population in quantitative research; the sample and context are typical of the target population;
b. *Nomological generalizing*: Principles that have universal applicability, which is not possible in social science;
c. *Grounded generalizing*: All relevant information about the generalization is considered. An exhaustive set of cases, negative cases, have been considered and eliminated as opposing to the generalization;
d. *Generalizing by means of syntheses and meta-analyses*: Agreement across research findings across studies based on similarity of research focus and approach; and
e. *Theoretical generalizing*: How the research findings from one study can be extended to another context and how these links and distinctions are relevant to the generalization.

There are three chapters in the book that make sample to population generalizing their focus: Shavelson and Webb (chapter 2), Solano-Flores (chapter 3), and Ercikan (chapter 10). The respective authors discuss the factors and limitations in sample-to-population generalizing.

The arguments in the grounded generalization are similar to those used in making validity inferences from assessments discussed by Mislevy, Moss, and Gee (chapter 5). The similarity of syntheses and meta-analyses in qualitative research to statistical meta-analyses is clearly evident. Similar types of arguments are used in both approaches, similarity of research and aggregation of research findings. Whereas the overall effect size from a meta-analysis may be a numerical value, the synthesis of qualitative research may result in generalizations that are more interpretive, conceptual in nature. The theoretical arguments in both approaches would be the same.

The Mislevy, Moss, and Gee chapter deals with making inferences from assessments. The chapter brings psychometric, sociocultural, and situated perspectives into making inferences from assessments. This is the first chapter in the book that compares and discusses *explicitly* the complementarity of "quantitative" and "qualitative" evidence. The three authors of this chapter focus on making inferences from assessments and emphasize that performance on assessments cannot be understood separately from their context and use. Mislevy in his part discusses the common belief that "psychometrics might work okay for assessment cast in trait, behavioral, and cognitive perspectives, but it cannot address the inferences that are important from a situative/sociocultural point of view." To determine whether this is possible, he poses a challenge for the two perspectives and requires the answer to: "Just what the targets of inference might be, the kinds of observations in the kinds of situations that might support them, and the warrants that would connect them." Jim Gee discusses two challenges to addressing this requirement. First, that there are a number of different sociocultural and situative perspectives. The second challenge is that sociocultural perspectives are not formulated to address "implications for assessment arguments" and in fact some sociocultural perspectives may be opposed to making inferences based on some testing. Vygotsky not only points out that thinking is a temporal process at historical, ontogenetic, and situational time scales but also that the relationship between thinking and speaking continuously changes at the three time scales. If this is so, then we cannot ever theorize thinking in terms of something stable, a substance or a structure, but have to think of it as a continuously changing and self-modifying process. It is a moving target and all we can ever do from such a perspective is to document how it expresses itself across changing situations, settings, times, social relations, and so on.

Jim emphasizes that any inferences specific to the individual student is incomplete and that the target of inferences should be students in conjunction with their environments, which goes in the direction of an argument that has been made recently about assessment like the one that identifies a student as learning disabled, if anything, assesses situations

(Roth & Barton, 2004). Given different situations, the same student may act in ways that are entirely consistent with the label "learning disabled" or "attention deficit" and be highly competent as student an as teacher of others, not only peers but adults in and out-of school alike. Gee's emphasis has significant implications on targets of inference shifting from individuals to models of students' "trajectories" through time and space. This brings up the issue of the utility and value of inferences that are targeted to single points in time on individuals without consideration of their histories and contexts. What does all this mean for making generalizations from assessments in real life educational contexts? Perhaps we have to change our perspective more radically and ask who profits most from education as it is, the form curricula take, and assessment as it is enacted. It often appears that assessment serves institutions and the middle class that most benefits from it; it does not serve students from the lower and working classes. If we were truly interested in using assessment to foster individual development, then we would have to engage with the observed variance that occurs in testing when the same person moves through different forms of tests, situations, settings, social relations, and so on.

Finally, Moss highlights two key aspects of inferences that have not been explicitly addressed by Bob or Jim—who is making the inferences and why are they making them. She makes the point that interpretations, models, and theories are applied in local contexts adapted to the particular intentions, contextual factors and limitations by the local players. Therefore one additional dimension of validity of inferences is "to be able to take situations and dynamic interpretations into account as well as interpretations that are the recorded result of extended inquiry."

The summary of points by Mislevy, Moss, and Gee highlight the connections between this chapter and the Solano-Flores chapter in the previous section. The intention of the Mislevy et al. chapter is not to create a single mathematical model to summarize the complexity of factors in generalizing from assessments, and these issues are not discussed in dichotomous terms. However, many connections can be made between the two chapters. The sociocultural perspective in the Solano-Flores discussions of generalizing is explicit and connections with Jim Gee's points are quite obvious. In particular Solano-Flores' sociocultural view of the student with her/his cultural, linguistic and educational histories aligns well with Jim Gee's view of trajectories through time and space. Jim Gee states "Interpretations are always social and cultural, that is, flow from people's participation in social and cultural affiliations." But once we adopt such a perspective, especially if we attempt to implement the dialectical perspective Vygotsky outlined in his process model of thinking and speaking, then we are far away from the kinds of considerations at the heart of G-theory, the purpose of which is to come to grips with various factors that may be contributing to the variability of scores.

Solano-Flores delineates what different factors are for the flow with his identification of student related factors such as cultural affiliations, linguistic differences, test related factors such as cultural and linguistic appropriateness and factors related to testing contexts such as whom, where and when. One distinction we may note between Gee and Solano-Flores is the difference in targets of inference. Whereas the latter highlights the complexities, the target of inference are the individual students with their unique sociolinguistic background, the former draws attention to the importance of making the whole trajectory as target of inference. Moss discusses the *who*, which is clearly part of the Solano-Flores generalizability model. However, one of Moss's points about *why* the inferences are being made is not covered by the stochastic model that Solano-Flores proposes. The target of difference (student versus the trajectory) and why the inferences are being made are two key differences in the two chapters.

The chapter "Generalizability and Research Synthesis" (Becker and Wu) highlights the fact that generalizability is tied to consistency of findings across studies. The findings captured in effect sizes are the data in meta-analysis. Becker and Wu discuss factors that affect generalizability of findings that arise in the effort of conducting research synthesis by means of meta-analysis: *problem formulation, data collection, data evaluation, data analysis*, and *interpretation and presentation*. Generalizing in research synthesis (meta-analysis) can in fact be thought of as making inferences based on other research findings where these research findings serve as data for the research synthesis. The formulation of the problem can then be thought of as being the initial step in research synthesis and therefore is analogous to formulating the research problem in an empirical research project. Becker and Wu argue for a broad view of this initial step, the formulation of the problem. They draw attention to the limitation of generalizability that comes with a narrow problem formulation. In research synthesis, a narrow research formulation might be in the form of specific outcomes, types of treatments, or formulations that allow considering research based on specific designs only, such as experimental designs. For us, this raises a host of questions, including: How does the formulation of research problem affect generalizability of research findings? Does research based on a narrow focus limit generalizability of findings? Would a broader research problem lead to better/ stronger/wider generalizations?

Consider the example Becker and Wu present, the instructional approaches and interventions aimed at increasing reading ability. What would be a narrow versus broad view of research problem? A narrow view of research investigating instructional practices and interventions aimed at increasing reading ability would have a narrow definition of reading ability, instructional practices, and interventions. A narrow definition of reading ability may be similar to the one adopted by the National Reading Panel, which specified seven skills as related to decoding. A broad definition of this variable may be one that is more holistic and may include other components of reading ability such as comprehension. It is clear that a broader definition of the outcome should allow research findings regarding effectiveness to instructional practices and interventions to be applicable to this broader view of the outcome.

For a second example, consider broad versus narrow definitions of independent variables such as instructional practices and interventions. A broad definition of instructional practices may include teacher classroom strategies, interaction style, books and materials, homework and assessments. A narrower definition of instructional practices, however, may involve teaching of phonics and phonemics. Keeping the definitions broad is more challenging for operationalizing these variables. Operationalizing these variables means that data need to be constructed to capture these broader definitions. This is similar in synthesizing research, that is broader problem formulation will lead to more relevant data being captured and greater likelihood that some relevant effects may be captured.

These examples show how already in the stage of formulating the problem a narrow versus broad definition changes the level to which educational researchers can generalize from their studies. Similar analogies between *data collection, data evaluation, data analysis,* and *interpretation and presentation* as factors affecting generalizability in research synthesis can be made with those in education research. These five considerations therefore cover many issues concerning the extent to which orientation mediates the level to which educational research can be generalized. The next section opens up a whole new dimension by articulating *research use* as a major element that any effort in generalization needs to take into account.

References

Roth, W.-M., & Barton, A. C. (2004). *Rethinking scientific literacy.* New York: Routledge.

Section III

How Research Use Mediates Generalization

Overview

> Philosophers have hitherto only interpreted the world in various ways; the point is to change it. (Karl Marx, "11th Thesis on Feuerbach")

In his famous aphorism, Karl Marx suggested that philosophers were concerned with understanding rather than with the use and application of knowledge to bring about changes in the world. The underlying issue he thereby addressed was the fundamental difference between human beings to be able to change the world rather than being subject to it and the environmental conditions it constitutes for life. Marx also addresses a theme familiar to educators: the gap between theory and praxis. What is the origin of this gap, and how does the gap elucidate issues of generalization of knowledge from research to use?

In cultural-historical activity theory—fathered by the work of the Russian social psychologist Lev Semenovich Vygotsky—all societal activity is theorized in terms mediations (Roth & Lee, 2007). Thus, the subjects of the activities (farming, producing tools, researching, educating) never are directly related to the objects used in the activities (materials) and the collective motives of activity; rather, the means (tools, instruments, discourses) mediate, shape, and are embodied in future outcomes (Figure III.1). That is, for cultural-historical activity theorists, it does not come as a surprise that the use of different methods—i.e., *means* of knowledge production—produces different forms of knowledge; and these forms of knowledge are marked by the means that were used to produce them. Outcomes are also shaped by the society-based and -generated motives that drive the activity, which has as a consequence that an activity producing knowledge (educational research) and an activity teaching kids (educating) produce very different forms of knowledge given that they are associated with very different means, objects, and motives.

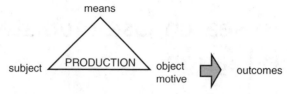

Figure III.1 Means of production mediate the relation between subject and collectively motive, including objects and outcomes of activity..

It therefore is the case that knowledge production in itself does not ascertain that the knowledge produced meets the needs of those people for whom the knowledge was designed or whose work this knowledge was intended to support. If the knowledge needs of future users are to be met, the system of knowledge production has to be chosen accordingly, including the means of production. These means have to be chosen such that they lead to the production of the desired knowledge. This, in essence, is the argument that the three chapters in this section make: methods have to be chosen such that they lead to usable knowledge on the part of those it is designed for. Or, to express this in other words, future knowledge use—as the motive of activity—needs to drive the selection of objects and means in the production of knowledge.

Cultural-historical activity theorists also explicitly theorize the uptake and use of the products of activity, which become entities that are taken up by society as a whole or by sections thereof because they satisfy some need. In the past, much of academic research has been conducted for the sole purpose of being used in subsequent academic endeavors. It is therefore not surprising that those aspects of knowledge brought about by the particular means of production employed were not questioned at all. Yet increasing demands by practitioners, policy makers, funding agencies, and politicians for knowledge that practitioners can actually use also has to lead us to ask questions about the means of production that we employ in research. If these means lead to knowledge that cannot be used, then questions have to be raised. There is precedent in the AIDS case, where the scientific protocols for testing new drugs, which up to that point were solely based on double-blind studies, were changed as AIDS activists and AIDS patients interacted with scientists (e.g., Epstein, 1997). As an outcome of these interactions, medical researchers abandoned what they had held to be "the gold standard" for testing new drugs and elaborated new means of testing where willing AIDS infected individuals were provided access to new drugs if they so desired. This shows that even those "hard" sciences where controlled experiments were the only standard for establishing internal and external validity were able, upon reflection, to improve their research designs and evolve means of establishing generalizability without requiring double-blind experiments.

Further light has been thrown on the problematic of general statements of knowledge and practical action by the research that studied the gap between general prescriptions and the situated work of acting in ways so that the prescriptions become appropriate descriptions of what has been done (Suchman, 1987). General, abstract prescriptions for getting work done—in education, these are curriculum statements, lesson outlines, prescriptions for teaching methods—cannot ever *guarantee* what will happen when real people attempt to act in accordance with the prescriptions. General knowledge that researchers produce may not be relevant at all to guide the actions of those most concerned. What we therefore need to know better is the nature of knowledge that relevant stakeholders require to get their jobs done in the best way possible. The knowledge requirements, as per the framing of a cultural-historical approach to activity, will be different for different stakeholders. A one-size-fits-all approach to knowledge, therefore, will not produce relevant knowledge, nor does a one-size-fits all approach to knowledge production generate the different forms of knowledge that users actually need. In Allan Luke's words, what is important is not that something works, but the responses to questions such as "What works with whom? Where? When? With alignments of which enabling policy flows? With what collateral effects in different local ecologies?" These questions parallel the focus of the Solano-Flores chapter 3, of *Who*, *Tests*, *Language*, *By Whom*, *When*, and *Where* as well as the Mislevy, Moss, and Gee chapter 5 focus on *context* and *use*.

All three chapters address the same issue of research use in arguments about the selection of research methods. Lyle Bachman constructs a general argument about why and how research use should drive method selection and discussions about generalizability. He suggests transcending the qualitative-quantitative opposition and to make use of the method that produces the kind of knowledge users actually need to improve on what they do—teachers require knowledge about how to mediate learning, learners need knowledge for learning-how-to-learn, principals need knowledge about how administrative and organizational issues mediate classroom learning, and policymakers need to know how the outcomes of their work mediate—positively, negatively, or not at all—classroom teaching and learning.

The two authors that follow Bachman approach the research-use argument from very different angles, though both draw on historical/biographical genres to make their argument. Allan Luke is concerned with policy and its mediation of educational processes. His account of how testing and assessment mediate classroom teaching and learning are, necessarily, at a societal macrolevel. For example, he repeatedly links knowledge and policy to particular forms of government, whether this pertains to the U.S. government under George W. Bush or the Australian

government under the leadership of John Howard. The chapter is interesting in the way it traces—consistent with a cultural-historical activity
theoretic approach though not articulated as such—the history of the
relation between methods, types of knowledge, and policy.

Also using a historical approach, Ken Tobin uses his autobiographical account to articulate how his research methods changed with the
kinds of knowledge and interest needs: He began as a researcher using
the most powerful statistical tools available at the time—his dissertation included a chapter on generalizability theory as discussed in chapters 1 (Shavelson/Webb) and 2 (Solano-Flores)—to using ethnographic
methods and to using critical ethnography to produce, together with
users (teachers, students), knowledge that they can employ to change
their lives in the *then-and-there* of their situation. The kinds of knowledge produced allow these individuals and groups, in the way figured
in Marx's aphorism, to produce knowledge that allows them to change
the world that they inhabit, and thereby gain the level of control necessary to turn events for the better. That is, the knowledge created in this
way expands their agency (room to maneuver) and thereby *is* relevant in
and to their lives. It is knowledge that holds up to the "gold standard"
of fourth-generation evaluation (Guba & Lincoln, 1989), a standard
that is concerned with the *ontological, educative, catalytic*, and *tactical
authenticity*. These different forms of authenticity aim at the understanding of the participants (users) and the people they interact with develop
in and as of the research process, how the knowledge enables actions on
the part of the participants, and how the knowledge enables participant
to expand their room to maneuver to engage relevant others in gaining
control. The forms of knowledge generated in this way therefore do not
only pertain to the situations lived but more importantly to situations
in the future. It is a form of generalization that operates diachronically
into the future.

References

Epstein, S. (1997). Activism, drug regulation, and the politics of therapeutic
evaluation in the AIDS era: A case study of ddC and the 'Surrogate Markers' debate. *Social Studies of Science, 27*, 691–726.
Guba, E. G., & Lincoln, Y. S. (1989). *Fourth generation evaluation*. Newbury
Park, CA: Sage.
Roth, W.-M., & Lee, Y. J. (2007). "Vygotsky's neglected legacy": Cultural-
historical activity theory. *Review of Educational Research, 77*, 186–232.
Suchman, L. A. (1987). *Plans and situated actions: The problem of human-
machine communication*. Cambridge, UK: Cambridge University Press.

Chapter 7

Generalizability and Research Use Arguments

Lyle F. Bachman

Empirical research in education can be described as an activity in which the researcher observes some phenomenon in the real world, interprets this in some way, and then uses this interpretation to reach a decision or generalization. If one accepts this description, then educational researchers would appear to have in common both the research activity in which they engage and a concern with generalizability. However, despite these general commonalities, educational research has been factionalized over the years by a debate over differences between so-called "quantitative" and" qualitative" approaches to research. Quantitative research, on the one hand has been derided as "reductionist," while qualitative research has been characterized as "unscientific," on the other. (I will refer to this "quantitative-qualitative" debate as the "Q-Q debate.") What is lacking, in my view, is a common conceptual framework for both conducting research in education and for justifying the use of this research.

In this chapter, I discuss some general issues about the nature of research in education and about generalizability, illustrating these throughout with references from my own field, applied linguistics. I first discuss the nature of educational research, and particularly how it differs from research in the natural sciences. I then present a broad view of generalizability in terms of inferential links from observed performance to an observation report, to an interpretation, to the use and consequences of that interpretation. I argue that in addition to considering generalizability as consistency, or reliability across observations and as the meaningfulness, or validity of the interpretations we make from these observations, we also need to consider the uses that may be made of our research results, and the consequences of these uses for various individuals who may be affected by them. I then describe a "research use argument" and propose this as a basis both for guiding the conceptualization or design of research in education and for providing the justification for interpretations and uses of research results. Finally, I offer some observations on the viability of combining multiple approaches to research in education.

The Nature of Research in Education:
Qualitative and Quantitative

Empirical research in education exhibits a rich diversity in the method-ological approaches that are used. Educational researchers use every-thing from tests, measures, assessments, elicitation tasks, and surveys, to ethnography, conversation analysis, verbal protocol analysis, and hermeneutic and critical analysis. Despite this diversity of approaches, it is common to categorize these as either "quantitative" or "qualitative." The origins of the different approaches to research in education can be traced historically to research in a wide range of disciplines outside of education. Much of what is generally referred to as "qualitative" research has drawn on approaches to research from a wide variety of fields, such as anthropology (ethnographic research), philosophy of science (inter-pretive research), biblical interpretation (hermeneutic research), social theory and literary criticism (critical research), and history (historical research).

"Quantitative" approaches to research in education, on the other hand, can be traced to methods that were originally developed in the natural sciences.[1] Certainly, from the perspective of what researchers *do* (observe, interpret, generalize), empirical research in education would appear to be very similar to that in the physical and biological sciences. However, when we consider the ways in which educational researchers report and interpret the phenomena they observe, and the entities that are of interest to them, it becomes clear that the research enterprise in education is quite different from that in the natural sciences.

Phenomena and Perceptions in Education and the Natural Sciences

In a recent paper, Ercikan and Roth (2006) argue that the ways phe-nomena are represented in both the natural sciences and in education have characteristics that are both quantitative and qualitative. Drawing on the research in such diverse fields as perceptual processes, dialectical philosophy, phenomenology, and neurophenomenology, they conclude that "all phenomena and all knowledge simultaneously have quantita-tive and qualitative dimensions" (p. 22). I would note that Ercikan and Roth also conclude that the distinction between subjectivity and objec-tivity is essentially irrelevant to the Q-Q debate and that generalizabil-ity is not limited to research that uses statistical analyses. The part of their argument upon which I wish to build, however, is that which deals with phenomena and perception as these apply to empirical research in education.

I interpret Ercikan and Roth's argument as beginning with the propo-sition that the phenomena that are observed in both the natural sciences and education are largely the same, comprising natural objects, processes, or behavior that can be directly perceived by our five senses. The operative term here, I believe, is "perceived," and Ercikan and Roth explicitly state that these perceptions are the data with which researchers work: "Data are *representations* of phenomena in nature, society, education and culture" (pp. 15–16). I agree that it is our perceptions of phenomena rather than the phenomena themselves, that are critical, not only to the Q-Q debate, but to a fundamental understanding of empirical research in education. I would thus propose to extend the discussion of perceptions in three ways. First, I argue that we need to recognize perception as an active process that is shaped by factors in addition to physical and physiological ones.[2] Second, I argue that empirical research in education is fundamentally different from that in the natural sciences. This is because in educational research our perceptions of phenomena are represented in language as both indices and symbols, whereas researchers in the natural sciences represent phenomena primarily as indices. Third, I argue that in educational research we are very seldom if ever interested in the phenomena themselves, but in our representations of these, most often in language.

Factors that Affect the Researcher's Perceptions

The ways in which a given researcher records and interprets the phenomenon he or she observes is shaped by a number of different dimensions. Although I do not frame his discussion in the view of perception that Ercikan and Roth adopt, the acts of recording and interpreting the phenomena that are observed could be seen as operational realizations of perception in educational research. Of particular relevance here are the dimensions I describe that are associated with the researcher (What are the researcher's ontological and epistemological views or beliefs? What is his or her ontological stance towards the observation? What is his or her purpose in conducting the research?), the way the researcher defines the entity of interest, or the construct (What are constructs? Where do they reside? Where do they come from?), and the context the researcher has chosen in which to make the observation (What is the relationship between the context and the construct? What is the range or scope of the construct?). These dimensions affect not only the ways in which researchers perceive, report, and interpret the phenomena they observe, but also the ways in which they deal with issues of generalizability.

Representations of Phenomena

The way humans perceive and represent phenomena, as well as how they perceive and respond to these representations can be seen, from an evolutionary perspective, as conditioned by language. Drawing on the research in neuroscience, evolutionary anthropology, and social cognition, Schumann (2003) argues that human beings inhabit several domains of reality, two of which are particularly relevant to the discussion here. One domain is that of the physiosphere, which includes all objects, processes, and behavior whose existence can be directly confirmed by the senses.[3] The other domain is the symbolosphere, which is the "nonphysical conceptual and symbolic counterpart to the physiosphere" (Logan & Schumann, 2005, p. 204).

Signs: Indices and Symbols

Schumann's distinction between the physiosphere and the symbolosphere draws on Peirce's (1992) theory of signs. In very simple terms, Peirce distinguishes three types of signs: icons, indices, and symbols.[4] *Icons* represent physical objects essentially by imitating them, and are icons by virtue of someone's perceiving them as icons. Thus, a particular bear, or other bears, if interpreted by someone as a category for all bears, serves as an icon. If I make sounds or gestures to imitate a bear, or draw a figure depicting a bear or show someone a picture of a bear, these all can serve as icons of the object, bear.

An *index* is a sign that refers to an object, generally in terms of a time and a place or position that are known to the interpreting individual. If a naturalist shows some tourists the tracks a bear has left in a riverbed or a cave where a bear hibernates during the winter, these can serve as indices referring to the object, bear. Similarly the strong smell of a bear or a sign in a park warning tourists to beware of the bears can be indices referring to the object, bear. Finally, and most relevant to the discussion here, words that refer to objects in the natural world can also serve as indices. (On this point see also the discussion of the metonymic character of signs to lived experience in chapter 11.)

A *symbol* is a sign that stands for, or represents another sign. That is, a symbol does not imitate an object as does an icon, nor represent an object, as does an index. Rather, a symbol is a sign that has, through habit or usage, acquired a conventional signification. Thus, whereas the word "bear" can serve as an index, referring to the object, it can also serve as a symbol, invoking a whole semantic network of other words, such as *beast, grizzly, carnivore, hungry, polar,* and *teddy,* not to mention those that might be associated with the homographic verb *bear.* Symbolic relationships can be formed not only via semantic networks among words, but also by abstraction, higher-level categorization, and predication.

The Symbolosphere

The distinction between the physiosphere and the symbolosphere provides a means for understanding what I believe are fundamental differences between research in education and the natural sciences in terms of what researchers observe and what they are interested in. The symbolosphere emerged and developed as language itself evolved through the interactions of prehistoric hominids as they first used single sounds to refer to objects in the physical environment, then joined words together to make utterances, and eventually used these words as symbols to refer to other symbols. Thus, as language emerged among humans, the symbolosphere also evolved as "a set of relations among words that is as real as the inorganic physiosphere and the organic biosphere" (Schumann, 2003, p. 5). Over time the symbolosphere, which was initially based in oral language, has been expanded through technologies such as writing, print, audio and visual media, and the Internet. Furthermore, this symbolosphere influences us just as strongly as does the physiosphere. With the symbolosphere, "it is possible to create a virtual world that has no physical reality but which we inhabit as profoundly as we do the physical biosphere. In Deacon's (1977) words we are 'the symbolic species,' and the symbolosphere is our econiche" (Schumann, 2003, p. 16).

Entities of Interest

The implication of the distinction between the physiosphere and the symbolosphere for empirical research in education is that the entities in which we are interested are different, in a very elemental way, from those that are of interest to researchers in the natural sciences. Constructs, or the entities that are of interest in the natural sciences reside in the physiosphere, which includes the biosphere. These constructs can be defined by "consensual indexicality," by which is meant that "words unambiguously index entities in the environment that can be verified by the senses or the senses plus some amplifying technology (e.g., the electron microscope)" (Schumann, 2003, p. 16). Schumann illustrates this with an example from anatomy, in which hypotheses about the relationships among certain neuroanatomical entities and processes can be tested by using a physical procedure. In educational research, as with the other social sciences, however, the entities in which we are interested reside in the symbolosphere, where words are symbols referring to other symbols, and consensual indexicalization is a near impossibility. We might think that we are indexing entities such as "aptitude," "intelligence," and "language proficiency" when we define them operationally as measures. However, very few, if any, researchers in these areas would still hold to the strict operationalist interpretation that the measures *are* the construct. Furthermore, as a century of research in these areas clearly demonstrates, we are far from any consensus on what these terms mean.

Because of this difference in the entities that are of interest, Schumann concludes that researchers in the social sciences should "just understand the nature of the symbolic world in which such research must be conducted. Social science is largely carried out in the symbolic world where words do not have unique references or indexes. Therefore, precision, closure and unique solutions are much more difficult to achieve" (pp. 7–8). I reach a slightly different conclusion. I argue that rather than accepting the fact that our research may not be able to achieve the "precision, closure and unique solutions" that our colleagues in the natural sciences accept as a standard of practice, we should recognize that such criteria are inappropriate for empirical research in education. This is because in educational research, our purpose is not to discover truths or laws about the physical world but rather to convince or persuade various groups of stakeholders that the results of our research are useful for some purpose, whether this be advancing our understanding of some phenomena in our socially mediated symbolosphere or helping stakeholders make decisions that will benefit our educational systems and society.

Commonalities across Approaches

In my view, there are four very fundamental commonalities to virtually all approaches to empirical research in education. Two of these pertain to the *purpose* of empirical research and how we achieve this purpose. First, most educational researchers would agree that empirical research is aimed at the creation or construction of knowledge. Second, most researchers would agree that we create knowledge by observing phenomena. I note, however, that despite these two points of general agreement, there are nevertheless differences among researchers in what constitutes "knowledge," in how we go about creating or constructing it, what counts as "phenomena" and how to observe these, and in the values and assumptions that underlie our different approaches to conducting empirical research.

The third commonality that underlies empirical research in education is the fact that virtually all of the entities in which we are interested exist in the symbolosphere, and consist of symbols, rather than indices. Thus, although we observe physical phenomena in the physiosphere, we are generally interested in entities that can only be inferred from observing what people do or say in a given setting. For this reason, the purpose of empirical research in education should be properly viewed as that of convincing our peers and other stakeholders of the usefulness of our results.

Finally, empirical researchers share a common concern for generalizability, that is, a desire to find meaning for our research results beyond the particular study itself. The chapters in this volume all discuss issues that have to do with the generalizability of results, the appropriateness of inferences, and dependability in the research process. The authors in this volume consider these notions from a variety of research perspectives within educational research. The approach to generalizability that I take derives from a view of educational research as a series of inferential links from an observation to a use.

Generalization as Inferential Links in Empirical Research

In most empirical research in education, we want to infer interpretations on the basis of our observations of phenomena. That is, we want to attach meaning to our observations (see also Mislevy, Moss, and Gee, chapter 5 of this volume). In my field, applied linguistics, for example, these observations are typically of language use, or the performance of language users. In addition to attaching meaning, to an observation of performance, in much educational research this interpretation is used, sometimes by the researcher, sometimes by others, to make generalizations or decisions that go beyond the observation and its particular setting. Thus, in much of our research we need to make a series of *inferences* that link an observed phenomenon to use. Each inference has an outcome, and with each outcome there will be a need to address a particular aspect of generalizability. The inferential links between an observed phenomenon and the use of the research are illustrated in Figure 7.1.

The *observed phenomenon* in the bottom box in this figure is an instance of the phenomenon that we observe in our research. In applied linguistics, for example, this phenomenon might be a conversation, a "collaborative dialogue," a group interaction among members of a speech community (e.g., family, classroom, the workplace), a grammaticality judgment, or performance on an assessment task. The *observation report* in the next box up, is the outcome that is inferred from the observed phenomenon, and consists of an initial extraction, or "filtering," by the researcher, of the phenomenon that is observed. This observation report might consist of, for example, a score, a verbal description, a transcription, a picture or a video clip, or any combination of these. I say that the observation report is *inferred* from the observation, because, to arrive at the observation report, the researcher makes decisions about what to observe and how to record it. These decisions "filter" the phe-

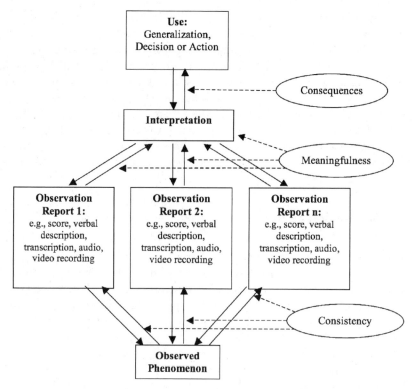

Figure 7.1 Generalization: Inferential inks from an observation to use (after Bachman 2004, p. 725).

nomenon to be observed out of all the possible phenomena that might be observed, as well as filtering the observations themselves, since even the most detailed observation report will necessarily reflect the selective perceptions of the researcher. Other researchers might make different decisions, filter the phenomenon differently, and hence arrive at, or infer, different observation reports.

The researcher arrives at the observation report by deciding what to observe and by deciding to use observation and analytic procedures that are consistent with and appropriate for the particular methodology that underlies these observations and procedures. These decisions about what and how to observe, and what and how to transcribe or report, will be informed by the researcher's own methodological and theoretical perspectives, or biases (Ochs, 1979). The method of conversation analysis, for example, will include the way in which the particular conversation is selected and the medium with which it is recorded, and the procedures employed to transcribe the details (e.g., words, non-verbal sounds, pauses) of the conversation. The method of language assessment will include how the assessment developer has defined the ability or attribute to be assessed, the kinds of assessment tasks that are presented to the test takers, the administrative procedures, and the scoring method used. The rigor with which the observation and analytic process are described and followed by the researcher provides the primary justification for the link between the phenomenon that is observed and the observation report.

If we assume that a given observation report is but one instance of a number of possible observation reports based on the observed phenomenon, then we might be interested to know whether this particular report might generalize to a theoretically infinite universe of all such reports, as illustrated in the three boxes in the middle of the figure. (On the variation of tests and test items and its influence on test scores see the chapters in section I.) Other similar reports might be transcriptions of a conversation by different researchers or scores obtained from different forms of a test aimed at measuring the same ability. The aspect of generalizability that is of concern with observation reports is that of the *consistency*.

The next box up in the chain is the *interpretation*, or the meaning that we want to infer from our observation report. This interpretation might consist of the recognition of a recurring pattern in the observations to which the researcher might assign a label, such as "adjacency pair" or "knowledge of L2 vocabulary." Deriving meaning from an observation report involves a broader type of inference: from symbols—verbal descriptions or narratives, visible images, or numbers—to other symbols or inferred meanings, which are generally understood to be abstract concepts. (See discussion of symbols above.) The aspect of generalizability that is of concern with interpretations is that of *meaningfulness*.

The top box of Figure 7.1 is the *use* the researcher or consumers of the research make of the interpretation. The inference from interpretation to use typically consists of a generalization to a larger group or to other situations, or a decision that the researcher or consumers of the research make on the basis of the interpretation. The aspect of generalizability that is of concern with uses is that of the *consequences*, or impact, of the use of the interpretation.

In summary, I argue that in educational research, the links between an observed phenomenon, an observation report, an interpretation, and a use consist of a chain of inferences, or generalizations, from one level to the next. Each inference in the chain must be supported both by coherent arguments and empirical evidence in support of these arguments. Furthermore, the inferential and evidentiary burden increases as the researcher's purpose moves from that of describing the performance in the observation report, to interpreting that report, to using this interpretation in some way.

If the researcher's objective is to provide a careful and detailed *description* of the phenomenon, she will need to consider the consistency of that description, with respect to how it might differ from those of other researchers. Two conversation analysts, for example, might differ in how they transcribe particular details of a conversation, and different participants in a speech event might provide different reports of that event. Similarly, scores for an individual from two different forms of a language test intended to assess the same aspect of language ability, might differ. The extent to which such inconsistencies are considered problematic, and how they are resolved, differ across the different research approaches that are commonly used in educational research. In some approaches, inconsistencies may be regarded as beneficial, in that they provide differing perspectives. The building up of multiple observations into a thick description in ethnography, for example, enables the researcher to report both commonalities and differences in the observations of different participants. In other approaches, such as experimental and quasi-experimental designs or language assessment, lack of consistency is generally considered to be a serious problem; and various statistical procedures have been developed to estimate this and to minimize it.

If the researcher's purpose is to generalize beyond a particular observation, to *interpret* the observation report in a way that gives it meaning within the framework of an existing body of research or a theory, she needs to consider both the consistency of the observation report and the meaningfulness of her interpretation. She will need to articulate an argument that she can, indeed, generalize from the observation report (or from multiple observation reports) to the intended interpretation, and then provide evidence to support this argument. The links described above provide the scaffolding she needs for developing an argument that the meanings she attaches to her observations are valid. The links also provide a guide for identifying the kinds of evidence she needs to gather in support of this argument. As with consistency, the way the researcher provides support for the meaningfulness of interpretations varies from one research approach to another. In some approaches, this consists essentially of achieving a well-grounded interpretation based on multiple sources of information, whereas in others, it may also include the statistical analyses of numerical data.

Finally, if the purpose of the research is to provide a basis for a *decision* or an *action*, or if it is highly probable that the research results may have implications for actions that might be taken by the consumers of the research, then the researcher needs to consider the consequences of that decision or action. She, or the consumers of the research, will need to articulate an argument that the interpretation of the observation report is relevant to the intended use, that it is actually useful for the intended use, that the consequences of the intended use are beneficial, and that the probability of potential unintended adverse consequences is minimal.

Generalizability in Empirical Research in Education

Researchers in education address issues of generalizability from a variety of perspectives, and use the term "generalizability" in a number of different ways. For example, the term is frequently used to refer to an inference from the observation of a single case or sample to a larger group. However, it is also used to refer to the inferential link between an observation and an interpretation and it sometimes refers to the dependability or consistency of the observations themselves. Many researchers have pointed out the limitations of viewing consistency as a desirable quality of observations, and discuss other qualities, such as trustworthiness, credibility, verisimilitude, authenticity, and comparability, as being equally, if not more, important (e.g., Lincoln & Denzin, 2000). In this chapter, I take a broader view that generalizability includes three different inferences: (a) from the observed phenomenon to the observation report, (b) from the observation report to the interpretation, and (c) from the interpretation to the use of the research. Associated with each of these inferences is a set of issues that need to be addressed: consistency of observation reports, meaningfulness of interpretations and consequences of research use.

Consistency of Observations and Reports

Consistency has to do with the extent to which any given observation report provides essentially the same information, or generalizes, across different aspects, or facets, of the observation and reporting procedure (e.g., instances, events, observers, ethnographers, categorizers, analysts, raters). When considering the consistency of research results, we need to question both the desirability of consistency and the level of consistency that will be acceptable. Is consistency of observation reports necessarily desirable? It is well known that consistency is an essential quality of measurements.[5] If a score is not a consistent measure of anything, how can it be a measure of something? However, concerns with *internal* consistency may limit the capacity of measures for providing information about the construct of interest. In the literature on writing assessment, some researchers view different "readings" of a composition by different raters as a positive outcome. Likewise, the "thick description" of ethnography is built up by bringing together multiple perspectives of a given event, all of which are likely to vary in some details, as well as in their emphasis or stance. So whether consistency is viewed as desirable or necessary will reflect the researcher's approach and perspective, as well as her purpose. If the researcher's purpose is to interpret different observation reports, or scores, as indicators or descriptions of essentially the same construct, as is the case with language assessment, then consistency among reports is essential. If, however, the purpose is primarily to describe the phenomenon in all its richness, as in conversational analysis and ethnography, then variations in reports may be viewed as adding to and enhancing the description of the phenomenon.

If consistency is considered desirable or necessary, then another question that we need to address is, "What level of consistency is acceptable?" How consistent, and in what ways, do the observations, or data collection procedures need to be? How consistent, and in what ways, do test scores, transcriptions, ethnographies, analyses, or reports of different observers need to be, to be reliable, trustworthy, or credible? The answer to this question depends, of course, on the importance and types of decisions or actions to be taken. If one is making potentially life-affecting decisions about people, as in high-stakes testing, we need to have highly reliable measures. However, if we are testing a theoretical hypothesis in research, how consistent do our reports need to be? What if were are primarily interested in providing a description of a particular phenomenon? How trustworthy does this description need to be? The way we answer these questions in educational research will determine how we view and operationalize generalizability as consistency in our research, whether this is in the form of a statistical estimate of reliability, or a consensus of researcher observations.

Meaningfulness of Interpretations

When a researcher interprets her observations, she is, in effect, attaching meaning to these with respect to some domain of prior research or experience, or a theoretical position, in the field. Thus, the research may enrich her understanding of general processes involved in interaction, or of co-constructing discourse, or it may lead to a new generalization about these. But while the researcher may feel very confident about the meaningfulness of her interpretation, how do other researchers evaluate her claim of meaningfulness?

Meaningfulness in Quantitative Research

Within quantitative approaches to research, meaningfulness has been conceptualized from two perspectives: research design and measurement. In a classic article, Campbell and Stanley (1963) describe two types of meaningfulness, or validity, in experimental and quasi-experimental designs: external validity and internal validity. *External validity* is what might be called generalizability or extrapolation from the results of a study based on a sample, to a population or to other similar settings. External validity thus has to do with the extent to which the research results generalize beyond the study itself. *Internal validity,* on the other hand, is the extent to which the causal connection between treatment and outcome that is inferred from the results is supported by features of the research design itself (e.g., randomization, distinctiveness of treatments, non-interaction between treatments). In measurement, *validity* refers to the meaningfulness and appropriateness of interpretations. Validity is sometimes seen as a unitary concept, and evidence in support of the validity or meaningfulness of interpretations can be collected in a variety of ways (e.g., content coverage, concurrent relatedness, predictive utility). However, recent argument-based approaches to conceptualizing validity in educational measurement have taken a view that validity depends on the coherence of the validity argument, and quality of the evidence, both qualitative and quantitative, that is collected to support that argument. I extend this argument-based approach so as to link not only observations with interpretations, but also to provide a means for linking interpretations to intended uses—the decisions or actions that may be taken on the basis of interpretations—and the consequences of these decisions or actions.

Meaningfulness in Qualitative Research

Within the approaches to research that are broadly referred to as "qualitative," meaningfulness, or validity, is also of concern, although the way it is conceptualized and implemented in practice differs, understandably, from that of quantitative research design and measurement. As with quantitative research, validity within the qualitative research tradition has been conceived from several different perspectives.

Kirk and Miller (1999) define the issue of validity in qualitative research as "a question of whether the researcher sees what he or she thinks he or she sees" (p. 21). In a similar vein, Lynch (1996) defines validity as "the correspondence between the researcher's ëaccount' of some phenomenon and their 'reality' (which may be the participant's constructions of the phenomena)" (p. 55). Lynch discusses several different types of validity: descriptive validity (the factual accuracy of the research account), interpretive validity (how accurately the account describes what the phenomenon means to the participants—excluding the researcher), theoretical validity (how well the account explains the phenomenon), generalizability (internal generalizations within the group being studied and external generalization to other groups) and evaluative validity (how accurately the research account assigns value judgments to the phenomenon). Lynch also discusses validity in terms of "trustworthiness criteria": credibility, transferability, dependability and confirmability. Lynch describes a variety of techniques for assessing and assuring validity in qualitative/naturalistic research (e.g., prolonged engagement, persistent observation, negative case analysis, thick description, dependability audit and confirmability audit) (p. 57). Lynch also discusses the use of triangulation, which he describes as "the gathering and reconciling of data from several sources and/or from different data-gathering techniques" (p. 59). Citing the limitations of the navigational metaphor of triangulation, Lynch discusses another metaphor for this approach, that of detective work. In this metaphor, the researcher sifts through the data collected from multiple sources, looking not only for agreement, but also searching for examples of disagreement. In this way, triangulation is not a confirmation of the meaningfulness through the collection of research results that converge, but is rather "the search for an explanation of contradictory evidence" (p. 61).

In summary, meaningfulness, or validity, is of paramount interest and concern in both quantitative and qualitative/naturalistic approaches to educational research. For both research approaches, the essential question is the extent to which the researcher's interpretation of, or the meaning he attaches to the phenomenon that is observed, can be justified, in terms of the evidence collected in the research study. In evaluating the meaningfulness of his interpretations, the researcher is, in effect, constructing an argument that his interpretation is justified, and collecting evidence that is relevant to supporting or justifying this interpretation. Whereas the structure of the validity argument may well be essentially the same irrespective of the research approach used, the types of evidence collected and the methods for collecting these will vary considerably across different research approaches, and will be highly specific to any given research study.

Decisions and Consequences

The research that we conduct may lead to a decision based on the meaning that is attached to the observation. These decisions will have an impact on, or consequences for, different groups of stakeholders. If, for example, the interpretation of our observation report leads to placing in question a particular hypothesis or proposition that might be part of a theory or widely-held view in the field, it may result in a reformulation of the theory or view, or in its rejection by the field. This, in turn, may affect the research that is subsequently conducted, and that gets published by other researchers, or the ways in which the results of other research are interpreted. In much educational research, however, the intended use is to produce findings with implications for addressing real-world issues, such as the impact of class size, classroom organization, student interactions on learning, or the effects of accommodations in standardized achievement assessments for students with disabilities and English language learners.

Consequences of Decisions

In much educational research, the use that is made of an interpretation takes the form of an action or an implication for action in the real world. These actions will have consequences for individuals beyond those whose performance was part of our research. For example, language educators may use interpretations of research on classroom interactions to implement changes in language curricula and pedagogical practice. Or, test users may use our interpretations of performance on a language test to make decisions about certifying individuals' professional qualifications, about issuing them a visa, or about hiring them. When our interpretations are used to make decisions or actions beyond the research itself, we need to extend our notion of generalizability to include the consequences of the way we use our results. That is, we need to consider the *impact* of our research on those who will be affected by our decisions or actions. This is of particular importance when the lives of other individuals, such as students, teachers, or of institutions, such as schools and school districts, may be affected by the uses that are made of our research results.

Responsibility of the Researcher

If the results of educational research do, indeed, have consequences, or impact, beyond the research itself, then it would be reasonable to consider the question of the extent or limit of the researcher's responsibility for the way research results are used. It is in the field of assessment, where measurement specialists or assessment users are most often held accountable for the ways in which the results of their tests are used, that the issues of responsibility for consequences has been discussed most extensively. In the language testing literature, for example, there has been an expanding discussion of ethics and consequences. As some others, Hamp-Lyons (1997) discuss the language tester's (researcher's) responsibility for the way the results of a given test (research study) are used. She finesses the issue of the tester's responsibility for making himself aware of or anticipating possible misuses of tests. I have taken a more proactive stance toward the language tester's responsibility for anticipating unintended consequences, arguing that the language test developer should "list the potential consequences, both positive and negative, of using a particular test" and then "rank these [potential consequences] in terms of the desirability or undesirability of their occurring" (Bachman, 1990, p. 283). In Bachman and Palmer (forthcoming) I take this a step further, arguing that unintended consequences need to be anticipated and that statements about their potential seriousness, and the likelihood of their happening need to be articulated by the test developer as part of an assessment use argument. Then, depending upon the potential seriousness and likelihood of these happening, the test developer may need to allocate appropriate resources to minimize these. These discussions of consequences and the responsibility of the language test developer are also relevant to research in education.

If we accept this line of reasoning, then educational researchers should articulate, as part of their research design, an argument supporting the intended uses of their research results, in which they indicate what they believe would be appropriate uses and beneficial consequences of their research results, and what they would consider inappropriate, or would have detrimental consequences for different groups of stakeholders. It is currently quite common for funding agencies to require researchers to provide a statement of the possible impact of their research on various individuals, groups, or institutions. What is not so common, is asking researchers to anticipate what the possible detrimental impacts of their research might be.

Research Use Arguments

The inferential links between an observed phenomenon, an observation report, an interpretation, and the use of the educational research results were discussed and illustrated in Figure 7.1 above. But whereas the researcher may *claim* that these links are justified, if she wants to *convince* the various audiences to whom the research is directed, the inferences that constitute these links need to be supported by a coherent argument and evidence. Whereas the specific details of that argument and the kinds of evidence that will be acceptable or convincing will vary across different research approaches, I propose that the basic *structure* of these arguments is essentially the same for all, and can be characterized more generally as a "research use argument."

A *research use argument* (RUA) employs the reasoning of informal arguments to explicitly state all the claims and assumptions that are entailed in a particular research study. As such, it provides an overarching framework for guiding the design and implementation of empirical research in education, and for the interpretation and use of research results. An RUA is essentially a generalized form of an "assessment use argument," which I describe as a framework for linking assessment performance with scores, interpretations, and uses (Bachman, 2006). Unlike formal logic, in which conclusions are certain, following regularly from the premises according to the rules of inference, in informal arguments, support is provided for the plausibility of, or "presumptions in favor of conclusions or decisions" (Kane, 2006, p. 27). Kane argues that evaluating the interpretations and uses of test results involves a wide range of judgments about appropriateness, relevance, and value, which cannot be fit into a formal logical syllogism. Thus, real-world arguments must consider how well they fit with the data of our observations, experience, and prior knowledge, and how appropriate they are to a particular use.

The structure of an assessment use argument that I describe follows Toulmin's (2003) argument structure. At the center of an assessment use argument is a link between some *data*, or observations, and a *claim*, or an interpretation of those observations. This link is supported by various *warrants*, which are statements that we use to justify the link between the observation and the interpretation. These warrants are in turn supported by *backing*, which consists of evidence that may come from prior research or experience, or that is collected by the researcher specifically to support the warrant. In addition to these parts, the argument also includes *rebuttals*, or potential alternative interpretations or counterclaims to the intended interpretation. These rebuttals may be either weakened or strengthened by *rebuttal data*.

I suggest that an RUA can provide a framework for guiding empirical research in education. Such an argument can provide a principled basis for linking observations of phenomena to intended interpretations and uses. An RUA can thus be used not only as a guide in the design and development of specific research studies, but can also inform a program of research for collecting the most critical evidence in support of the interpretations and uses for which the research is intended. The primary function of an RUA is *not* to falsify a theory, in a positivistic sense, but rather to convince or persuade one or more specific audiences—fellow researchers, journal reviewers, funding agencies, tenure committees, teachers, school administrators, curriculum developers, policy makers— that the researcher's claim or interpretation is useful for some purpose.

The criterion by which educational research should be judged is not the extent to which it captures a glimpse of the "Truth," but by its usefulness. The usefulness of a given research study will be determined by the cogency of the RUA that underlies the research and the quality of the evidence that is collected by the researcher to support the claims made in the RUA. In order for the research to be useful, the RUA and its supporting evince needs to be convincing to relevant audiences or stakeholders.

Using an RUA as a rationale and organizing principle for research enables educational researchers to break away from attempts to emulate "scientific" research in the natural sciences, and from the never-ending paradigm debate between the so-called quantitative and qualitative approaches to research. In addition, as discussed next, I believe that an RUA can provide a conceptual framework and rationale for the appropriate use of multiple approaches, or mixed methods, for collecting evidence to support the claims made by the researcher.

Combining Different Perspectives
and Approaches in Research

Is the complementary use of multiple approaches in a single study desirable or even possible? What is the value added of attempting to use complementary approaches? Is it possible to gain important insights about a phenomenon through multiple approaches? There are examples too numerous to mention of research in education that have productively combined qualitative and quantitative approaches to yield richer and, in my view, better supported interpretations and insights into the phenomena they have investigated. (On combining qualitative and quantitative methods, see the contributions to section II.) The metaphor of triangulation is often used to describe a viable way to obtain converging evidence from multiple approaches. However, multiple approaches can also be used to investigate possible alternative interpretations, or what Lynch (1996) calls "negative case analysis," the search for instances in the data that do not fit with an interpretation suggested by other data in the study. Thus, with respect to using multiple approaches, we need to ask, "at what level are the approaches combined—philosophical perspective, approach to defining the phenomenon or construct that is of interest, procedures for observing and reporting, the researcher's ontological stance?" In many studies, it is not always clear that there is a genuine combining of approaches; rather, the combination appears to be opportunistic and unplanned. For example, quantitative research with a qualitative "add on" to hopefully help make some sense of the quantitative analyses, or counting frequencies of occurrences of categorizations based on naturalistic observation, and then using a test of statistical significance, might superficially combine aspects of different research approaches, without integrating these into a single coherent study. There is thus a need for a principled basis for determining, for a particular study, whether to combine approaches, and if so, at what level, how, and why.

There is a rich literature, going back to the mid 1980s, in the social sciences and education, discussing multiple approaches, or what is more commonly referred to now as "mixed methods" research, and several collections and handbooks of mixed methods research are available. Recently, Johnson and Onwuegbuzie (2004) have argued for a pragmatic and balanced or pluralist position to inform the use of qualitative, quantitative, or mixed approaches to research. Drawing on the work of the American pragmatist philosophers Peirce, James, and Dewey, they arrive at a pragmatic principle that is essentially the same as the criterion of the usefulness of research that I have discussed above: "when judging ideas we should consider their empirical and practical consequences" (p. 17). Extending this principle to research methods, they argue that the decision on what research approach to take—quantitative, qualitative, or mixed—for a given research study should be based not on doctrinaire or philosophical positions, but rather on the consideration of which approach is the most appropriate and likely to yield the most important insights into the research question.

Consideration and discussion of pragmatism by research methodologists and empirical researchers will be productive because it offers an immediate and useful middle position philosophically and methodologically; it offers a practical and outcome-oriented method of inquiry that is based on action and leads, iteratively, to further action and the elimination of doubt; and it offers a method for selecting methodological mixes that can help researchers better answer many of their research questions.

Johnson and Onwuegbuzie go on to describe a typology of mixed research methods, along with a process model for making decisions about research methodologies in the design and implementation of research. Empirical research in education has much to learn from the literature on mixed methods research. It is clear that such research is not only feasible, but is also highly desirable, in that it expands the methodological tools that are at the researcher's disposal, thereby increasing the likelihood that the insights gained from the research will constitute genuine advances in our knowledge.

Conclusion

For at least the last quarter of a century research in education has been seriously compromised as well as that of many others, by a "paradigm debate" between so-called "quantitative vs. qualitative" or "positivist vs. constructivist" approaches to research. Writing in 1989, after what Gage then referred to as the "Paradigm Wars" between "naturalist, positivistic" research and its critics, the "anti-naturalists," the "interpretivists," and the "critical theorists," had, in his view, "come to a sanguinary climax," Gage engaged in a thought experiment, looking ahead 20 years to 2009. In one scenario of his thought experiment, the objectivist-quantitative researchers were utterly defeated by the onslaught of criticism, which ushered in a new era in which students no longer took courses in measurement and statistics, research grants, and contracts were almost never given to quantitative researchers, and journals shunned articles that reported tests of statistical significance, effect sizes or correlations. Furthermore, these changes had beneficial effects on teaching, as teachers began to realize that "small changes in teaching made a big difference in student achievement" and in teaching history, "pupils were sensitized to the ways in which their previous history courses had neglected almost everything done by people who were not white men, political leaders, military heroes, or industrialists" (Gage, 1989, p. 6).

In Gage's second scenario, things turned out quite differently. The interpretivists and critical theorists continued to do research and did bring about the kinds of improvements in curriculum and teaching their views and research implied. But positivistic research did not decline. Rather, the field recovered from its confusion and "came to a great awakening" (p. 6). Researchers came to realize that "paradigm differences do not require paradigm conflict" and that "nothing about objective-quantitative research precluded the description and analysis of classroom processes with the interpretative-qualitative methods" (p. 7). So the world of educational research was the happiest place on earth.

In Gage's third scenario, the wars raged on.

> The invective and vituperation continued.... Some ... suggested that the wars continued because they were rooted in deep-seated differences in human temperament and values ... were embedded in the ethos of *communities* of researchers, who huddled together in embattled camps and fought off the aggressions of their opponents. (p. 9)

Gage ends his thought experiment with the almost wistful but hauntingly prophetic rhetorical question, "How long the war will last, and whether it will lead to the demise of social and educational research . . . are questions that cannot be answered in the year 2009" (p. 9).

Gage eventually ends his discussion on a positive note, challenging educational researchers to reach "recognize the foolishness of these paradigm wars on the way to an honest and productive rapprochement between the paradigms" (p. 10). But here we are, nearly at 2009, and a recent report produced by the National Research Council on research in education (Towne, Wise, & Winters, 2004), with its unapologetic and unqualified endorsement of "scientifically based" research, and the flurry of responses this raised in our field demonstrates to me, at least, that the wars smolder on.

In this chapter I outline a broad view of the research enterprise and of generalizability in empirical research in education. According to this view, generalizability is a concept that has different aspects—consistency, meaningfulness and consequences. Articulating these aspects as part of a research use argument can provide empirical researchers in education of all philosophical and methodological persuasions a basis for interpreting their observations, and for considering the possible uses and consequences of these interpretations. I suggest that we adopt an epistemology of argumentation that moves away from one that seems to be driven by a preoccupation with our differences (e.g., quantitative, positivistic, theory falsification vs. qualitative, naturalistic, descriptive; "science" vs. "non-science") and toward one that admits a wide range of empirical stances and methodologies. I further suggest that adopting such an epistemology enables researchers in education to break away from attempts to emulate "scientific" research in the natural sciences, and from the never-ending paradigm debate between so-called quantitative and qualitative approaches to research.

Notes

1. Although there are obvious differences between the physical and biological sciences in terms of what they observe and what they are interested in, for purposes of my argument, I use a single term, "natural sciences" to include both.
2. The term "percept," which has a long history in philosophy of language and mind and more recently in theories of perception, captures, I believe, this level of perception. On perception see chapter 11 of this volume by Wolff-Michael Roth.
3. Note that Schumann includes the "biosphere," the domain of living things, within the physiosphere.
4. For Pierce, a sign involves three elements: the *sign* itself, the characteristics of the *object* that the sign signifies, and the *interpretant*, or the person who recognizes the relationship between the sign and the object. The precise characterization of these three elements, however, is not relevant to my discussion here.
5. I am using "consistency" as a broader term than psychometric "reliability."

References

Bachman, L. F. (1990). *Fundamental considerations in language testing.* Oxford, UK: Oxford University Press.

Bachman, L. F. (2006). *Linking interpretation and use in educational assessments.* Paper presented at the National Council for Measurement in Education, San Francisco, April 2006.

Bachman, L. F., & Palmer, A. S. (Forthcoming). *Language assessment in practice* (2nd ed.). Oxford, UK: Oxford University Press.

Campbell, D. T., & Stanley, J. (1963). *Experimental and quasi-experimental designs for research.* Chicago: Rand McNally.

Ercikan, K., & Roth, W.-M. (2006). What good is polarizing research into quantitative and qualitative? *Educational Researcher, 35*(5), 14–23.

Gage, N. L. (1989). The paradigm wars and their aftermath: A "historical" sketch of research on teaching since 1989. *Educational Researcher, 18*(7), 4–10.

Hamp-Lyons, L. (1997). Ethics in language testing. In C. Clapham & D. Corson (Eds.), *Encyclopedia of language and education* (Vol. 7: Language testing and assessment, pp. 323–333). Dordrecht, The Netherlands: Kluwer.

Johnson, R. B., & Onwuegbuzie, A. J. (2004). Mixed methods research: a research paradigm whose time has come. *Educational Researcher, 33*(7), 14–26.

Kane, M. (2006). Validation. In R. L. Brennan (Ed.), *Educational measurement* (4th ed., pp. 18–64). New York: American Council on Education and Praeger Publishers.

Kirk, J., & Miller, M. L. (1999). *Reliability and validity in qualitative research.* Newbury Park, CA: Sage.

Lincoln, Y. S., & Denzin, N. K. (Eds.). (2000). *The handbook of qualitative research* (2nd ed.). Newbury Park, CA: Sage.

Logan, R. K., & Schumann, J. H. (2005). The symbolosphere, conceptualization, language and neo-dualism. *Semiotica, 155,* 201–214.

Lynch, B. K. (1996). *Language program evaluation: Theory and practice.* Cambridge, UK: Cambridge University Press.

Mathison, S. (1988). Why triangulate? *Educational Researcher, 17*(2), 13–17.

Ochs, E. (1979). Transcription as theory. In E. Ochs & B. B. Schieffelin (Eds.), *Developmental pragmatics* (pp. 47–72). New York: Academic Press.

Peirce, C. S. (1992). *The essential Peirce: Selected philosophical writings,* Vol. 1. N. Hauser & C. Kloesel (Eds.). Bloomington: Indiana University Press.

Schumann, J. H. (2003). *The evolution of the symbolosphere.* Center for Governance, University of California, Los Angeles.

Toulmin, S. E. (2003). *The uses of argument* (Updated ed.). Cambridge, UK: Cambridge University Press.

Towne, L., Wise, L. L., & Winters, T. M. (Eds.). (2004). *Advancing scientific research in education.* Washington, DC: National Academies Press.

Chapter 8

Repetition, Difference, and Rising Up with Research in Education

Kenneth Tobin

[G]enerality expresses a point of view according to which one term may be exchanged or substituted for another. The exchange or substitution of particulars defines our conduct in relation to generality. That is why the empiricists are not wrong to present general ideas as particular ideas in themselves, so long as they add the belief that each of these can be replaced by any other particular idea which resembles it in relation to a given word. By contrast we can see that repetition is a necessary and justified conduct only in relation to that which cannot be replaced. Repetition as a conduct and as a point of view concerns non-exchangeable and non-substitutable singularities.

Deleuze, 1968/1994, p. 1

As I first encountered it, generalizability was a useful construct whereby something I learned from research was applied with due caution in a different context. In the social sciences generalizability arises from statistical analyses in which samples are drawn and statistics are calculated based on data from the sample. Then, what is learned from the sample is generalized to the population. What I have not said so far is that the "something learned" arises from an empirical investigation involving human participants and is "applied" to different others—arguably like those in the study. In the excerpt that begins this chapter, Deleuze notes that for generality to other fields to be possible, participants in the new field must be identical to those in the original study. However, since participants in social life are individuals who are different, whereas it makes sense to substitute one molecule of oxygen with another, it seems like a stretch to substitute any person with another. Even when the same individuals are involved, in the same spaces, substitution is not warranted, because as individuals grow older, even by a few seconds, they change.

At the heart of generalizability in the social sciences is confidence that claims are dependable, implying substitution across time and space. Since this is not feasible, perhaps the construct that best fits research in the social sciences, and social life at large, is repetition, rather than generality. A central question in empirical research in the social sciences is—what confidence do I have in a claim that some cultural pattern will repeat in fields similar to those applicable to a study? Although this question maps nicely on to situations that generalize from sample to population, there are broader concerns about the veracity of knowledge claims.

In the following sections of this chapter, I present an autobiography that traces the ways in which I have encountered generalizability in my research and a growing realization that viability of research findings is an essential factor associated with the uptake of educational research. Increasingly my concerns focused on the beneficence of research to participants, and used research design favoring activist genres. An integral part of the approach I take in the chapter is to show how my changing theoretical frameworks were associated with different research goals and methods.

An Autobiographical Approach

The issue of generalizability has particular salience to me because over a career of more than 30 years as an educational researcher, my ideas on generalizability have changed dramatically. Also, as a teacher, I have had the experience of putting generalizable research findings into practice, initially with considerable success and then with unexpected failure when I applied what I knew in urban science classes. This personal experience assisted me to see shortcomings in the generalizability construct. In this chapter I examine events selected from my career as a researcher in relation to the bottom line for generalizability, that is, how to repeat desirable outcomes from a research field in my professional practice as an educator. I describe my understandings and uses of generalizability, repetition, and difference in a historical autobiography, a trajectory that includes the following road stops: skepticism about research in the social sciences; doing quasi-experiments; participating in forms of inquiry grounded in social theories such as hermeneutics and phenomenology; and enacting activist forms of research. In so doing I address the ways in which generalizability was salient to my research and, often tacitly, how I was oriented to inform my own practices by what I learned and accepted as credible from research, and efforts to educate others based on my learning, including empirical research and understandings of theory and its possible applications. As my experience as a researcher expanded, my changing epistemology and ontology afforded a continuously evolving understanding of the purposes, potential, and nature of educational research.

Before commencing an autobiographical journey, in the next section I address what is involved when there is an endeavor to repeat research outcomes in another educational field. My perspective is grounded in cultural sociology rather than the more familiar psychological and philosophical frameworks that have dominated educational scholarship. To assist readers unfamiliar with some of the specialized concepts that are central to my work, I provide a glossary of terms in the appendix to this chapter.

Perspectives on Repetition

This section provides an overview of a theoretical framework for repetition of research outcomes in three parts, which address research as culture, creation of thought objects, and doing thought experiments, and the structuring of repetition in the reproduction of research outcomes that bear a family resemblance to those anticipated by theory or that were obtained in previous research.

Research as Culture

Educational research is a study of culture, which I consider to be experienced as patterned actions (i.e., practices) and dialectically related schemas. Alfred Schutz (1962) noted that "Action may be covert (for example, the attempt to solve a scientific problem mentally) or overt, gearing into the outer world; it may take place by commission or omission, purposive abstention from acting being considered an action in itself" (p. 20). I regard differences between covert and overt actions as arbitrary, since schemas mediate experiences with the outside in much the same way that schemas I produce in thought are grounded in experience. As a researcher, this issue is important because there is a tendency to separate theoretical, empirical and everyday knowledge (e.g., in claiming that research outcomes are generalizable). From my perspective, differences between theoretically and empirically derived knowledge are not salient, since, with repetition as a goal, viability of knowledge is the central issue. To be considered viable, knowledge must fit with what else is known, not clash with experience in the outside world and, when it is put to overt and covert tests, remain tenable by continuing to produce expected outcomes.

Creating Thought Objects

Doing research (i.e., seeking to learn from research) involves a search for patterns and associated contradictions as culture is enacted in fields germane to education. What is learned from research is adapted by peer review, initially involving participants within a research squad and, gradually involving others more distant from the research. In the process, others' perspectives refine research outcomes, which are presented at conferences and published as proceedings, journal articles, pages on the World Wide Web, chapters in books, and books. Based on what is heard and read, research outcomes and salient details of the research context are produced as thought objects, which become foci for critical reflection in conversations with others and internal (i.e., covert) actions. Thought objects can be elaborated by thinking and writing about them and in dialogues with others.

Thought experiments arise when knowledge is put to the test on the inside, that is during covert encounters when a person applies thought objects in selected imagined contexts. For example, a science teacher learning about a new questioning strategy can imagine herself asking questions in ways that cohere with her understandings of the research outcomes and project whether her students would conduct their roles as others did in the research field. This can be one part of a social process of deciding whether or not knowledge claims from research are viable. If thought experiments and interactions with others support an endeavor to apply knowledge in an educational setting, that is, if the knowledge remains viable, repetition may be attempted as knowledge is put to the test on the outside. As participants enact their plan, that is put their knowledge to the test, their praxis (i.e., enacted knowledge as it unfolds with time), is structured partly by the thought objects previously referred to and other dynamic structures of the field.

Structure and Repetition

As culture, knowledge is produced through praxis within fields, which are structured by resources to support the agency of participants. My research priority is to understand the dynamic flux of structures (i.e., resources to support action), since enacted culture anticipates structures and contributes to them. The structural flux of a field is dynamic and changes continuously over time and space, as culture is produced. Accessing and appropriating the structures of a field affords agency, which is the power to conduct social life. Structure and agency presuppose one another and are mutually constitutive and dialectically interrelated.

If I consider agency|structure[1] relationships in terms of repeating what is learned from a study, the likelihood of reproducing particular research outcomes seems greater when similar structures occur in the field in which repetition is to occur. Using matrix algebra as a metaphor to illustrate this claim, S represents the structures associated with research outcomes, R, in a field of study. That is, S is an affordance for R. Because structures are dynamic, there is no certainty that outcomes obtained from earlier research and theorizing will repeat as hypothesized. If the goal is to repeat R in a new field, Schutz (1962) notes, "'repeated' action will be something else than a mere re-performance" (p. 21). Repetition is experienced as cultural reproduction (and associated transformation), evident in patterns of coherence with ever-present contradictions. In the new field, the repetition of R is experienced as family resemblance, R'. The likelihood of producing R' in the new field is higher when structures like S are reproduced, here denoted as S'. That is, S' provides a resonant condition to "bring to hand" dispositions to enact R'. Viability does not imply determinism because of the dynamic nature of cultural fields and, repetition involves the reproduction of family resemblance, not substitution (i.e., R' rather than R).

Having presented a theoretical framework for considering repetition, I now turn to autobiographical episodes and examine their salience to generality and repetition in educational research.

From Skeptic to Quasi-Experimenter

There was a time when I did not think there could be any such thing as credible research in education. I was finishing up the coursework component of a master's degree in physics, while teaching high school physics, chemistry, and biology. My goals were to study for a doctorate in physics and obtain a university position as a physics professor. Because of my experiences as a science teacher and physics student, I understood physics through the lenses of positivism and solved many problems in terms of variables and causal relationships. I could not see social life through the same lenses and in comparison with physics, social science (including education) seemed unpredictable and virtually impossible to control.

In 1974 I got a job as a science teacher educator, involved in preparing teachers of science in elementary and middle school grades. As distinct from my science disciplinary focus of just a year earlier, I was exploring issues about teaching and learning, and accessing science education research journals, especially those that explored problem solving and inquiry from a Piagetian perspective. I wanted to identify teaching strategies that were effective in producing higher science achievement. As a new consumer of education research, I quickly realized that whether or not research would make a difference to my practice depended primarily on whether I regarded it as credible and relevant. Though I did not yet use the term "viability," I considered it a priority to consider whether what I learned from a study was potentially viable.

What Makes Research Worth Doing?

An insightful moment occurred during a colloquium when a science educator gave a presentation on the relationship between teacher wait time and the incidence of verbal inquiry in students' talk. As he spoke, my mind was focused on the bottom line—would the use of an extended wait time create environments conducive to higher science achievement? By the time the colloquium finished, I had completed a thought experiment, figuring out that the teacher and students would use additional time to make sense of their experiences, and improve the quality of their encounters. I concluded that teacher wait time would probably increase student achievement by creating classroom environments in which inquiry would occur. Also, I hypothesized that the patterns of social conduct associated with using a long wait time would be repeated and improve the quality of science learning environments in grades 5 to 7 in suburban schools in Western Australia. I asked a few questions and, when the colloquium was over, I approached the speaker to ask whether or not he thought the study I contemplated was worth doing. He remarked, "Everything that needs to be researched in wait time has been done already." These words capture my recollections of what was said—he was discouraging to say the least. What was he assuming? First, the patterns he identified in his research in the United States would be repeated in Australia. Second, the production of particular patterns of verbal interaction would produce higher science achievement irrespective of geographic location. Third, the study I proposed would replicate some of what had been done already and would not produce new knowledge.

I disagreed with his stance, its shaky assumptions, and failure to acknowledge the necessity, in the changed social contexts, to test the robustness of his claims and extend the scope to include science achievement. Although I regarded his research claims as credible and applicable to my practices, the fields of education in Australia and the United States were (and are) so different; hence, replication and extension were desirable, expanding what we knew about wait time and science education. My colleague's perspectives seem grounded in a view of research as discovering truths that transcend context, bolstering an argument that replication is unnecessary, even in another country. The position that "everything has been done already" reflects over-generalizing, a frequent problem in the social sciences with dire consequences for learning from research, building research programs, and creating policy grounded in research outcomes. His perspectives miss an important point. It does not matter what he, as a researcher, believes or regards as truths about generalizability. As a consumer, researcher and teacher educator, I believed that what had been done already was just the tip of an iceberg of what needs to be done. Accordingly, I began a long journey of research on wait time in science classes.

Doing Research on Wait Time

My first study was quasi-experimental, incorporating the manipulation of teaching practices in an investigation of students' science achievement. At the design stage, my concerns were to ensure that I did not limit the study's objectivity and detract from the generalizability of the results. I identified 30 teachers and invited them to participate in the study. Their classes were grades 5 to 7. One teacher taught all subject areas to the same students for the academic year. I randomly assigned the teachers and their classes to one of two groups—a treatment that used a long wait time, and a control in which wait time was not manipulated. During a relatively long study of 15 weeks, in which three related science topics were taught, seven teachers withdrew. I ascertained that attrition was unrelated to the assigned treatment group, analyzed the data, rejected the null hypotheses, and concluded that my research hypotheses were supported. I regarded the research outcomes as viable and was confident in recommending that teachers use a long wait time if they teach science in schools like those involved in my research. As a science teacher educator, I ensured that new teachers and those involved in professional development knew about wait time and practiced using longer wait times when they taught.

I regarded the knowledge from my research as viable and that it could be reproduced in contexts like those involved in the study. That is, thought objects could be enacted, producing structures (S') and outcomes (R') bearing a family resemblance to S and R that applied to the conduct of the original research.

Expanding the Scope of My Research

Limitations to my first study that warranted changes in methods included theoretical incompatibilities in the use of: Piagetian psychology to underpin the research questions; positivism to frame the research design and associated methods; and, to justify generalizing the results, assumptions that participants were replaceable objects. Peer review from other scholars (including thesis examiners and dissertation advisors[2]) led me to expand the research foci to explore how relationships between teacher wait time and science achievement were mediated by student participation.

Studies of student participation tended to dichotomize students' actions as on or off task. I realized that a dichotomy would not be useful in science education and developed an observation protocol to code participation of the teacher and students in terms of a cognitive hierarchy of participation categories. Similarly, I investigated science achievement as a hierarchy of process skills. Accordingly, the research design was more sophisticated than my first study, including many more variables and their hypothesized relationships. For example, the teacher variables were dependent in relation to teacher wait time, which was manipulated, and independent in relation to student engagement. The inclusion of more variables and the use of a more sophisticated model supported my belief that the research was more likely to produce outcomes that were potentially useful for teachers to improve the quality of science teaching and learning. I used multivariate statistics to estimate a network of relationships, but I was bothered by the causation embodied in my theoretical model. One of my advisors queried the unidirectional aspects of my arguments and research design, especially in regard to wait time affecting teacher variables such as questioning clarity, cognitive level, and relevance. He encouraged me to incorporate a level of complexity that involved multidirectional paths between variables, arguing, for example, that what students did was just as likely to affect wait time as wait time was to affect what students did.

Although statistical models at the time were developed to calculate path coefficients in complicated models like those suggested by my advisor, there were few published studies that included such analyses. I did the analyses but did not publish the paper, mainly because my priorities were changing. I was concerned with reductionism in my research. Leading researchers like Mary Budd Rowe (1974) argued against the reductionist turn in education research alluding to research that addressed macrolevel questions such as the impact of high stakes testing on enacted curricula. Her concerns encouraged me to consider researching macrostructures, such as epistemology and ontology, in relation to teaching and learning.

Over-Generalizing

During a colloquium I was disseminating what I learned from a 10-year program of research on wait time in the United States and Australia. A colleague who did research with Australian Aboriginals, asked me whether an extended wait time would be effective in cross-cultural settings. I assured him it would, clearly extrapolating beyond the limits of the external validity of the research that had been done. The basis for my confidence in generalizing was probably grounded in a quick thought experiment conducted as the question was asked. Although my colleague was committed to the idea that teaching had to be culturally adaptive and that one size would not fit all, I was convinced by the universality of the research I had done and I represented wait time as the penicillin of education—good results when administered appropriately, and no harmful side effects. I did not seriously consider that an assumption was that participants in a study could be substituted for one another—an assumption I should have rejected as nonsense since, as a science teacher, I knew better. What seems clear two decades after the event is that my response had more to do with viability than generalizability. As I formulated a response to the question, more than likely I examined what I knew about wait time, teaching, and learning in relation to educating Australian Aboriginals. In providing a response, I synthesized all I knew, not differentiating between theoretically and empirically grounded knowledge. In the moments prior to and during the praxis of responding, I endeavored to communicate what I regarded as viable knowledge. Undue weight was not given to research outcomes, though they were the topic of the colloquium.

Generalizing from Ethnography

When I commenced ethnographic studies, my goal was to explore the big questions that had been so elusive in my statistically oriented research. The move to ethnography was intended to overcome some of the reductionist aspects of classroom research in which I had engaged. While doing ethnography, it was no longer necessary to look at social life in terms of variables and a huge advantage for me was to investigate questions arising during the conduct of a study. Hence, if my concerns were with improving the quality of science teaching, I could commence with broad questions and focus on issues arising in the research field. The project was interpretive and my purpose was to find out what was happening and why it was happening from the perspectives of the participants.

The relatively small number of participants in a study was a striking difference compared to my quasi-experiments. I did not use random selection, opting instead to involve participants intentionally, serially, and contingently (Guba & Lincoln, 1989). This was quite a change and it took me a while to let go of the idea that I needed to study a relatively large number of randomly selected participants in order to learn anything worthwhile. However, having too many participants can be a logistical nightmare and I had to reconsider the purpose of including participants in research in relation to the goals of ethnography. If the emphasis was to be on interpreting data in an ongoing way, then a serious question regarding division of labor was why have more than one participant involved at a time? This question catalyzed new ways of thinking about participants and took me beyond ever thinking of participants as subjects or a sample. Describing participants in terms of $N = 1$ was simply buying into a paradigm of research that did not apply to interpretive research.

I made every effort to provide details to allow readers to decide what aspects of my research might be applicable to their lifeworlds. The essence of my approach was to figure out what was happening from the perspectives of the participants and to look for and make sense of contradictions. At the time, my view of culture was that social life was experienced as patterns with thick coherence, discernible as practices and schema. Contradictions, when they occurred, had to be fully understood—not regarded as errors to be explained away. Because culture was enacted in fields regarded as having solid boundaries, the studies were highly contextualized and an imperative was to use thick description to describe patterns of coherence and make explicit the structures of fields in which the research occurred. It turned out that my view of culture being enacted as thick patterns in fields with solid borders was a significant constraint on the way I conducted and learned from interpretive research. In later sections of this chapter, it becomes clear that different ways of conceptualizing culture afforded fresh research methods and emphases.

What is apparent in this section is that designing a study with generalizability as a goal can lead to serious distortions in the focus of the research, the methods used, the outcomes, and the perceived relevance of the work to those involved in the study and the education community in general. Breaking away from the reductionism of doing research that involved variables and statistics was only a partial solution to a goal of conducting worthwhile educational research. It was necessary for me to carefully consider the humanity of participants and my purposes for involving them in research. Among the puzzles that needed to be resolved were how many participants to include in a study, when to include them, the nature of what could be learned from research, and how to handle diversity within a data set. Before addressing these issues, I turn to questions arising from others appropriating my research through presentations at meetings and in journals and books. As a researcher, it is not for me to decide whether others regard what they learn from my research as viable knowledge. In my writing I endeavor to fully describe the structures of the research field and the research outcomes. Then, it is for readers to create thought objects, do thought experiments, dialogue with others, and decide whether to apply what they have learned to their professional practices.

Does Generalizability Trump Plausibility?

In a recent publication Mansoor Niaz (2007) explores generalizability and, as part of his research, uses a paper I published with Sarah LaMaster, a teacher researcher. Niaz focuses on Sarah's use of a metaphor to reconstruct her practices regarding how she assessed science achievement in her class. Based on a social constructivist framework and ongoing research in her classroom, Sarah figured out that she could resolve many of the interpersonal conflicts in her class if she assessed the students differently, essentially focusing on what they knew rather than what they didn't know. Furthermore, Sarah was aware of her tendency to make sense of social life metaphorically, including how she taught. Accordingly, she created a metaphor, used it as a referent for teaching, and changed her classroom practices. Her action research produced viable knowledge for her and our research squad. That is, we found the research outcomes plausible. In writing the paper, our expectation was that educators would consider the viability of what we had learned. It seems as if this is what happened in Niaz's study. He reported that: "Almost 91% of the teachers agreed that generalization (external) in a different social context is feasible" (p. 442). It is a shame that Niaz framed the questionnaire used in his research in terms of generalizability. Perhaps the respondents found the study credible, felt that what they learned was viable, and were confident they could enact teaching differently to repeat the outcomes of our study.

Consistent with my goals for doing research to catalyze educational improvement, I hope that many of the teachers in Niaz's study successfully applied what they learned from our research to education in Venezuela. My stance is that what can be learned and possibly repeated from a study is not for a researcher to determine, but a professional decision necessarily left to potential consumers. More is involved than accepting what is claimed from research when considering whether research outcomes are viable. Other social truths are considered and contextual factors weigh into whether knowledge is considered viable in other fields. Furthermore, even if research outcomes are regarded as viable in given fields, they may not be enacted there until some later time, due to cultural lag. Whether culture is enacted in a field may not be consciously determined, when structures having a family resemblance to those of the research field arise (i.e., S'), resonances can occur, bringing to hand culture to be enacted in ways that cohere with research that was at some earlier time considered viable (i.e., R that would be reproduced|transformed to be experienced as R').

Producing Kernels for Thought

I undertook ethnographic research expecting triangulation to point toward social truths on which participants' experiences converged. Hence, the outcomes of my research at the time consisted of assertions (claims associated with patterns having thick coherence), evidence for and against them, and an imperative that evidence in favor would outweigh evidence against a viable assertion. I regarded assertions as grounded theory linked to the structures of the research fields. Repetition would be probable, that is outcomes would be repeated, when structures recurred. However, in arriving at assertions I had to make decisions on how to address difference. I regarded patterns of coherence as social truths and exceptions to them as invitations to learn more about social life in the research field. I was not pushed on whether I regarded deviations as social truths or errors, but it seems likely that I regarded them as anomalies or outliers rather than an expected characteristic of social life. It took many years for me to attain a level of comfort with the many ways in which to treat difference in my research, and especially to assign others' ontologies the same weight as my own. Learning from difference remains an ongoing challenge. Presently, I consider my research outcomes as kernels for others' actions and focus on making a compelling case about social life, allowing others to apply what they learn to fields in which they conduct their professional practices.

Research for Change

Throughout my career as a researcher, I adapted methods depending on what I believed about knowledge, teaching, and learning. For example, as I learned about radical constructivism I became uneasy about epistemological and ontological issues and the purposes of research in education. Guba and Lincoln's (1989) research methods became an appealing extension to interpretive research, especially the desirability of including the perspectives of all stakeholders and learning from them. My use of Guba and Lincoln's authenticity criteria to design, enact, and judge the worth of research focused my attention on a necessity for research to improve the quality of social life in the institutions participating in the research, thereby redressing a tendency for Western philosophy to undervalue human action in favor of theory. In the following subsections I examine the potential of research to improve the quality of social life by producing theoretical knowledge and improving praxis in the research field.

Producing Theory

I embrace a polysemic perspective on social life in which difference is acknowledged and learning from difference is valued. Adopting this perspective supports a goal of improving the social lives of participants through their involvement in research. A priority is for difference to be a resource for educating all participants in the research fields, thereby increasing understandings of advantage, disadvantage, equity, agency, affordances, and oppressive structures. A symmetrical process can be established to ensure that, across salient social categories (e.g., institutional position, ethnicity, gender, native language), each participant learns about and from the ontologies of others. As a result of participating in research, participants' ontologies should change, evident in the ways in which they give meaning to their educational experiences and the knowledge they consider viable.

Improving Praxis

How can the institutions and people involved in research be advantaged through their participation? Rather than focusing solely on theoretical knowledge, there is much to be gained from critically reflecting on what is learned and making changes to effect improvements. That is, theory produced can be used educatively with the goal of improving the praxis of all participants. It goes without saying that some individuals are placed in a field such that they are better positioned than others to take advantage of the benefits of being involved in research. Researchers can ensure that individuals who cannot autonomously benefit from research are assisted to overcome actual and possible disadvantages. The conduct of research can produce structures to expand the agency of all, not just participants who can reposition themselves to appropriate structures emerging during a study. Special efforts are made to help those who cannot readily help themselves because of oppressive structures, about which they are unaware, especially those that produce disadvantage passively (Roth, 2007). It is a priority for researchers to assume roles to assist disadvantaged participants to identify sources of hegemony and inequity, affording those from non-dominant groups learning and rising up against sources of their domination and disadvantage. Unless researchers are proactive in addressing sources of inequity, some individuals may not benefit from research and, if repetition is a goal, the extent to which it occurs might be uneven.

Beyond the Research Field

A primary goal is to expand participants' social possibilities by doing research, not just for the duration of a study, but beginning there and continuing thereafter. In disseminating what is learned, difference can be described and interpreted, respecting the rights of participants to be and remain different. People in other fields, not involved in research, also can benefit through their encounters with research participants. Like the ripples in a pond, the benefits from a study can extend outward, expanding the collective agency of participants and of those with whom they have encounters. Repetition occurs because social fields are unbounded, and culture from a field moves into other fields as research participants conduct social life in multiple fields, often restructuring them by reproducing culture initially produced in the research field.

Improving Social Life

In this section I show how desirable changes arise through active participation in a project built on good ideas. Rather than originating in formal research, this project grew from critical reflections on lived experiences and a search for improved social opportunities for people living in poverty, amidst crime and violence. Dialogues about the contradictions of social life and possible solutions produced a plan for improved social conditions to allow participants to actively participate, "rising up" against oppression and thereby expanding their horizons of possibility.

Favela Rising

Anderson Sa is a Brazilian activist and a member of the Afro Reggae band and cultural foundation, a movement that seeks to change the social lives of youth from the *favelas* of Rio de Janeiro. *Favelas* are shantytowns, largely inhabited by Afro-Brazilians who live in conditions of poverty—communities in which drug trafficking, violence, and crime are rampant. The rise of this social movement was depicted in *Favela Rising*, a film biography of Sa and José Junior (Zimbalist & Mochary, 2007), who collaborated in 1993 to create Grupo Cultural AfroReggae (GCAR, 2007) with the goal of providing youth with alternative ways to participate in society and thereby lessen the effects of violent oppression from corrupt police and youth drug armies. GCAR, which was established in a *favela* known as Vigário Geral, began by producing a newspaper and then adding a community center. The goal was to reproduce Black culture through participation in music genres such as reggae, soul, and hip-hop, thereby changing participants' identities and horizons of possibility. Over time, the repertoire of activities in which participants engaged expanded to include martial arts, literary expression (e.g., creating comic strips), sports, circus, and environmental issues such as recycling.

Individuals who joined GCAR practiced together at their community center and, through active participation, created new forms of culture and identity. From the community center the group moved into the *favela* to conduct live concerts, thereby entertaining others and creating recruitment incentives for potential members. The movement recognized that its slate of activities would be dynamic, changing to meet the interests of youth and providing forums for the growth of solidarity. Collectively, the group fought against racial prejudice while seeking to improve the quality of life in *favelas*. The activities of GCAR were disseminated, first throughout Vigário Geral and then through ripple effects to neighboring *favelas*, such as Parada de Lucas, "where rival narco-traffic factions have been living at war since 1985" (GCAR, 2007). According to the movie and the GCAR Web site, community support is widespread and even includes drug lords. As planned, the focus in new *favelas* differs according to local interests and priorities.

The possibilities for transforming social life emerge from active involvement in a project in which participants collaborate to produce new forms of culture. The planners of GCAR began with goals and a plan to overcome oppression and the lure of crime and violence—getting youth involved in activities in which they would experience success, contribute to society, build solidarity with others, and forge new identities. The creation of a sense of purpose through participation in GCAR projects fuelled production of social, symbolic and cultural capital that repositioned participants in social space, providing new vistas of possibility. One such possibility is to identify schemas and practices that produce inequities, thereby affording critique and possible change. Through dialogue among participants, agreements can be reached on what changes can improve *favela* life, including divisions of labor and rules to support trajectories toward equity.

In this example an activity was planned to produce desirable outcomes in a community, and then, based on what happened, the activity was repeated within the same *favela* and in new *favelas* with the goal of producing similar outcomes bearing family resemblances to those previously produced. Activist projects such as GCAR raise the possibility of enacting genres of research to produce desirable changes in education.

Efficacy-Oriented Research

Good ideas can be a resource for planning projects that will likely do more good than harm and thereby improve social life. Research can then be designed to figure out what is happening, why it is happening, and coordinate the production of theoretical knowledge with the improvement of praxis and expansion of social possibilities. Systematically producing thought objects associated with projects such as GCAR allow for peer review and integration with other theoretical knowledge. As theory is produced, it can illuminate GCAR in ways that show coherences and contradictions that were not previously visible and explicate problems to be resolved in ongoing activity.

Favela Rising is a powerful reminder of the importance of collective participation in activities that produce inscriptions of belonging, self-worth, and success. Assuming the participants are receptive to learning together by being together, it seems as if much of what is learned is accomplished without participants having control over their actions. That is, part of participants' actions enacted in the field are beyond individual control. Lévinas associates such actions with passivity, which is dialectically related to agency (Roth, 2007). Hence, whenever culture is enacted, the associated praxis is due to agency and passivity. In GCAR passivity occurs as culture is produced by being with others while doing reggae, producing beat, rhythm, and verve as part of the givenness of the field. Others are transcendent (i.e., unknowable) to a given individual, constantly disrupt the unity and coherence of an individual's experience, and their actions produce a continuous flux of structures that perturb an individual's actions and hence cultural production and repetition. Receptivity to others is one salient aspect of passivity, the elaboration of which is a priority for work in progress.

Activism in School-Based Research

Activist research is possible when thought objects regarded as viable (R) are enacted in an institution with the purpose of repeating the advantages reported from research. The activity is described as research rather than (merely) a project because of the intention to learn how the particular thought objects are reproduced and transformed while producing research outcomes (R') and structures that afford them (S'). Two examples of activist research are provided, involving teachers and students as researchers of their own practices and using cogenerative dialogues to catalyze improvements in schools and classes. In these examples, participation affords reproduction and transformation of advantage.

Teacher and Student Researchers

The involvement of participants in action research, in which they describe what happens in educational settings, can produce foci for critical dialogue among them. Through critical analyses of what happens and why it happens, participants can consider possibilities for improvement in terms of changes to structures such as physical resources, rules, and roles. Often this process involves dialogues among participants and analyses of short excerpts of videotape that capture events that represent salient patterns and contradictions (i.e., what's happening?).

In my research squads, the purposes of including teachers as researchers was to increase their autonomy for what happens at their sites, avoid ethical concerns about doing research on others' practices, and learn from multiple ontologies. Currently, teacher researchers are principal investigators at their own schools and involve others in their research as they desire. They meet regularly with me and other teacher researchers to ensure their studies are informed by what is done and learned in other schools. However, teacher researchers and others with whom they do research decide on all aspects of the design. The primary goal is repetition, by enacting knowledge considered viable, to improve learning in the school and, through ripple effects, expand the social possibilities for students and communities.

In the early 1990s I used students as researchers in a study with Stephen Ritchie and Karl Hook, the latter a teacher researcher in a middle school. At the time, we did not know enough about collaborating with youth as researchers to attain our goals of doing better research and expanding the student researcher's social possibilities. It took about a decade to figure out how to work with students such that they shed their student roles and adopted autonomous roles as researchers. The development of cogenerative dialogues was a giant step forward in this regard as we learned to listen and learn from students while expecting that they would listen and learn from other participants. Once we realized that students could understand and use new theories and methods, we made significant progress in creating research designs in which student voices informed what was studied, how we studied it, and what we learned.

By including teachers and students as researchers in a chapter on generalizability, I re-emphasize the value I assign to participants in a culture undertaking research to improve the quality of social life in a field. My approach is consistent with activism through research in which the production of theory is coordinated with improvement of praxis as participants do research and continuously expand, refine, and attain their motives.

Catalyzing Educational Improvements

Cogenerative dialogues were developed with the purpose of improving social life in schools by learning from participants' diverse points of view, reaching consensus about changes to be made, and adopting collective responsibility for agreed to changes in subsequent lessons. We adapted similar activities to those we had employed in science classes in urban schools in which we acknowledge and endeavor to learn from the perspectives of participants from the class, selected to maximize diversity by including representatives from salient social categories such as institutional role, ethnicity, gender, and achievement level.

The rules for cogenerative dialogues structure participation in as much as all participants have roughly equal turns at talk, equal time talking, and share responsibility for everyone being involved. Issues on the table are resolved before new issues are introduced, and there is group buy-in to solutions of emergent problems. Attentive listening of all participants is highlighted as desirable and each person shows respect for others by listening and dealing substantively with what they say. Part of the rule structure for cogenerative dialogues is to acknowledge each person's rights to be different and endeavor to learn from different perspectives. To the extent possible, participants in cogenerative dialogue do not regard differences in perspectives as errors, but as tangible evidence that individuals who are situated differently in social space experience social life in ways that reflect their experiences. Acceptance of difference is regarded as essential for a polysemic view of social life—a perspective that represents social life as contextualized and legitimizes differences as well as similarities. In each cogenerative dialogue something has to be cogenerated, hence consensuses are forged while respecting and retaining differences. Through participation in cogenerative dialogues participants become knowledgeable about different perspectives, learn from them, and change personal ontologies. We decided that a good place to start in cogenerative dialogues was in the resolution of contradictions that arose from a recent lesson. Often this was accomplished by critical dialogues about video segments selected by participants because of their salience.

Initially, cogenerative dialogues were small in size, including the participation of well-chosen representatives from a class. For example, a teacher and four students might be selected with student representation attending to gender, ethnicity, and achievement level. Gillian Bayne (2007) successfully used and uses large group cogenerative dialogues in an ongoing three-year longitudinal study in a public school in New York City. A move toward larger sized cogenerative dialogues occurred because the class as a whole had to agree with changes recommended by smaller cogenerative dialogue groups and, as the advantages of being involved in cogenerative dialogues became evident, an ethical imperative was to allow all students to gain the advantages that accrue from participation.

Students involved in cogenerative dialogues show considerable evidence of changes in identity and expansion of their agency. Also, through their efforts in the school and larger community, students show an acute awareness of their concerns for collectives and willingness to act in the interests of the collective. Theoretical ideas discussed in cogenerative dialogues, such as communalism as a disposition of African American youth, were debated, adapted, and applied in school wide projects, after consultations between students and school administrators. Bayne's research shows how students enacted knowledge that can be traced back to being produced in cogenerative dialogues in numerous fields and over several years. In so doing, the students expanded their roles and enacted coteaching roles spontaneously, thereby showing evidence of accepting responsibility for collective motives. For example a recommendation arising from cogenerative dialogue was to use a buddy system, a form of peer tutoring, in the science class. Students decided to expand the system in several high school classes and, when it was successful, they assigned buddies in all middle and high classes to produce a higher degree of communality and address hot button issues identified by students and school administrators. During cogenerative dialogues there is evidence to suggest that students arrive at consensus in ways that acknowledge and accept difference. The solutions they agree to usually do not require them to be something they are not. That is, there is willingness to make use of each person's capital to improve the learning of all. At the same time, there is an expectation that all students will continuously change their identities and benefit from school life.

Addressing macrostructures that might produce disadvantage also is an important goal of cogenerative dialogues. If the human resources needed to solve specific problems do not exist among the students and teachers, then others can and should be invited to participate in cogenerative dialogue. For example, if school policy changes need to occur, then school administrators, such as principals and department heads, might be invited to participate in arriving at solutions to problems. Participants in cogenerative dialogues in which I have been involved include university researchers, teacher educators from a university, school and district administrators, and parents. Obviously members from the business community and former students also can participate in cogenerative dialogues.

Representatives from key stakeholder groups participating in cogenerative dialogues can avoid a common problem of outside-in—where administrators and policy makers judge and decide about schools and classes without having direct experiences with the fields to be transformed. Creating schemas as mandates (e.g., policies) to be enacted by others, with accountability consequences for failing to meet established benchmarks, ignores individual|collective relationships and the dynamic complexity of social life. While participation in cogenerative dialogues does not completely overcome the potential coercion of outsiders ruling over participants in socially distant fields, regular participation in cogenerative dialogues raises the hope that cultural production will directly advantage the participants of the class and school concerned, with the possibility of repetition occurring through ripple effects and dissemination of outcomes.

Most research has shown impressive benefits for participants engaging in cogenerative dialogues. Evidently, cogenerative dialogues are seedbeds for capital production. Research suggests that all participants, including teachers and students, produce capital that affords success in multiple fields. Active participation, success, and solidarity produce new roles, structures, and possibilities for individual and collective agency. Outcomes such as these suggest that the use of cogenerative dialogue as a research method expands the possibilities of the collective, produces equity in patterns of attainment, and disseminates improvements through ripple effects to the classroom, school, and lifeworld generally. Cogenerative dialogue is a research method belonging to activist research genres that produce potentially viable knowledge while benefiting participants and institutions involved in research.

Rising-Up with Educational Research

At the heart of generalizability is the premise that the knowledge arising from research can be used to benefit the quality of social life. Through the events I chose to illustrate my changing understandings of generalizability, I conclude that educational research can serve education in numerous ways that follow from changing what can be expected from questions about generalizability to focus on the feasibility of repetition in which family resemblances are produced in processes in which reproduction and transformation presuppose one another. Once the focus shifts to the desirability of research reproducing and transforming benefits, research designs can address authenticity, ripple effects, and repetition in other fields. I contend that these ideas are central to the purposes of educational research and always have been. However, concerns with generalizability, considered in terms of substitution, have fitted well with oversimplified neo-positivist theories that have supported the retention of reductionist views of social life. Not surprisingly, what was learned from this research movement and claimed as generalizable, did not map credibly on to social life. Educators often rejected educational research as lacking relevance or found that when they tried to apply it, the expected favorable outcomes did not occur. Put simply, the generalization did not apply.

As an urban educator, my concern is with education in cities, and I have experienced the folly of outsiders setting mandates for the accountability of others. Also, I have felt the sharp edge of deficit-laden research describing what is wrong with urban education and illustrating what has to be the end state. Furthermore, in my efforts to do what I know has to be done, I have experienced first hand the futility of trying to be a lone hero working to resolve problems in an urban science class. So much for generalizability! I have known what research has said about best practices, and like my teacher education students I have learned that what we know from research really does not generalize to urban students, teachers, and schools. What has mattered most has been what has happened when the rubber has hit the road. Unless face-to-face encounters are successful, there is little chance to build and sustain high quality learning environments in which the learning that should occur does occur. However, if encounters are to succeed, all participants need to acknowledge individual|collective relationships and the necessity for continuous efforts from all participants to afford fluent participation of others. Rising up is not due to the efforts of one individual acting alone, but to every individual acting in concert. So, in my exhortation to rise up, I invite all participants to engage in educational research designed to catalyze desirable changes in the institutions involved in the research, and to repeat successes in other institutions through effective dissemination and planned ripple effects.

Navigating the Future

In making a case for activist forms of research, I do not deny the value of learning from many different genres of inquiry, including interpretive research, critical ethnography, conversation analysis, and studies that hypothesize and test multivariate models to represent social life. What I insist on, as an educator, is to decide for myself what is viable and potentially useful to my professional life. To be sure, each research genre has its own quality criteria and I would consider these as I make a decision on the viability of the research outcomes. As a scholar, I am open to learn from different genres and seek the chance to contribute evidence through my own research.

Numerous research methods are used in education, each characterized by rationale supporting a plurality of methods. Within each research genre is a sizable mass of highly credentialed scholars, working hard to produce unprecedented numbers of refereed publications. Scholars and the methods they embrace differ in terms of the explicit and implicit theories that underpin action and issues of epistemology and ontology create divisions that have been described as possible grounds for incommensurability. Those who accept incommensurability may take the traditional stance of philosophy; tearing planks from the boat one by one, highlighting problems with frameworks on which claims rest, until the boat sinks to the floor of the sea. This approach can involve stance taking and marginalizing others, creating a dismal landscape in which no boats remain floating. In contrast to this approach, learning from multiple research methods is a priority. Rather than taking oppositional stances, a goal is to find grounds for effective encounters with others, creating interstitial culture to afford success, affiliation, and motivation to rise up. How can we learn from difference, show respect to others who differ in their stances, and create viable claims supported by different and seemingly incommensurable frameworks? An alternative to sinking others' boats is to take what is promising from their work, see how it fits with other knowledge considered viable and, if it appeals as a potential solution to a problem in a professional field, repeat what has been learned in the external world making whatever adaptations seem desirable.

Notes

1. Consistent with research undertaken within our research squad and by colleagues such as Wolff-Michael Roth, I use a vertical stroke (|) to denote a dialectical relationship between the constructs shown on either side of it.
2. My first study was evaluated as a thesis by two external examiners who also participated in an oral defense. My follow-up study in the United States was presented as a doctoral dissertation.

References

Bayne, G. (2007). *Cogenerative dialogues: Aligning culture and expanding student roles inside and outside of the urban science classroom.* (Doctoral dissertation, The Graduate School and University Center, The City University of New York).

Deleuze, G. (1994). *Difference and repetition* (P. Patton, Trans.). New York: Columbia University Press. (Original work published 1968)

Grupo Cultural AfroReggae. (2007). *History.* Retrieved August 23, 2007, from http://www.afroreggae.org.br/sec_historia.php.

Guba, E., & Lincoln, Y. S. (1989). *Fourth generation evaluation.* Newbury Park, CA: Sage.

Niaz, M. (2007). Can findings of qualitative research in education be generalized? *Quality & Quantity, 41,* 429–445.

Roth, W.-M. (2007). Theorizing passivity. *Cultural Studies of Science Education, 2,* 1–8.

Rowe, M. B. (1974). Reflections on wait-time: Some methodological questions. *Journal of Research in Science Teaching, 11,* 263–79.

Schutz, A. (1962). Common sense and scientific interpretation of human action. In M. Natanson (Ed.) *Collected papers I—The problem of social reality* (pp. 3–96). The Hague: Martinus Nijhoff.

Zimbalist, J., & Mochary, M. (2007). *Favela rising.* West Hollywood, CA: Voy Pictures/Stealth Films.

Appendix

Glossary

Action is human conduct devised by the actor in advance—that is enactment of culture (or social life) according to a conscious decision by an actor. An act is what is accomplished by an action. I refer to acting in progress as praxis. Action is experienced "after the event" when an actor "stops to think."

Agency is the power to conduct social life and is a principal framework for understanding identity. Dialectically related to structure, agency involves access to and appropriation of structures and pertains to the fields in which culture is conducted.

Capital consists of the stocks of knowledge available to conduct social life. I adapt Bourdieu's forms of capital in the use of three forms of capital: cultural, social, and symbolic. The forms of capital presuppose one another and capital is produced when symbolic, social, and cultural capital afford successful encounters and the production of positive emotional energy (a form of cultural capital).

Conduct includes an actor's subjectively meaningful experiences, may be overt or covert, and does not imply intent.

Dialectical is used in several ways in this chapter and elsewhere in my research project. If A and B are patterns applicable to social life, a dialectical relationship can be recursive; a continuous flow from A to B and back to A. In this instance A and B might be considered opposites. In our research we soon came to realize that for any assertions there are contradictions, not due to measurement error, but because in social life there always are enactments that do not conform to patterns of (thin) coherence. Often these contradictions are cultural resistance to norms or transformative culture that reflects newcomers in a field. That is, when considering a dialectical relationship between A and B there would be patterns to support A, patterns to support B, and patterns that support neither A nor B. A dialectical relationship between reproduction and transformation, which we use to define production, can be thought of as parts constituting an inseparable whole, that is, a both/and relationship. In production, both reproduction and transformation occur.

Encounter occurs when an actor interacts with a social object. I regard interaction as dialectically related to transaction, an acknowledgement that during an encounter, production occurs. Just as I see action as a progression that occurs over time, so it is with encounter. Encounters are experienced "after the event" in the same way I describe for action. Hence, they can be thought of as they happened and can be projected or planned. In examining encounters they are temporally bounded, seen in relation to purpose, and involve conduct consistent with an individual|collective relationship.

Field is a site for the conduct of social life. Fields are structured and culture is enacted in them. Like an electric field, there is no boundary around a field, though the dynamic structures afford characteristic forms of production, but not in a deterministic way. Because there are no boundaries, culture produced in another field can be enacted, thereby changing the structures and the potential for conducting social life.

Hegemony arises when participants within a subculture are disadvantaged by structures, regarded by the oppressed as the way things should be. The disadvantaged accept their relative disadvantage as normal rather than rising up to identity and remove hegemony and disadvantage.

Macro, meso, and **micro.** I analyze and give meaning to social life in terms of three levels: **macro, meso,** and **micro.** Social life is not experienced in terms of these categories. The categories are heuristic, useful in research, and dialectically interrelated with each presupposing the others. I use field to distinguish macro from meso, arguing that a macro focus involves multiple fields in an analysis whereas a meso-analysis occurs in a single field. Ethnography is ideal for macro and meso level research. The micro level is distinguished from the meso level by manipulating time in the analysis, either by slowing down video and audio tape or speeding it up. The focus is on the appropriation of resources and in making sense of the anatomy of encounters. In contrast, even though meso level analyses might involve videotape, they are done without changing the timescale. Making sense of encounters usually involves coordinated analyses at all three levels.

Passivity involves encounters in social life in which an actor cannot exert any power. Passivity is similar to receptivity—it is not the opposite of activity and concerns acting without power, with no possibility of taking situations in hand.

Structures are the resources of a field. Structure may be schematic and material, and include participation. I regard structures as a continuously dynamic flux that structures, but does not determine social life. As social life is conducted resources are appropriated in the production of culture (i.e., reproduced|transformed).

Chapter 9

Critical Realism, Policy, and Educational Research

Allan Luke

In this chapter, I make the case for a critical realist approach to educational research and policy making. Such an approach enlists the full range of educational research tools to generate as broad an empirical picture of educational practices, patterns, and institutional outcomes as possible. Its aim is to establish a comprehensive picture of an educational system at work, not just classical input/process/output descriptions, but also models of the life trajectories and capital of teachers and students to and through schools. The empirical work sets the table for theorizing and modeling educational practice, for the interpretive and discursive work of policy formation. The translation of critical realist research into policy formation requires historical narratives and scenario planning, explanations about how things came to be, and about how alternative normative scenarios might be constructed. Here I provide a historical backdrop to the links between critical realism and a broader agenda of social justice and educational equity. Noting the parameters of current and recent research on pedagogy, achievement, and social class, I emphasize the need for new sociological directions in pedagogy and in educational assessment and evaluation—but new directions built squarely on the foundations of social reproduction theory. In so doing, I suggest a way past the critical/empirical, qualitative/quantitative divide that has arisen in the context of neo-liberal educational politics in the United States, United Kingdom, and Canada. To address questions of generalizability, such an approach entails a shunting back and forth between levels of scale in a system. But moreover, it requires a sociological imagination and critical hermeneutics for reading and interpreting evidence and research.

My case here is that the last three decades of work on the social class, cultural, and gendered bases for social reproduction have tended to move away from quantitative research paradigms—with the resultant position that there is limited generalizability for claims about marginalization, disadvantage, and inequality based on the critical ethnographic traditions. To address these critiques and to redress the move towards a narrow quantitative base for policy basis requires a much stronger and well-theorized linkage between qualitative and quantitative, as other chapters here argue. This entails both a turn towards larger scale sociological studies to provide the empirical bases for a critical hermeneutics, and a reinvigorated qualitative paradigm that raises and approaches issues of the scale of reform and provides a rich case-based description of the enacted curriculum. For if the classical epistemological and methodological questions remain— those of validity in all its forms and generalizability—the salient and correlative policy question focuses on matters of scale, of how systemic larger scale educational policies can enable high levels of "informed" and "adaptive" professionalism at the school and classroom level. My case is that the bridging of the binary divides of educational research is required for effective policy that can address issues of both recognitive *and* redistributive social justice in educational systems.

The myth underlying the current approach to scientific evidence is that there is something like a hypodermic effect between (a) scientific identification of a particular educational treatment, however construed, (b) its articulation in policy or curriculum discourse, (c) its implementation and application in the complex fields of an educational system, and (d) consequential student outcomes, broadly defined. That is, the prevailing assumption of a gold standard is that findings from experimental and quasi-experimental designed research are generalizable across space, time, human populations, and cultural ecology of region, school, and community. This invokes also questions of scale and contextual level (Luke, 2007): that is, that an educational phenomena that has demonstrated efficacy in a particular context can and should be replicated via larger-scale policy in another local, variable context.

This is to say nothing of the intrinsically messy ecologies of educational bureaucracies and policy-making contexts, and those of the lifeworlds of schools and classrooms. Even where we have the capacity to analytically isolate and identify a particular pedagogy or curriculum intervention that appears to have efficacy, systemic prescription can only set enabling and disenabling conditions for changes in teaching and learning. It cannot, as in a laboratory, be replicated with detailed precision—and is always remediated through the intersubjective capacities and material social relations of communities, staffrooms, and classrooms. These, much to the perplexity of policy makers and teacher-proofers of all orders, tend to be archetypal cases of Foucault's (1972) axiom about the local contingency of discourse: teachers and students consistently generate idiosyncratic and unpredictable interactional face-to-face and text-generative action. Not only does this confound the attempts of policy to generalize putatively generalizable curriculum and pedagogic action; it also troubles the patterns of deliberate hegemony. Even where curriculum can attempt to establish dominant ideology and behavioral control, empirically this constitutes at best a paper-thin hegemony.

Educational policy that attempts to steer from a difference on this basis without a multi-leveled empirical data base on teachers' and students' work, everyday lives, and interaction in classrooms is inherently limited and prone to "collateral damage." It is limited in terms of its capacity to re/present teachers' and students' work and classroom lives, and thereby to reconstruct, shift, mobilize, or transform teaching/learning relations. It is limited in terms of its actual analysis of the individual and social consequences of teaching and learning, restricted to those conventional outcome measures of high-stakes systems. If the issue facing qualitative studies of pedagogical innovation and school reform is one of scaling up through systems into enabling policy, then the issue facing quantitative studies is the degree to which the "complex ecologies" of schools and classrooms are altered by larger scale policy with collateral local effects in specific curriculum contexts. Nichols and Berliners' (2007) qualitative study of the effects of the U.S. No Child Left Behind Act and accompanying policy is an exemplar of this kind of work, where the enacted curriculum or the curriculum-in-use generates a host of institutional effects that run counter to policy goals and directives.

The folk narrative of neoliberal U.S. public policy discourse is that the educational research community is populated by "soft" researchers, that too much case-based educational research is qualitative, local and nongeneralizable, and, worse yet, anecdotal and unscientific. Further, the rich trove of case-based, descriptive and interpretive work in educational ethnography, sociocultural psychology, discourse and interactional analysis—much of it participatory and intervention based—is left by the side of the road in state policy formation. By this logic practical repair of schooling requires a return to rigorously empirical research from what is often portrayed as an apocryphal fall from a prior era of research dominated by quantitative criteria. In the last two years under the conservative government of John Howard, this view spread to Australia via ongoing attacks on schooling in the national press, even while those debates tend to shift the grounds for evidence arbitrarily, are often based on superficial or misleading interpretations of data sets, are dismissive of data that does not suit particular ideological positions, and rely upon anecdotal claims about the effects of particular approaches to curriculum and assessment on students.

Whereas the former claim about the softness of educational research is spurious—given the ongoing extensive debates within the educational community about the comparative value of different methods the call for rigorous research bases for the formation of policy is partly right. As many who have worked as policy bureaucrats attest, decisions about curricula, resource flows, and assessment are often made based on a

range of criteria—fiscal, political, and, indeed, anecdotal/personal—
without recourse to *any* educational research. The belief that education
ministries and departments are faceless, numbers-driven technocratic
regimes is a myth: they are complex, intersubjective social fields. At the
same time, a new rigor is required in research design. But this is a multidisciplinary and interpretive rigor that goes far beyond and around some
mythical gold standard of quasi-experimental design and can be part of
a renewed focus on issues of educational access, social and economic
equity and new life pathways. Here I describe how this might be done.

My aim is to both reconnoiter the historical bases of *critical* educational research focused upon redistributive social justice, and outline
some programmatic directions for future work. For a principled and rigorous approach to issues of educational equity should sit at the heart of
current debates, popular claims about the dated nature of such concerns
notwithstanding, and it is a renewed focus on equity and social justice
in education that holds the key to finding effective and targeted policy
interventions. The problem is how we move past binary debates between
qualitative and quantitative, archetypal trade-offs between validity and
generalizability, local reform, and bids at larger-scale educational policy.
This also requires that we not be distracted by public debate that would
narrow, rather than widen our theoretical and empirical resources.

Remaking Policy

Having spent two decades opening and expanding the methodologies
and epistemologies, discourses and practices of educational research
beyond the boundaries of the Thorndike tradition—it is fitting that the
task of defending and justifying the redefinition of educational research
should fall to the current generation of critical researchers. For the
debate over what counts as research sits within explicitly political con-
troversy over what should count as evidence in educational *and* social
policy. For those of us working from materialist sociological perspectives on differential and stratified educational effects, this translates into
a concern with what counts as evidence for the analysis of social reproduction and possible ameliorative reform agendas *after* two decades of
critique.[1] These remain significant epistemological, political, theoretical,
and practical and programmatic decisions.

Any debate over educational research is a debate over what counts
as pedagogical practice and, therefore, over what should count as the
normative purposes, experiences, and consequences of education. The
current debate over evidence is a struggle over the fundamental character and direction of schooling and education and over which fields
constitute its foundations. It is not, nor should it be construed as, a narrow debate over scientific versus non-scientific or quantitative versus

qualitative research. The matter at hand is one of policy, philosophy, and political economy; it also is one of educational science, epistemology, and methodology *per se*. Nothing less than the foundational purposes, practices, and consequences of state schooling are on the line.

It could be no other way. Self-understanding in science is a matter of understanding the complex historical lineages, structural constraints, and social relations that comprise a field and its resident researchers. Nor is policy making as straightforward a matter as the generalization of scientific findings into larger-scale systems interventions, however ideological or overtly political such a process might appear. The making of the social and moral order goes beyond issues of the accuracy or rigor of science per se, entailing the difficult hermeneutic task of translating "facts into norms" within and around the available discourses of particular state formations and economies. This, as all policy formation, is a textual and interpretive task. Contrary to the claims of fundamentalist approaches to understanding the world, policy makers by definition cannot simply read the numbers and then extrapolate these to intervention. Just as questions of method inevitably are resolved on epistemological and teleological grounds, questions of science in any applied form necessarily generate questions of norms, ideology, and ethics. This is a particularly important link in a scientific environment where the boundaries between scientific and ideological truth claims, between technocratic and civic society, between scientific and civic literacy are blurred—and where the claims of corporation and state morph into more general premises that connect scientific truth and the civic good. Of course, the use of high science to legitimate social and educational policy is nothing new—with powerful precedents in American educational research, but as well in the more sordid European social engineering projects of the past century.

Despite the claims to ethical neutrality of behaviorism and many other approaches to what have come to be called *the learning sciences*, and the approaches of some genealogical analyses—a non-normative educational practice is logically and practically impossible. The formation of state educational policy is intrinsically normative, entailing three moves:

1. *Narrative function*: The establishment of a state ideological narrative and critical counternarratives over the purposes and outcomes of schoolings.
2. *Resource flow*: The purposive regulation of flows of human resources (e.g., teachers, students), discourse resources (e.g., policies, syllabi, curricular materials, professional development), and fiscal resources (e.g., infrastructure, materials, artifacts, and convertible capital) to realize the aims of these narratives.

3. *Pedagogical alignment*: Central and local bids to focus the resources via alignment (or misalignment) of the message systems of curriculum, instruction, and assessment.

Whereas at the strategic, ideological level (a) educational policy is about socially and culturally consequential narratives, in bureaucratic practice (b) it entails the selective regulation of flows of material and human resources, knowledge, and discourse. These flows, in turn, are translated by teachers (c) into the enacted curriculum, the face-to-face construction of versions of subjectivity and identity, skill and practice, knowledge, and competence with material consequences for students and communities. Accordingly, the current policy context returns us to a foundational argument about which developmental meta-narratives, which material practices, which official discourses actually *should be made to count* in the reshaping of schools and classrooms, teaching and learning for new cultures and economies. It also asks the practical administrative and systemic questions about which centrally and locally governed flows of resources might realize these goals. Third, it returns us to questions about the evidence and generalization; it asks which alignments of educational discourse actually have different material effects and outcomes in what schooling does with human beings, societies and economies.

To appraise the complex effects and possibilities of evidence-based educational policy formation on state schooling and practice requires that we reconsider the recent history of research in the postwar era—a history that has, in part, led us to the current impasse, but one that also provides intellectual and methodological resources for redressing matters at hand. This may be old hat to some but will be new for many of the next generation of researchers working in critical and social justice traditions. I then briefly note alternative approaches to evidence in New Zealand and Australia as having the potential for tactically redefining debates around equity and social justice in more generative ways than academic critique of empiricism in and of themselves enable. It is only with this kind of research base, one better aligned to address and critique questions about the grand narratives of state educational policy in the contexts of globalized capitalism, that systems can begin to enable the systematic manipulation of resources that might alter practical alignments and their material consequences.

A Brief History of the Present

In the last four years, there has been an official push by the U.S. and U.K. governments to narrow research to quasi-experimental research, calling for a reinstatement of traditional criteria of validity and reliability. As part of its version of evidence-based policy, the Bush administration has enforced a medical model by tying all Title I funding for lower-socio-economic schools to the use of scientifically tested reading programs. In its first iteration, double-blind drug testing was cited as an exemplar of a gold standard of experimental evidence. The National Reading Panel, National Science Foundation, and other research organizations generally have moved in these directions—and there is a noticeable strategic shift from professional organizations like the International Reading Association to accommodate the change in government discourse. To its credit, the American Educational Research Association has quite strategically and critically engaged with these moves, as has AARE leadership via rigorous internal debates, various conference forums and its publications and journals. In the United States and United Kingdom, there also is a systematic attempt to reorient official recognition of evidence to a gold standard of randomized experimental field trials (e.g., the various *What Works* clearing houses and ERIC Websites). Many federal and state governments now prefer to fund those programs that can claim to have verification of efficacy by quasi-experimental design. The press and conservative educational lobbies in Australia have enlisted similar claims. The press in Australia has tended to use what evidence suits (e.g., declining test scores) and has tended to ignore other evidence where it portrays a successful system and where it suggests more complex, deeper-seated educational and social problems around the effects of neoliberal policy in exacerbating stratified educational performance.

Consequently, small- and medium-scale case-based research, larger-scale survey and interview studies, interactional analyses, ethnography, discourse analyses, action research, even design experiments, but as well sociometric, economic, and demographic analyses have been written out of many important decisions on school reform, program adoption and implementation. Even data from quantitative coding of classroom teaching and tracking studies—key to understanding how, where, and in what ways teaching and learning occurs, and its consequences for students—does not figure in the U.S. or Australian policy debates. It is notable that the U.S. National Reading Panel's initial report, considered the benchmark for scientific policy formation, did not include the many studies with large minority and second-language speaking populations because the population/demographic variables made it more difficult to meet their strict criteria of randomized field trials.

To find a way forward, it is worth reconnoitering how we arrived at what to the naïve observer appears as a qualitative/quantitative, case/generalizable, interpretive/empirical binary divide in research methodology—with advocates of equity and social justice supposedly lined up on the left and advocates of scientific evidence and free markets on the right. What follows is a brief sketch of the qualitative and critical turn of educational research. My aim is to reframe and re-enlist these methods as part of a multidisciplinary, interpretive educational research agenda that is both critical and empirically rigorous, while taking what I here want to suggest is a more forensic approach to the complex problems around educational achievement and poverty, stratification, and reproduction.

A major achievement of work of the last two decades was an expansion of what counts as educational research beyond the longstanding boundaries established in the tradition of educational behaviorism. This distinctively American legacy, coupled with the industrial design and expansion of the educational system, translated into a large-scale focus on pre-post experimental design, with norm referenced standardized achievement tests as the principal indicator of educational efficacy. The ascendancy of the model, abetted by Thorndike's skirmishes with Dewey at Teachers College and Skinner's long tenure at Harvard, led to very strong parameters of design established through organizations like the American Educational Research Association across the postwar period (the 1950s and 1960s National Society for the Study of Education annual handbooks are historically illustrative). Well into the 1970s, the pre-post design stood as the benchmark for doctoral studies in most major U.S. and U.K. institutions—with powerful legacies still operating internationally (e.g., such traditions have powerful half-lives in those parts of Asia and the Americas where postgraduate training was founded by graduates of these programs sponsored by postwar aid programs).

The model owed as much to industrial assembly line, time, and motion studies of Frederick Winslow Taylor and to agricultural crop-yield studies as it might have to medical models. There is a strong historical relationship between the industrial and urban reorganization of work and civic life in the United States, and the emergence of early 20th century behaviorism as an explanatory template for worker behavior, consumer behavior and, indeed, large-scale militarization of the body politic. The spatial/temporal and bureaucratic organizational features of the contemporary high school follow a factory model. As revisionist histories argued, the push towards fairness through test-driven streaming and placement systems had substantive roots in race-based eugenics and class-based social Darwinism. These formed the basis of early testing, tracking, and placement systems that are at the heart of a performative meritocracy, as readily as early behaviorist or developmental models of mental measurement might have been.

Neo-Marxian and social control theory critiques of the mid-1960s began to focus on the reproductive effects of this model, its claims to aim towards scientific meritocracy notwithstanding. These critiques came from several sources—in the reanalysis of demographic, achievement and test score data; in critical revisionist histories of the role of schooling in urbanization, industrialization and reform, and in curriculum theory based on ideology critique. Note here that the former two traditions of analysis, including the social historical school, relied extensively on quantitative analysis, sociodemographic, and the critical reanalysis of archival census, population demographic, school achievement, and performance data.

The prototypical findings set the grounds for a generation of research theory and practice. It began with a radical critique of traditional psychometric models. The result was a compelling quantitative and qualitative database that indicated that the test-driven meritocracy had created a stratified division of educational outcomes strongly aligned with existing relations of social class, gender, and race and culture. The terms were set for three decades of critical educational research strongly focused on qualitative, case-based, discourse analytic, and narrative models. This amounted to a hermeneutic push to explain the patterns that the test score, socioeconomic class and minority achievement data demonstrated. The prototype for qualitative explanations of minority failure is framed in *Functions of Language in the Classroom* (Cazden, Johns, & Hymes, 1972), where essays by the editors, Basil Bernstein, Susan Phillips, and others launched the ethnography of communication. Courtney Cazden states that at the commencement of much of this work in the 1960s, a small group of researchers focusing principally on child language development began a qualitative investigation of social class and cultural variation in interaction, simply because the only available accounts and research paradigms were based on structural functionalist and behaviorist models of deficit (Cazden, personal communication, June 2008). For critical research, the new standard became Willis's (1981) *Learning to Labor,* and the numerous curriculum studies undertaken by Michael Apple and colleagues. In this way, the impact of qualitative work in Birmingham cultural studies was notable in both U.S. cultural studies and educational studies, with audience ethnography and ideological analysis featured prominently. Both of these models—ethnographic and ideological text analysis, acted as concrete explications of the broader mechanisms of social reproduction identified in the larger scale empirical social historical and political economic analyses.

In this regard, the critical qualitative turn of the last three decades was not a simple anti-positivist reaction to the Thorndike tradition; it was as well an attempt to instantiate and to understand with some depth the mechanisms of class stratification of educational outcomes. Discussing this history with Cazden, Dell Hymes, Vera John-Steiner, and other historical participants, I came to understand that their efforts were spurred both by a strong commitment to questions of educational equality, but as well by the inability of traditional psychologically based quasi-experimental research models to explain the institutional and cultural processes of educational inequality. Then, the social and institutional construction of deficit, disadvantage and difference was undocumented territory—as were such interactional and microsociological phenomenon as resistance, ideological control, and face-to-face power. While for Bernstein (1990) this meant a three-decade elaboration and refinement of structuralist sociology—for Cazden, Hymes, and colleagues this entailed the development of a range of what were then unprecedented applications of qualitative and descriptive classroom and community research.

There are various explanations for the historical move from quantitative research, despite the historically empirical foundation of social reproduction theory, correspondence models of economic reproduction in the aforementioned sociodemographic analyses. First, there was a general backlash against behavioral psychology and assessment as having founded and legitimated systems of inequality—exacerbated by the politics of race around IQ testing and the bell curve that continue to this day. Second, there was increasing attention to emergent, post-1968 theoretical work in both mainstream fields including sociology, cultural anthropology and literature studies, French discourse theory, and new fields of feminist and gender studies, cultural studies, semiotics, communications, and media studies. These included a powerful critique of the ideological construction and manipulation of scientific knowledge using feminist, poststructuralist, and postmodern theories. Third, the documentation of large-scale historical processes of social reproduction and ideological control raised a series of provocative questions about the implications of countability for purposes of social surveillance and legitimation of state power. These processes had new material grounds in the political economy of postwar corporate capitalism. But whereas a generation of educational researchers took it for granted that social and cultural reproduction worked to generate stratified intergenerational effects, we did not fully grasp the mechanisms through which these larger patterns of reproduction translated into everyday institutional life, face-to-face social relations, identity formation, and so forth.

Without an empirical and interpretive understanding of these nested and interwoven levels of mediation, we wind up advocating and experimenting with pedagogical and curricular interventions across a broad spectrum (from critical pedagogy to cooperative learning, from explicit teaching to project work) without a concrete estimation of how they might or might not alter tenacious patterns of inequality. In this regard, the empiricists who argue that only scientifically generalizable empirical research should count in policy formation and adjudication have a point. Indeed, we do need evidence on the differential and idiosyncratic local material effects of particular resource flows and alignments, despite the dangerous limitations of their preferred answer: that only the randomized field trials of traditional experimentalism will do the job.

The uptake of critical models was accelerated during the 1980s and early 1990s in Australia, where expanding educational research and development rode on the back a strong Labor government funding commitment to educational equity and social justice, gender equity, multiculturalism and reconciliation. There are different historical accounts of the development of these models in Australia. Bill Green (2005) documents the emergence of educational progressivism in the 1960s through the "New Education," and subsequently attributes the shift to the work of later progressives like Garth Boomer. Through government organizations like the Curriculum Development Commission, led by Boomer, strong policy-maker/researcher/teacher coalitions were formed, with large-scale university and government commitments to participatory action research, curriculum interventions in gender equity, indigenous education and programs for the disadvantaged. A range of leading Australian researchers began their work through participation in these programs. Applied research was disseminated through various national professional development programs and supported through programs like the *Disadvantaged Schools Program.*

This shift altered the patterns of training and reproduction within faculties of education and university social science more generally. During the last two decades, the orientation of PhD theses and research methods courses shifted—with an increasing focus on students of at risk and disadvantaged backgrounds, an increasing application of neo-Marxian, poststructuralist and feminist theory, and a broad movement towards qualitative case-based, action research, critical ethnographic, and discourse analytic methods. In this regard, Australian (and perhaps Canadian) educational researchers were ahead of their U.K. and U.S. counterparts. These trends were supported by federal and state-funded research projects. They were represented in Australian Association for Research in Education (AARE) theses awards and increased rates of publication by Australian researchers in national and international journals. At the same time, a great deal of prototypical work that lagged behind in the more traditional U.S. environments—on gender equity, critical policy analyses, critical literacy, citizenship education, larger-scale participatory action research, active citizenship, digital media, and literacies—marked a distinctive Australian watermark to educational research. Partly because of coalitions between researchers and government, teachers and universities and the distinctive intellectual economy of Australia, the critical turn pushed Australian research forward as an international counter-balance to traditional quantitative positivism. Early 1990s citation searches and impact studies would bear this out, as do the chronology of contents of the annual AARE Radford Lectures on Australian education. Simply, Australian work in key areas like participatory action research, gender and education, literacy education was setting new precedents in the field.

Internationally, major paradigm shifts within the mainstream social sciences further destabilized the Thorndike tradition. These included cognitive, schema-theoretic psychology, psycholinguistic models of linguistic competence, the revision of developmentalist growth models, structuralist sociology, and, most recently, sociocultural psychology. They arose in response to the problems of new contexts and conditions: the cultural and linguistic diversification of the populations of countries of the postindustrial north and west; the emergence of new technologies and their affiliated discourses, practices and skills; and, most recently, visible shifts in the formation of identity and agency, generational and life pathways. Just as behaviorism was so strongly affiliated with the formation of the new human subject in early 20th century industrialism, these new social sciences and psychologies offered salient models for explaining and constructing new forms of subjectivity, discourse, and practice. In education, they had the effect of shifting psychologists' attention to models of prior knowledge, to the significance of student error, to cognitive and metacognitive processes, to constitutive contexts of culture, and recognition of the complexities of longitudinal growth and development, beyond models that focused on the psychometric measurement of skill acquisition—more on this momentarily.

The linguistic turn in the social sciences placed further critical caveats on traditional psychological experimentalism. The debates between Chomsky and Hymes over the nature of linguistic competence began from a critique of behaviorist models of learning. The object lesson was that all models of research could only proceed on the basis of linguistically mediated and produced evidence of growth, development, and, indeed, learning—and these might involve other forces, both the visible ones of cultural scripts and discourse formation and the less visible ones of language acquisition devices and prior knowledge. At the same time, this broad focus on language and linguistic processes as constitutive of learning, development and, indeed, cultural practice provided new grounds for analyzing intergenerational social, cultural and economic reproduction, culminating in benchmark ethnographies of educational inequality like Shirley Heath's (1983) *Ways with Words*. The focus on language, culture and social relations was consolidated in the rapid development and expansion of models of sociohistorical psychology in the 1990s, when Vygotskian models began to supplant traditional structuralist developmental and cognitive models in the explanation of teaching and learning. The result was a strong orientation towards cultural explanations of social reproduction.

Taken together, these shifts can be viewed as reflexive responses to new social, cultural, and educational phenomena—Kuhnian anomalies that defied existing paradigmatic definition and solution. The two most significant social facts facing schooling in the mid to late 20th century concerned the unequal and highly stratified performance of students from socioeconomically and culturally marginal communities, and the increasing linguistic and cultural diversity of student bodies in established state educational systems. Psychologies and sociologies were forced to explain social class, race/cultural, linguistic and gender stratified performance.

The shifts can also be taken as emergent discourses began to systematically rename and redefine education, educational practices, teachers, learners and others in ways that enabled different policy and pedagogical foci and reforms. It was indeed the Foucauldian, feminist and postcolonial discourse turn in literary, historical, and cultural theory that expanded the theoretical vocabulary of educational research while simultaneously treating that vocabulary as discourse. Among other effects, this enabled the merging of a materialist critique of reproduction with phenomenological models of subjectivity and discourse. This opened the possibility for a layered, nested analysis of how reproduction occurred, whether via the macro-formation of state policies, or the face-to-face microlevel exchanges in families and children, classrooms, and staffrooms. Discourse-based educational research refocused on the constitution of identity and culture via discourse.

If there is a common point to the recent history of critical educational research, it lies both in (a) normative reframings of the aims and possibilities of educational practice and research, and (b) the radical expansion of the epistemological and methodological toolkits of educational research. The very idea that research by definition acts in the interests of particular constituencies, and that it can be undertaken with explicit attention to these normative goals was disruptive and enabling—and continues to serve the interests of indigenous peoples, linguistic and cultural minorities, women and girls, and others. The normative models focused on issues of recognitive justice: from pedagogic models of empowerment, voice, and identity in the classroom, revisionist approaches to curriculum content, to culturally appropriate curricular and pedagogical foci looking to alter the achievement patterns of historically marginalized working class, linguistic, and cultural minority groups. In terms of the former, this work yielded an expanded range of explanations of the unequal production of educational outcomes: including foci on home/school cultural and linguistic transition, models of identity and capital, studies of exclusionary classroom discourse practices, tracking and the politics of labeling and naming, and so forth. In terms of the latter, it yielded an expanded range of legitimated approaches to explaining educational phenomenon: from macro to micro, quantitative to qualitative, empirical to hermeneutic, realist to discourse analytic. My point here is that far from narrowing or softening educational research, limiting its validity and generalizability, the last two decades of work have given us a vastly expanded toolkit for approaching current policy problems, one that has the potential, at least, to offer rich, triangulated, multidisciplinary evidence around both residual problems facing schools—most notably, the intransigence of unequal social reproduction—and emergent challenges raised by new life pathways and identities, new technologies, and new conditions of work and community life.

Recovering a Critical Realism

Evidence-based policy is a logical, viable, and productive route for the governance of educational systems and, more generally, for social and economic policy. But many of us in the international educational research community have also argued that such an approach must be based on broad, rich, and disciplinarily diverse data, on contending and varied analyses and interpretations of the meaning of and connections between this data. How do we reconcile this broad critical, qualitative turn with the current demands for empirical verification, experimental design and replicable, generalizable evidence? We can begin from three interwoven propositions, taken from three very different methodological and epistemological traditions:

- That there are material, cognitive, and social conditions, interactions and processes in educational worlds that can be studied, tracked, and examined scientifically, through rigorous observation and careful theorization;
- That these can be optimally studied through a rigorous multidisciplinary social science—and not a narrow, selective psychometrics—that examines sociodemographic data, data on the contexts of schools and teachers, studies of face-to-face pedagogy, and a broad array of educational outcomes; and
- That these processes can be interpreted and represented in ways that are mindful of the politics of representation, both in terms of how they define, position and represent particular communities and practices, and in terms of their uptakes by particular constituencies, media, politicians, and policy makers.

Debates about what constitutes research evidence have varied by national context. In the U.K., policies have led to the development of multilevel statistical procedures that assess, at the school level, the value added by schools to student learning (as measured by key national performance indicators, including national examination results), taking into account prior achievement levels and family background characteristics. In Australia, the debate has also moved towards the development of comparative testing measures, pushed by a federal government that has progressively expanded funding for non-state schooling and state governments working for curriculum reform. To date, interschool and cross-systems comparisons in Australia have been checked by lack of consistent and comparable datasets within and across states and the technical limits of existing test instruments. In Queensland, New South Wales, and Singapore, systematic observational data on teachers' work and classroom interaction has been used as the basis for curriculum and policy reform. Further the utilization of longitudinal pathway studies of student capability, identity, and engagement with increasingly volatile social fields of employment, civic, and community life has begun.

Yet the research and data-analytic capacity within many state ministries of education in Australia and internationally is limited. This is in part because of the concentration of resources within systems on the everyday deliverables required to run school systems, and in part because of a tendency of many ministries to adopt reforms based upon ostensible patterns of innovation in what appeared to be the leading U.S. and U.K. educational systems. The assumption was, therefore, that educational research would have an indirect or mediated impact upon educational policy. We in educational faculties, corporate think-tanks, non-government organizations, and transnational organizations (ranging from ETS to the OECD), would do the research. Governments selectively would draw from this research, where needed and expedient, to generate policy. As many of us continue to find, government–researcher collaboration is potentially a vexed affair: with issues of academic freedom, intellectual property ownership, and vested interests on the table, and the continual specter of research findings that might contradict or critique previous or prospective policy directions always looming. On the surface, at least, the United States pushes towards scientific evidence in an attempt to solve this problem.

Internationally, the most comprehensive approach to building synthetic, multidisciplinary is the New Zealand Ministry of Education's *Iterative Best Evidence Synthesis Programme*. Its director, Adrienne Alton-Lee (2004) defines this as a "collaborative knowledge building strategy to draw upon and synthesize … valuable but inaccessible and fragmented research literature in education" (p. 2) on both English and Maori-medium settings in New Zealand. It weighs quantitative and qualitative research data case by case, depending upon the policy questions at issue. International and local studies—qualitative and quantitative—are reviewed and assayed, with a specific focus on evidence about changed student outcomes and educational consequences broadly defined. Unlike many systems, the focus is not simply on testing and curricular reform. Ongoing work in New Zealand focuses on finding best-evidence exemplars of teacher professional development, school leadership, and policy making. Not surprisingly, such work is sometimes taken as a potential threat not just to longstanding ministry commitments and ongoing policy directions, but as well to tertiary institutions and consultants with substantive investments in particular approaches to pre- and inservice training.

The model is based upon a fitness-for-purpose approach, focusing on contextual validity and relevance—on "what works, under what conditions, why and how" (Alton-Lee, 2004, p. 1). What is distinctive about the New Zealand approach is the willingness to consider all forms of research evidence regardless of methodological paradigms and ideological rectitude, and its concern in finding contextually effective, appropriate, and locally powerful examples of what works. Its focus is on capturing and examining the impact of local contextual variables (e.g., population, school, community, linguistic, and cultural variables). Indeed, what *authentically* works in educational interventions may be locally effective with particular populations, in particular settings, to particular educational ends.

These principles stand against the base assumption of the U.S. model: that there are instructional treatments that can be shown to have generalizable and universal efficacy across and despite contexts, that this efficacy at the production of educational outcomes can be assessed solely through standardized achievement test results, and that the matter of reform of systems requires the "hard prescription," standardization and implementation of these approaches. A strong advocate of the new empiricism in the United States recently restated this position (Radenbush, 2005). The author argues that quasi-experimental design findings always are but a first step, opening the door to a host of other questions about the mediation of approaches through the multiple complex layers of educational systems into everyday practice. Simply put, classrooms and schools are not laboratories, but complex, messy, and idiosyncratically local, social ecologies. The lesson for policy is that no matter how generalizable the science of the evidence may purport it to be, educational reform is a complex, local phenomenon requiring a range of enabling conditions—policy, material, cultural, and institutional.

Many quasi-experimental approaches to evidence in the US and UK fail to capture these variable processes and practices adequately. This is principally because they adopt a black box approach, controlling inputs and variables, with a reductionist quantification of educational outcomes. There is little emphasis on the close study of pedagogy, face-to-face classroom teaching, where the work of teaching and learning occurs. This precludes a finer grained, contextually valid set of analyses and interventions that can address the host of cultural and institutional variables that might influence performance and indeed, make elements of them valid and replicable in local sites. Finally, there is no attempt to systematically study the full range of cultural and linguistic, social and economic outcomes, including quality of life, psychological health, values, and social ideologies, identities and affiliations, and other non-cognitive educationally related outcomes. This is particularly ironic given the shift in educational policy internationally to claims that schools should build the dispositions and generic skills necessary for new economies and technologies.

These are all matters that we attempted to address in the Core Research Program of the Centre for Research in Pedagogy and Practice for the Singapore national system (e.g., Luke, Freebody, Gopinathan, & Lau, 2005). At its establishment, we framed the central questions about Singapore education in general and open terms, using a simple black-box model of inputs, processes, and outcomes.

- What are the sociodemographic, community, cultural and linguistic, and institutional factors contributing to academic achievement?
- What is the experience of teaching and learning in Singaporean classrooms? How can teaching and learning in classrooms be enhanced?
- What are the consequences of education for Singaporean students? How does education have an impact not just on school achievement per se, but upon employment and citizenship, upon attitudes, beliefs, aspirations, identity, upon social and economic capital? How are educational outcomes translated and mediated into life pathways?

The Singapore research design aims to generate a rich database that is multilevel, cross-sectional and longitudinal, and quantitative and qualitative. It does so by nesting micro-qualitative work within larger-scale quantitative datasets on student social class and linguistic background, teacher background, and student and teacher surveys. It treats school test and examination scores as but one set of outcomes but by no means the single or sole indicator of institutional or individual efficacy. In so doing, it goes beyond the acceptance of conventional indicators of success (e.g., test and exam scores, school-assigned marks) to explore the question of what might count as an outcome in the evaluation of educational efficacy. That is, the design makes problematic the conventional measures of success to look at both alternative accounts of achievement thereby following the prototypes of the Wisconsin CORS studies. Its classroom coding observational scheme builds upon previous schemes but makes more explicit use of curriculum theory and discourse analysis categories. The design also extends the conceptualization of outcomes to begin tracking the longitudinal consequences of schooling, tapping into the prototypes of the *World Youth Attitudes Study* and the *Longitudinal Study of Australian Youth* and previous studies of Singaporean youth and adolescent social and cultural capital.

Interpretations of the resultant data can provide the basis not only for policy development, but also for intervention and innovation in teacher education and professional development, school organizational capacity and leadership, curriculum development, and high stakes assessment. To date, descriptions of classroom practice and the relationship between pedagogical approaches and student artifact production have provided empirical grounds for ongoing and new curriculum reforms in language education, English teaching, and several other areas. Studies of the effects of population variables on high stakes test results and tracking systems have influenced future planning for reform of pathways and assessment approaches.

Policy making is in the first and final instance a hermeneutic activity (on research as hermeneutic activity see chapter 5 in this volume). As self-evident as it may seem, the notion that data itself can provide the ground for policy formation, for remaking educational practice is naïve in the extreme. The richer the datasets, the more triangulation and theoretical modeling is necessary to make sense of which patterns tell different stories of the processes and consequences for marginalized communities. We can extrapolate from empirical datasets various key systems indicators, from decreased predictive impact of social class and sociodemographic status on conventional achievement, to differential performance of best and worst achieving cohorts, to better achievement and post-school outcomes for specific marginalized cohorts, to improved retention and matriculation rates, subsequent tertiary participation, employment, and so forth.

Conventional equity targets and goals depend by definition on a given state's orientation towards and commitment to redistributive social justice. Yet they also depend on the robustness of its data. To generate policies that might begin to shift these patterns requires an analysis of which pedagogies recognize and enhance the resources of which groups of students to what cognate and substantive educational ends. The research toolkit outlined here indicates that it is possible to ascertain where curriculum and pedagogy can work together with enabling social and economic conditions to increase equality, shared and community identity, and mobility within and across life pathways. But unlike the quasi-experimental design approach, this richer research base also enables policy makers to consider the more nuanced and complex issues around generalization that haunt current approaches: not what works, but what works with whom? Where? When? From which alignments flows enabling policy? With what "collateral" effects in different local ecologies?

Expanding the Evidence—Shifting the Goalposts

Current systems indicators and evidence bases have their epistemological and technical limits. If states are to live up to their stated policy goals of preparation for new economies and cultural demands, there is a pressing need to begin shifting the goalposts of educational assessment: to develop valid and powerful indicators of the increase in student capital and capacity with durable, transferable effects in the social fields of work, civic life, and everyday life in communities. Current debates over evidence and public and media claims about systems failure tend to pivot on three historical models of what counts as an educational outcome. It is ironic that systems continue to measure the success of students, schools, teachers, and the system using instruments that have their historical genealogies in (a) classical British curricular examinations and (b) modern American norm-referenced standardized achievement testing. Recently, there also has been a shift towards increased use of (c) psychological survey instruments of student "non-cognitive" and social outcomes, including measures of psychological health, happiness, self-esteem, depression, and so forth.

There is no doubt that these three models of assessment do assess something of educational value: mastery of curriculum knowledge, skills and behavior measurable by pencil-and-paper instrument, and various psychological conditions and states. Further, the application of educational assessment and measurement standards offer assurances that, within their instrumental capacities, standardized tests and examinations are as technically precise and statistically reliable as possible. Yet there are persistent foundational questions around what might count as *validity* of current assessment models.

First is the problem of decontextualization and miscontextualization of knowledge and practice. A fundamental claim of sociocultural psychology is that both the learning and application of tool-making and using competence occurs in situ, that is in relation to scaffolded zones of proximal development.[2] The axiom that intrapsychological development is contingent on interpsychological relations applies here. Single-shot testing and examination situations in effect decontextualize practices from originary and subsequent social relations and resituate them in a different set of relations: those of the actual administration and taking of high stakes testing and examinations. The technical response is that skills are skills, regardless of context of acquisition, and that test-based recontextualization is an exercise in classical transfer of training. Where this argument holds, however, we could begin to view test results as indicators not of skill acquisition but rather of the transfer of training from one cultural site of learning (e.g., classroom interaction and myriad other learning zones) to the cultural site of the examination and test. That site, the scene of examination, all of its deliberate constructions of "neutrality" notwithstanding, constitutes an examination or test culture in itself, as studies of East Asian pedagogy suggest. The Singapore classroom pedagogy data, at the least, offers a plausible hypothesis that children score well on the standardized tests of international comparative studies because of the isomorphism between the zones of proximal development of classroom and test. Where this is shifted—for example, in more project-based, low-stakes curriculum settings—there is evidence that students' respond by producing cognitively richer and more complex intellectual artifacts.

A second problem concerns issues of what we might term *modal validity* raised by new media of representation. There is ample empirical, quantitative and qualitative demonstration that the current generations of students do a great deal of their learning in and out of schools using various forms and modes of digital technology. Recent studies of the efficacy of e-instruction use student performance on standardized print-based reading and writing tests as outcome indicators. Again, the assumption here is of transfer of training from screen to page, from digital image to print, from multimodal to unimodal system of representation. Yet in such studies, those distinctive cognitive and social achievements generated by human/tool interactions with new technologies are not adequately represented in the conventional pencil and paper assessment regime. To test knowledge and skill in one representational medium by means of another, then, potentially raises questions of *modal validity*, here referring to the distinctive medium of communication used for assessment.

The third and largest challenge to current measurement and assessment concerns the *policy relevance* of current assessment. Assuming the conventional validity and generalizability of said instruments, we could ask whether such instruments are actually testing and examining the knowledges, skills, and competences that will constitute capital for emergent life pathways through globalized economies and multicultural, digitalized cultures. Current claims around generic skills are that the employment volatility of knowledge economies requires transferable, transportable capacities and competences. At the same time, there are strong defenses mounted in current curriculum debates for various forms of basic and canonical knowledge, from grapho-phonemic awareness to knowledge of literary traditions. As in all curriculum debates, these questions are open to ongoing ideological contestation and empirical adjudication. But educational systems find themselves facing the curious millennial dilemma of aspiring to new skills, new competences, and new knowledges (from group work and critical thinking, to intercultural communication and bioethics)—while using longstanding measures of older industrial-era competences.

There are numerous possible responses to these issues facing assessment and, ultimately, the evidence-base on educational efficacy. First, we could argue that there are self-evident basics required of any human learner, upon which all subsequent learning depends. This is a defensible position, but given shifts in the modes and media of knowledge and representation, the blending of print and non-print modalities for learning, and new sites for learning and pedagogy in workplace, leisure, and across converging media—it would require at the least continual and rigorous empirical reexamination and theoretical reframing. Second, putting aside for a moment the self-serving rationale that these things have validity because they are required for further education by other institutions, we could argue that tests and exams test robust, longstanding knowledges and domains that readily transfer to new contexts of work and everyday life. This too is an empirically testable and contestable claim. But given the emergence of new workplaces and new trajectories, spurred by the deregulation of the workplace, the questions about what really counts in the new workplace, for which classes, and in whose interests these work will require a new wave of empirical study.

Yet the motive force and the Achilles heel of conservative educational policy is the validity and ongoing relevance of such instruments and the corresponding selective traditions of knowledge and skill they instate upon schools and classrooms, teachers, and students. Whether and how these instruments are the most currently relevant, technically accurate and ontologically valid means for assessing the complex forms of capital, dispositions, and resources that students actually acquire through everyday life and schooling, digitalized contemporary childhood is, at the very least, debatable. Whether they match well with the new requisites of the vaunted and mythologized "knowledge economies" that Australia and other OECD countries aspire towards are empirically and theoretically moot.

What is the goodness of fit between current measures of outcomes and the putative goals and challenges of education in contemporary conditions? I would argue that emergent contexts require a paradigm shift in educational assessment that moves towards the evaluation of new human resources, discursive and dispositional, and the varied and rich kinds of cultural, social, and symbolic capital that students require for these new contexts. This will require something other than century-old measurement paradigms that assume transfer of training of skills and knowledge from print to digital environments, from schools to communities and workplaces, even as these latter environments are under economic and cultural reformation. It will require an amplified effort and reframing of current work in the assessment-for-learning and authentic-assessment traditions to deal with new learner habitus, and to deal with new representational artifacts. The crude binaries of cognitive vs. non-cognitive, academic vs. social skills are, quite literally, remnant constructions of an industrial human subject. A new educational assessment will require due consideration of sociological models of production and reproduction (e.g., models of habitus and capital) and cultural psychological models of learning (e.g., models of cultural knowledge and situated practice). It would aim to assess those capital resources—literally, what people embody, speak, know and do, their material, social, and symbolic resources—when they enter educational environments, and how educational experience adds to their baskets of capital, and how these baskets are durably transported and deployed in social fields of various kinds and levels of discrimination. The possibilities for a grounded, materialist sociological assessment to the assessment of student-acquired cultural and social capital are open.

Triangulating Evidence

A critical realist approach to educational explanation can begin from and leads to and through theory. Obviously, critique and theory enable us to see the scientific truths and the epistemological limitations yielded by different instrumentation. Test scores or attrition rates or self-report data on educational experiences, for example, each tell us an epistemologically framed and delimited truth about what is occurring in the system. It is far trickier to see which patterns connect and which differences appear to make a difference in the production and reproduction of class and culture. The triangulating of multidisciplinary data can in turn enable us to build of narratives about how systems currently work, who traverses through them in what ways, with what material cultural and economic effects, and in whose material interests. Theory is needed to narratively model how we might change structural and interactional elements of these systems, building scenarios about how different policy moves might lead to shifts in outcomes, achievements or alteration in the patterns of achievement of normatively preferred educational goals.

In this regard, research-based policy analysis and formation bears some resemblances to forensic and epidemiological research. That work at once proceeds inductively from large, rich data sets—and simultaneously works deductively, generating hypotheses and making inferences from generalizable theoretical models. I refer to these fields cautiously, understanding the implications of using criminal and medical metaphors. But they are relevant considering the referents of the U.S. evidence-based approaches to policy, with Bush administration officials holding up the randomized field trial models of the pharmaceutical industry as the model for educational research and development.

In response to SARS and bird flu, the efforts of the Centers for Disease Control, World Health Organisation, and regional governmental and health institutions were rapid, comprehensive, and coordinated. They also were multidisciplinary. To address the problem has required classical scientific experimental work, with pre/intervention/post studies of treatment effectiveness, drugs, and so forth. But it also has entailed a range of other kinds of social scientific and scientific research brought together to build a comprehensive picture and, then, to normatively prescribe a series of governmental policy and practical interventions—both social and medical in kind. This involves case study and tracking of individual patients and their histories, epidemiological detective work tracking index cases to their sources, ethnographic and sociological analyses of habits and social practices, observational studies of hygiene, food-handling, and so forth and social and demographic analysis of population movement. Even the actual laboratory work of isolating the virus and determining its DNA structure—the Watson/Crick/Franklin stories about the dynamics of laboratory work would remind us—has involved intuition, guesswork, and high theorization, *as well as rigorous empiricism*. Modern epidemiology and medicine uses a broad palette of methods to acquire and triangulate different kinds of epistemological takes and data sets: these range from case-based work, observational ethnographies, and interviews to complex social statistical analyses. The palette of contemporary epidemiological research is far broader than the gold standard of quasi-experimental design invoked by advocates of policies like No Child Left Behind.

Educational problems likewise have complex social and cultural, psychological, and sociological dimensions. They cannot be solved exclusively or simply using randomized experimental trials. There is already evidence tabled by such senior researchers in the United States that the policy decisions made on the experimental research only rules of current U.S. policy have not solved a number of serious problems, including declining achievement and intellectual engagement in the middle years, and poor engagement with disciplinary knowledge at high school entry. One interpretation of the PISA studies is that increased curriculum specification and high-stakes testing run the risk of exacerbating the social class impacts upon and levels of stratification of achievement. We can term these unanticipated effects or collateral consequences—but the point is that similar phenomena occur when we extrapolate from, for example, simple drug trials to the social, institutional and cultural contexts where people put such medicines to work.

An Immodest Proposal

Schools and educational systems face complex problems of new student identities and increasingly socially stratified outcomes, new workplace and civic cultures, digital technologies and new dominant modes of representation, globalized economies and volatile patterns of work, and a new dynamics of shifting state, community, and religious value systems. These sit within a larger challenge of what might constitute a critical education for species survival, biosocial sustainability, and human justice in the face of a social, political, and economic order dominated by the new leviathan of the multinational corporation. The responses of educational systems—increasing micronization of the curriculum or a return to basics, increased basic skills testing, the scripting and surveillance of teachers' work, and the marketization of schools—would sit well in a Swiftian broadsheet on the amelioration of poverty in Ireland. Time is running out for a much more substantial vision of education and educational research.

I propose here a critical realist education research that blends quantitative and qualitative, cross-sectional and longitudinal studies, with a comprehensive sociodemographic and linguistic data base on student population, a central focus on descriptive and observational accounts of classroom pedagogy, and a multidimensional expanded definition of educational outcomes and pathways. Our focus would be to align rather than oppose distinctive approaches to educational research in the interests of identifying the core problem facing advanced educational systems: the enhancement of cultural and social capital in ways that empirically can be shown to contribute to economic mobility, social justice, and the development of sustainable human ethics in the face of new forms of corporatism and empire. This would be but a starting point for the reinvention of schooling.

As John Dewey (1923/2005) argued in *Art as Experience*, education, art, science, and other forms of human endeavor are problem posing and problem solving endeavors. Education is intrinsically goal-seeking. This was a core principle of James, Dewey, and Mead's philosophic and scientific pragmatism. Educational research is pragmatic, problem-solving, intellectual work. As such, it can draw upon and expand a rich palette of social scientific approaches and models—quantitative and qualitative, logico-analytic and critical-interpretive. In a world of fluidity and risk, indeterminacy, fuzziness, and contingency, the problems facing educational systems require a rich, rather narrow approach to educational research. An educational research for the 21st century must deal with complexity—and it must do so not by reverting to simple models. Unlike our predecessors a century ago—we have a broad array of tools, approaches, methods, and discourses to use to unpack educational problems, to hold them up to the light of different analyses, to triangulate, compare and debate the relationships between the findings yielded—and then to make the hardest move of them all: apply research to the improvement of teaching and learning.

For those of us whose philosophic and political stance is premised on the very possibility of an educational project of access and opportunity, and the equitable and fair distribution of educationally acquired and realized knowledge and power, the challenge remains one of normative institutional and social reconstruction, the philosophic and scientific task tabled by Dewey (1916) in the face of the last millennial economic and cultural shift. We can do so arguing that the failure to deal with achievement stratified by traditional lines of class, gender, and race may have potentially disruptive social and economic consequences; that narrow, reductionist versions of science will both misrecognise the complexity of the problems and risk one-dimensionalizing the educational variables and possible range of interventions. At the least, the task ahead will require:

- More rigorous approaches to the study of longitudinal educational effects of social class, race and ethnicity, and gender. The analysis of PISA data provides a starting point, as does reanalysis of matriculation and pathways data.
- A more rigorous approach to the analysis of teachers and teachers' work: Cochran-Smith (2001) recently pointed out that in spite of their push for evidence, U.S. state jurisdictions had a paucity of empirical data bases on their workforces, backgrounds, and career pathways. Although educational researchers have long had the quantitative and qualitative means for tracking cohorts of teachers to and across their working careers, little systematic longitudinal work is being done. This is hindering both workforce planning, the systematic redirection of resources to practicing teachers. However, again PISA and TIMMS studies do provide some data on relativities around teacher training and pay. These gaps in our knowledge about teachers' trajectories and work open the field to blame the teacher politics and media representation.
- A stronger focus on the variables of classroom practices: systematic ways of studying which pedagogical repertoires work to what cognitive and social ends for which groups of students. As argued here, the omission of systematic study of pedagogy is the most glaring weakness of current approaches to evidence.
- Richer definitions of student outcomes: it is ironic that while we talk about social policy around issues of capital, social, economic, community—we continue to assess students using 18th century and early and mid-20th century models.

- A persistent focus on new identities, new media, and new cultural formations and their affiliated knowledge/skill/power configurations. Current educational policy and curriculum planning works in relative isolation from studies of new youth culture, media and popular culture and empirical studies of workplaces. This is in part the result of the disciplinary isolation of many curriculum branches and their fields from work in cultural studies, sociology of work and other areas of emergent research. As importantly, it leaves curricular policy susceptible to two increasingly pernicious forces: first, a clichéd rhetoric about the alleged requisites of "knowledge economies" that lacks an empirical engagement with the new stratification of wealth, labor, and employment; second, the status quo of existing institutional capital/credential requirements as mandated by high stakes assessment, university and technical college entry requirements, and so forth.

These are but some of the research and development challenges in this transitional period of curriculum schooling. Two decades of attempts to name and appropriate policy and curriculum discourses around race, class, and gender to date have struggled to alter substantively the actual flows and distribution of educational capital in more equitable ways. By making new coalitions and shaping possible alignments between governments committed to redressive and redistributive educational policy, and the critical educational research community—we are in a position to reappraise which combinations of research tools can return us to the table of state policy formation with a stronger and more programmatic case for remaking schooling in the interests of economically, culturally, and socially marginalized communities. This does not mean that the strategic engagement with policy analysis, ideology critique, and deconstruction that contests and defines state and civic narrative ideological function should be abandoned. The political, philosophical, and moral responsibility of the educational research community to critique remains. But by engaging with the debate on evidence we can also intervene programmatically at the level of tactics: debating, hypothesizing and postulating, and empirically and interpretively testing which flows of resources generate which alignments with which concrete material consequences for teachers and for students, for communities, economies, and nation states.

We should welcome the challenges. The push towards evidence cannot be written off as by definition a neoliberal, neoconservative, or technocratic move to define performativity in ways that a priori protect particular class and corporate privilege —however it may have been enlisted towards these ends in the US, UK and, most recently, in Canada and Australia. Indeed, comparative international social, economic, and educational evidence already makes quite a compelling case that neoliberal marketization of social and human services, including education, is concomitant with a historical widening of socioeconomic disparity and decrease in social mobility. The debate over educational science can lead us to recover some of the powerful research traditions that historically set out the terms of our analyses of social reproduction and class stratification. These remain the main game—especially as the very grounds, players, and rules redefine themselves.

Notes

1. Such critique often employs and is recognized by terms such as deconstruction, poststructuralism, postcolonialism, postmodernism, neo-Marxian, and Frankfurtian.
2. The zone of proximal development denotes the difference between aided and unaided performance, which constitutes the zone of possible growth.

References

Alton-Lee, A. (2004). *A collaborative knowledge building strategy to improve educational policy and practice: Work-in-progress in the Ministry of Education's Iterative Best Evidence Synthesis Programme*. Wellington: Ministry of Education. Retrieved May 25, 2008, from http://www.educationcounts.govt.nz/_data/assets/pdf_file/0005/6647/ibes-nzare-paper-2004.pdf

Bernstein, B. (1990). *The structure of pedagogic discourse*. London: Routledge & Kegan Paul.

Cazden, C. B., Johns, V. & Hymes, D. (Eds.). (1972). *Functions of language in the classroom*. New York: Teachers College Press.

Cochran-Smith, M. (2001). The outcomes question in teacher education. *Teaching and Teacher Education, 17*, 527–546.

Dewey, J. (1923/2005). *Art as experience*. New York: Peregee Books.

Dewey, J. (1916). *Democracy and education*. New York: Macmillan.

Foucault, M. (1972) *The archaeology of knowledge and the discourse on language* (A. Sheridan-Smith, Trans). New York: Harper & Row.

Green, B. (2005). Curriculum inquiry in Australia. In W. Pinar (Ed.), *International handbook of curriculum research* (pp. 123–140). Mahwah, NJ: Erlbaum.

Heath, S. B. (1983). *Ways with words*. Cambridge, UK: Cambridge University Press.

Luke, A. (2007). Curriculum in context. In F. M. Connolly, M. F. He, & J. Phillion (Eds.), *The Sage handbook of curriculum and instruction* (pp. 145–152). Thousand Oaks, CA: Sage.

Luke, A., Freebody, P., Lau, S., & Gopinathan, S. (2005). Towards research-based innovation and reform: Singapore schooling in transition. *Asia Pacific Journal of Education, 25*, 5–28.

Nichols, S., & Berliner, D. (2007). *Collateral damage*. Cambridge, MA: Harvard Educational Press.

Raudenbush, S. (2005). Learning from attempts to improve schooling: the contribution of methodological diversity. *Educational Researcher, 34*(5), 25–33.

Willis, P. (1981). *Learning to labor.* New York: Columbia University Press.

Section III

Highlights

All three chapters in section III advocate orienting the questions of generalization and generalizability along the dimension of use and usability. Who is going to make use of the research results? For what purposes are the research results being used (local transformations, policy)?

All three authors advocate (Luke, Bachman) or at least accept (Tobin) the use of multiple forms of methods to generate the knowledge that is to be of use by one or another stakeholder in the educational enterprise. However, because the means of production leave their marks on and mediate the nature of outcomes, different research methods will determine the content and structure of the knowledge they produce. This then raises the question about how the different forms of knowledge can be articulated. In our reading, Tobin advocates accepting a patchwork of knowledge, whereas the two other authors (Luke, Bachman) argue for some form of process in which different forms of knowledge are triangulated.

Some concerns that may be voiced relate to the underlying epistemology according to which different forms of knowledge can be triangulated. If this were the case, then we would accept an ontology of the world that remains unchanged however we look at it. There is one world, and different forms of knowledge merely provide us with different perspectives that result from the different points of view (positions) that the knowledge producers (users) take and hold. This is consistent with recent scholarship on the nature of science, which appears to show that different paradigms—which is how some educational researchers have framed the distinction between different approaches in educational research—are incommensurable not only in terms of method but also in terms of their ontology, that is, the basic ways in which the world is cut up into identifiable entities and processes.

The issue of scale is important in the question about how and if the results of different methods can be combined to yield something useful. This is a question that may have to be resolved in concrete situations. On the surface, there appears to exist no impediment to the assumption that research outcomes are used at different levels of scale where they are complementary but have little influence on one another. A policy maker needs different forms of knowledge than a school principal or a classroom teacher with her student. On the one hand, a policy maker or school superintendent may make available resources that impede with or enhance the efforts at the classroom level that would bring together teachers, students, and others concerned with changing the teaching–learning situation. This would be the case if Luke's social justice issues were to be on the front burner for the policy makers and the same if similar social justice issues were at stake in the work between teachers, students, and parents, for example. On the other hand, it might be the case that the two forms of knowledge have very little to do with one another. Knowledge associated with policy issues or distribution of funding may have little bearing on the knowledge teachers and students produce in Tobin's cogenerative dialogues and require for making theirs a better world.

In his text on "The Practice of Reflexive Sociology," Pierre Bourdieu (1992) inveighs against the "monomaniacs" of method, whether it is the method "of log-linear modeling, of discourse analysis, of participant observation, of open-ended or in-depth interviewing, or of ethnographic description" (p. 226). He argues against the use of one method and for the combination of methods. But, if this were so, it would not be in a simplistic manner. Thus, Bourdieu belittles simple combinations of methods into multi-method approaches: "the fact of combining discourse analysis with ethnographic description will be hailed as a breakthrough and a daring challenge to methodological monotheism" (p. 226). But he does argue for the need to "mobilize all the techniques that are relevant and practically usable, given the object and the practical conditions of the data collection" (p. 227). In any event, he exhorts us to be critical of concepts, objects, and methods, all of which are preconstructed, associated with ideologies, seeking to be reified in the reproduction of the field. More so than a simple multi-method approach would be a self-critical educational science that not only investigates phenomena "out there," but also concerns itself with its own presuppositions (parts of paradigm) that shield us from questions and questioning.

A common idea and thread running through the Luke and Tobin chapters is that of the role of cultural history and biography to understanding the specific needs of specific user groups, requiring us to conduct studies that allow us to understand the trajectories of systems to the point where they are today. Luke produces a historical account that allows us to see how the relationship between educational policy and research has changed in different Anglo-Saxon countries over the past decades. This approach then allows us to understand better how the Bush and Howard regimes in the United States and Australia, respectively, have influenced the use of research methods in ways that many educational researchers have experienced as repressive. Tobin, with his particular historically evolving focus on the needs of specific groups of traditionally underserved populations, is more concerned with the production and mobilization of knowledge on the part of the members of those populations. And he has gotten there, as his auto/biography shows, through a period that has seen extensive changes in theory and method of educational research. He has changed the methods on which he has drawn, beginning as a researcher who drew on statistical tools to produce knowledge considered being applicable across time and space, to doing ethnographic research that also was considered to be transportable to and relevant in different places in the world, to doing research with stakeholders and for stakeholders.

We begin this section with a quote from Karl Marx, who, in his eleventh thesis on Feuerbach states that changing the world is the real point of the human endeavor. Knowledge in and of itself, such as that created by the austere order of intellectuals at the center of Hermann Hesse's Nobel Prize winning *The Glass Bead Game* (also *Magister Ludi*) for the sole pleasure of knowing independent of the needs of the players or the people outside in society at large. The knowledge created within the order was to be universality of the highest order, transcending traditional faculties to create a single form of knowledge and associated language. Recent developments in many societies have moved away from this image of knowledge as transcendent and, supported by granting councils that ask for greater relevance of research knowledge to users, implicate the impact of knowledge on efforts for improving social and material life. *Knowledge mobilization* and *knowledge use* have become key concepts in the vocabularies of funding councils.

Human beings are not at the mercy of reigning conditions, but constitute the agential species par excellence, as it changes its conditions to better suit its needs. From this perspective, therefore, the primary motive for producing new knowledge is to improve the social and material life within schools and school systems specifically and in society generally. The use of knowledge, therefore, ought to stand at the center of its production. The question therefore may be raised whether a purely epistemologically grounded framework, such as the research use argument Bachman promotes, alone suffices to steer us toward greater applicability and usefulness of knowledge production. It may be that the kind of political arguments found in the Tobin and Luke chapters is required to orient knowledge production; in turn, Bachman appears to us as providing the kind of framework we need to assess the degree of plausibility that leads from situation through research to use.

Use needs to be investigated critically, because it could be used to serve an ideology and thereby simply perpetuate social inequality, injustice, and inequity. A good example for us is the research done in traditional psychology concerning the concept of motivation. According to the German critical psychologist Klaus Holzkamp (1993), the motivation concept is used and theorized to subjugate those students issuing from the working and disadvantaged classes, and those students who do not fit the mold. Accordingly, research results on motivation are used to make people (students, teachers) do what they do not normally do on their own or do not want to do on their own. This knowledge is used by those who have most interest (stakes) in maintaining the current societal-political and economic status quo, which is based on the exploitation of many (workers in the industrialized nations, third-world nations in their entirety) for the benefit of some, largely the bourgeois middle class. This is precisely the direction in which we see the political arguments heading that Luke and Tobin make at very different scales of the educational enterprise.

Allan Luke explicitly makes an argument for multi-method approaches grounded in a sense that some forms of knowledge generalize better to other settings than other forms of knowledge, where we include in generalization the notion of transportability, the alternative criterion Guba and Lincoln (1989) introduced for the qualitative-interpretive approaches in educational (evaluation) research. Luke's chapter appears to be consistent with traditional conceptions of research whereby the results from experimental, quasi-experimental, and survey research can be more easily applied in a greater variety of settings than other knowledge explicitly constructed for the purposes at hand (as in Tobin's cogenerative dialogues involving teachers and their students). Here, we are not so sure whether this is the case. When the board of a school system or district in despair hires a superintendent from another district or state (province), it assumes that the new administrator will transport his/her knowledge gained in one local context, marked by singularity and contingency, to another local context with its own singularity and contingency. When a school principal hires a new teacher from out of town, province, and even country, he or she assumes that what the teacher has learned in one or more contingent settings is transported into another contingent setting. This points us to an ongoing everyday practice of assuming the generalization of knowledge across space and time.

Luke and Tobin both point us to the difficult question of the *why* of education research and generalization. The research use argument may lead us to reevaluate this question. The answers will not come easy and may have to be resolved and understood in the context of democracies to come, where democracy is not understood as a constant but as something we want to change to make it more appropriate for all, including those millions currently underserved. Working toward the goal of social justice, then we have to consider the changing individual along the trajectory he or she takes through formal educational institutions. If our goal is to provide equitable opportunities to *all* individuals, our assessment procedures and models need to be such that they address the needs of the individual rather than that of groups and populations.

References

Bourdieu, P. (1992). The practice of reflexive sociology (The Paris workshop). In P. Bourdieu & L. J. D. Wacquant, *An invitation to reflexive sociology* (pp. 216–260). Chicago: University of Chicago Press.

Guba, E., & Lincoln, Y. (1989). *Fourth generation evaluation*. Beverly Hills, CA: Sage.

Holzkamp, K. (1993). *Lernen: Subjektwissenschaftliche Grundlegung*. Frankfurt/M.: Campus.

Rethinking the Relationship Between the General and the Particular

Overview

In the previous section, Allan Luke discussed the role of the United States and Australian governments in influencing from the outside the methodological and method-related discussions within the field of educational research. Rather than allowing the practitioners whose daily life and bread-earning pursuits concern the production of knowledge and the interrogation and critique of the means of production involved, politicians use their own presuppositions and agendas to hijack the scholarly debate and to infect it with ideology labeled "gold standards" and other catchy terms, when in fact their decisions are based on common sense, generalities, and abstractions—politicians may have advisors but *they* and not the advisors *make* the decision, and the grounds on which politicians evaluate available knowledge *is* common sense. Already in the early 19th century, G.W.F. Hegel (1988) warned his readers to watch out for those who think abstractly, for they are uninformed or ill-informed, with undeveloped knowledge not suitable to make wise decisions, and generally uneducated.

Within the field of educational research, the use of (quasi-) experimental and large-sample survey approaches has often been pitted against the careful interpretive analysis of single groups, small events, and episodes based on ethnography or various forms of language analysis. In the 1980s, scholars such as Yvonna Lincoln and Egon Guba (a former statistician, measurement scholar, and quantitative researcher) proposed various forms of *Naturalistic Inquiry* (1985) as methods within a different paradigm that they opposed to *positivism*. One of their axioms for a different, post-positivist paradigm, concerns two opposed versions for the possibility of generalization from educational research:

> *Positivist version*: The aim of inquiry is to develop a nomothetic body of knowledge in the form of generalizations that are truth statements free from both time and context (they will hold anywhere and at any time.)

Naturalist version: The aim of inquiry is to develop an idiographic body of knowledge in the form of "working hypotheses" that describe the individual case. (p. 38)

Educational researchers have come to understand that both versions are hyperbolic in their formulation. All forms of knowledge are realized in concrete situations and therefore require practical wisdom (phronesis), which consists "in inventing just behavior suited to the singular nature of the case" "by betraying the rule to the smallest extent possible" (Ricœur, 1992, p. 269). If we understand Guba and Lincoln's "individual case" in the same way as Ricœur's, then the naturalist version of the possibility for generalization provides us with only one part of the story, whereas the positivist version provides us with the other part of the knowledge required in the enactment of practical wisdom. We already encountered this approach of bringing together the general and particular in the relational thinking Pierre Bourdieu (1992) advocates: "a particular case is constituted as a 'particular instance of the possible'" (p. 234). Two comments are in order: The first deals with the role and nature of paradigms; and the second deals with the dialectical relation between general rules and exceptions required by solicitude.

First, Thomas Kuhn (1970) suggests that scientific revolutions arise from a growing sense within some scientific community "that an existing paradigm has ceased to function adequately in the exploration of an aspect of nature to which that paradigm itself had previously led the way" (p. 92). Although there may be a chasm within the scientific community, it generally is not the case that one of the two parallel paradigms will win out as all adherents to the previous paradigm convert to the new. Rather, paradigms die out with their adherents. In educational research, we currently observe no trends that would suggest the disappearance or dying of the two main approaches denoted as "quantitative" and "qualitative" research. There is, as Becker and Wu, Bachman, and Luke, suggest in their respective chapters (6, 9, 11), place and need for both.

Second, in his description of practical wisdom and wise action, Paul Ricœur brings together two very different forms of knowledge: general rules (ethics) and situated action characterized by solicitude and singularity. We therefore need both forms to inform action, though these two forms of knowledge differ to a great extent. The two chapters in this section speak to different aspects of these two forms of knowledge, thereby pushing the internal critique within each form of knowledge production.

In her chapter, Kadriye Ercikan exhibits limitations in sample-to-population generalizations that cannot be overcome by the methods of G-theory presented in chapters 2 and 3. In Kuhnian terms, her chapter shows how aspects of the measurement paradigm break down or cease to function adequately, making a rethinking or replacement necessary.

More so, perhaps as a kind of mini-revolution, Wolff-Michael Roth proposes in his chapter 11 to completely rethink the very relationship between the abstract and the concrete, the general and the particular, the rule and the case. He provides two cases—phenomenological and dialectical materialist research—that are both concerned with the detailed study of cases and, by means of careful analysis, derive a full sample of cultural possibilities, which, because they are available to all members of a group, constitute the general as such. Such rethinking is difficult, because this form of thinking, dialectical logic, has not been supported in Western scholarship, which has continued to adhere to classical logic. Dialectical logic, however, has a solid history in the work of philosophy (there is a lineage from G.W.F. Hegel via Karl Marx to modern day philosophers including Jacques Derrida, Evald Il'enkov, Jean-Luc Nancy, and Paul Ricœur) and cultural-historical activity theorists and sociocultural psychologists (in the lineage of Lev Semenovich Vygotsky, Alexei Nikolaevich Leont'ev, and Klaus Holzkamp).

In this fourth section of our book, the authors engage in critiquing and rethinking concepts from the inside of the discipline, a reflexive turn that is required for the development of a discipline, for one that does not question itself does not truly know what it is doing (Bourdieu, 1992). In this effort, however, educational researchers find themselves in a double bind articulated in the following statement that paraphrases Bourdieu:

> Without the intellectual instruments bequeathed by her scholarly tradition, the educational researcher is little more than an amateur, an autodidactic, self-taught, spontaneous [educational researcher] ...; but at the same time, these instruments constantly put on in danger of simply substituting for the naïve doxa of lay common sense the no less naïve doxa of scholarly common sense that parrots, in technical jargon and under the official trappings of scientific discourse, the discourse of common sense. (p. 248)

Other sociologists and social psychologists have launched similar critiques at the heart of their discipline, alerting their peers to the dangers that come with taking on traditional concepts and methods without engaging in a constant critique to elaborate, improve, and develop them. This requires not only our decentering and critiquing but also our willingness to abandon heretofore taken-for-sacred foundations of a discipline. Both chapters that follow are provided as contributions to this internal effort of taking our discipline further by both critiquing and opening up avenues for rethinking what we, as a profession, do in our everyday practice of educational research.

References

Bourdieu, P. (1992). The practice of reflexive sociology (The Paris workshop). In P. Bourdieu & L. J. D. Wacquant, *An invitation to reflexive sociology* (pp. 216–260). Chicago: University of Chicago Press.

Hegel, G. W. F. (1988). *Werke Band 2*. Frankfurt a/M: Suhrkamp.

Kuhn, T. S. (1970). *The structure of scientific revolutions* (2nd ed.). Chicago: University of Chicago Press.

Lincoln, Y. S., & Guba, E. G. (1985). *Naturalistic inquiry*. Newbury Park, CA: Sage.

Recœur, P. (1992). *Oneself as another*. Chicago: University of Chicago Press.

Chapter 10

Limitations in Sample-to-Population Generalizing

Kadriye Ercikan

Generalizability of research findings is one of the key criterion researchers use to determine the value and usefulness of research. Often research that utilizes larger samples of data is associated with greater degrees of generalizability. Research that uses large-scale data bases and statistical approaches to analyses (typically referred to as "quantitative") is associated with higher levels of generalizability than research that utilizes interpretive approaches with small samples (typically referred to as "qualitative"). In a recent article, my colleague Wolff-Michael Roth and I argued that generalizability of research findings cannot be judged based on sample size (Ercikan & Roth, 2006). We provided examples of research which use small samples, such as in the case of phenomenology, yet may identify universal relationships that have great degrees of generalizability. As well as examples of research that may use very large samples but focus on overall group results and have very little generalizability for key sub-groups. To demonstrate this point, we used research on gender differences in mathematics as an example:

> Gender differences based on typical statistical analyses of group results are, in fact, differences in group means. These differences reflected in the group means may have very different patterns for groups of students. Some students may have different mathematical skills, while others may have been taught different curricula using different instructional methods and their results do not provide any information about individual students. Therefore, the findings are neither informative about individual students, nor do they provide insights about subgroups of students (e.g., high performing students who may have differential patterns of gender differences) that are not the focus of statistical comparisons. They are only relevant for the overall group the analyses focused on. (p. 21)

Generalizing from education research, typically, refers to the extent to which research findings are applicable to a broader set of contexts.

Researchers tend to use three arguments in making generalizations: (a) extrapolation from sample to population; (b) analytic generalization; and (c) case-to-case translation. These arguments are broadly associated with three types of research respectively: sampling with research using representative random samples, analytic generalization with experimental and quasi-experimental methods, and case-to-case translation with qualitative methods.

In the sample-to-population generalization, researchers and consumers of research judge the generalizability of research findings by the degree to which sample of subjects, outcomes and contexts used in research are representative of the population the research is intended to generalize to. This type of generalization is one of the most commonly used arguments in judging generalizability of research findings and is also referred to as probability or statistical generalization. It is also considered as the strongest argument for generalizing. In other words, strongest inferences are made by generalizing findings from a representative sample to population. A commonly used education research methods text book by Gall, Borg, and Gall (1996) describes sample-to-population generalization as follows:

> The researcher starts by defining a population of interest. The population typically includes too many members to study all of them, so the researcher attempts to select a manageable sample, but one that is representative of the population. He then attempts to generalize the findings obtained from studying the sample to the larger population. Statistical techniques are available to determine the likelihood that sample findings (e.g., students in the sample who received Method A earned higher test scores than students who received Method B) are likely to apply to the population. (p. 23)

Analytic generalization involves making arguments that support claims in relation to a theory. These arguments are not based on extrapolations from sample to population instead research findings are generalized to support a theory. This argument in experimental and quasi-experimental research involves direct manipulation of a variable, often referred to as intervention or treatment, and control of extraneous variables. Analytic generalizations may also be used in supporting inferences in "qualitative" research. In qualitative research distinctions are made between two types of analytic generalizations: theoretical generalization and grounded generalization. Eisenhart (chapter 4, this volume) makes the distinction as follows: "The difference is that the goal of grounded generalization is to produce new theories or explanations whereas the goal of theoretical generalization is to make existing theories more refined and incisive" (p. 60).

Case-to-case argumentation involves providing logical arguments to support claims that findings in one particular research setting may apply to another setting (case). The degree of generalization from case to case depend on the similarity of contexts, samples, interventions in the research study to those in cases the generalizations are intended for. Eisenhart argues that "transferability" is more appropriate in case-to-case inferences and emphasizes the need for knowledge about the cases across which generalizations are made and quotes Erickson (1986) as follows: "The search is not for abstract universals arrived at by statistical generalizations from a sample to a population, but for concrete universals arrived at by studying a specific case in great detail and then comparing it with other cases studied in great detail" (p. 130).

In both the analytic and case-to-case generalization, the arguments supporting generalizations are expected to be explicit since with a well explained rational for generalization, such generalizations are neither obvious nor can they be assumed. In quantitative research that utilizes a representative sample of subject/participants/units, the generalizations to the population are typically assumed as a direct outcome of the research design. The purpose of this chapter is to draw attention to such assumptions and to describe and discuss limitations in sample-to-population generalization. I discuss the limitation of sample-to-population generalizability as an indicator of whether research provides meaningful guidance to policy and practice. I elaborate on the point that even research that uses nationally representative samples may have very limited value to inform policy and practice using two research studies I conducted. In the last part of the chapter, I discuss implications of these limitations.

Sample-to-Population Generalization

The sample-to-population generalizability is based on a statistical rationale. The rationale most simply stated is: if the sample is representative of the population then the distribution of variables in the sample is expected to be similar to those in the population. Statistics provides tools for estimating the degree to which the sample is representative of the population (bias) and the degree of error (sampling error) involved in drawing conclusions based on the sample with respect to the population. For example, a nationally representative sample of fourth-grade students may be drawn from each of the participating countries in an international assessment such the Trends in International Mathematics and Science Study (TIMSS). Performance of these students on mathematics and science are then used to draw conclusions about student achievement in these subjects in each country. The nationally representative assessment data are also used to examine group differences such as gender or language groups, to investigate relationships between achievement in mathematics and science and student attitudes, teacher instructional practices, or school resources.

The sampling errors are estimated and used in any hypothesis testing regarding group differences and calculation of correlations. The effects of possible bias in the sample are adjusted by using sampling weights in all statistical estimations. The notions of bias and sampling error are indicators of the degree to which group level statistics in the sample generalize to the group defined in the same way in the population. The mean performance of the sample of fourth graders is used to derive a confidence interval using the sampling error that is intended to make claims with known uncertainty (e.g., 95% confidence interval) about the expected range of mean performance in the population. For example, if we randomly selected 100 fourth graders from among all fourth graders in Canada (say 100,000), how well would the average score for the 100 fourth graders estimate the average score for all the fourth graders in the country? The claims regarding the population are not limited to overall group means. They may involve many other statistics such as differences in gender or language groups, correlations, and several other statistical summaries of variables or associations among variables. Confidence intervals are critical in evaluating the degree of error in generalizing from sample to population due to sampling of units such as students, schools, classrooms. However, confidence intervals have two key limitations as an indicator of generalizability of research findings. The first limitation is related to whether all factors that affect the claims are considered in evaluating generalizability. The second limitation of sample-to-population generalization lies in its ability to demonstrate value and usefulness of research, i.e., applicability of findings to education practice and policy. These two limitations are discussed below.

Consideration of Factors Affecting Generalizability

In evaluating generalizability of research findings, representativeness considerations are often limited to the degree to which individuals or units of generalization such as schools or classrooms from the sample are representative of the population. However, claims such as "50% of the fourth-grade students in Canada are achieving at proficient level" have many aspects other than representativeness of the sample of boys and girls that require consideration when evaluating generalizability of research findings. Cronbach (1982) identifies at least four classes of factors one would want to sample in a generalization: the units affected (students, classrooms, schools, etc.), the treatments (interventions), the outcomes (effects as conceptualized and as measured), and the settings, including culture, historical period, and a variety of other dimensions.

In the international assessments example, targeted inferences are related to evaluating the achievement of fourth-grade students in mathematics and science. In this example, the targeted generalization is about student learning and achievement of fourth-grade students in the country. In such a generalization, sampling of students is only one of the factors that need to be taken into account in evaluating generalizability. The other key factors that need to be considered are outcomes, measurements and settings. How these four factors affect generalizations in international assessments are described below.

Sampling of Students

To what extent does the sample represent relevant characteristics of the population that is the target of inferences?

In international assessments, similarly to national assessments, students are sampled based on a systematic probability sampling design. The overall group level generalizations are determined by the degree to which the selected sample deviates from the sampling design. There are many challenges in implementing a complex sampling design in international assessments. For example, in many countries, selected schools are not required to participate in the assessment and they may decline. Replacement or non-replacement of the declining schools results in biased samples that have limited representativeness of the characteristics of the population. In addition to within country generalization, in international assessments, there are key intended generalizations that focus on cross-country comparisons such as ranking countries based on overall country level performances. One of the key factors that affect generalization across countries is whether the same sampling design is used across countries. For example, even though all the countries are required to use "nationally representative" samples, they may vary in their exclusion rules, such as whether and which special needs students are excluded from the assessments and whether they include private schools. These would constitute differences in sampling designs across countries.

Outcomes

To what extent is the targeted learning outcome the appropriate learning outcome for individual countries and to what extent does this appropriateness generalize across countries? In TIMSS, outcomes may be very broadly defined as learning outcomes in mathematics. Ss is evident in the changing goals of mathematics learning identified by the National Council of Teachers of Mathematics (NCTM), mathematics learning may be defined in many different ways, In addition, in the context of international assessments, this definition of mathematics may vary from one country to another. For example, in some countries, statistics may be included in elementary school mathematics curricula, in others it may not be. In addition, differential emphasis may be placed on different components of curricula. In some countries, problem solving may be integral to all of mathematics teaching, whereas in others, it may be covered as part of certain topics only. In making generalizations about learning and achievement, the "universe" of mathematics learning and outcomes may be identified as all possible definitions of mathematics learning. The representativeness of the mathematics included in the assessment will then need to be considered in evaluating the generalizability of findings from the assessment. In many large-scale assessments conducted at the national and international levels, test developers in fact do make an effort to include a very broad content of mathematics learning by using multiple test forms that are administered using a matrix sampling approach. In other words, an overlapping set of test forms are administered to randomly equivalent groups of students but a single student takes only a small number of test items that correspond to a narrow range of mathematics content. However, the extent to which the targeted domain is appropriate for each country and across countries is critical to any generalizations regarding learning outcomes within and across countries.

Measurements

What is the generalizability of the specific measurement (e.g., a combination of multiple-choice and constructed-response item) used in research? How different would the results be if a different type of measurement (e.g., all constructed-response items) was used?

Measurement is the operationalization of the sampled content domain of the assessment. There has been much discussion among measurement researchers during the last three decades about formats of assessments, such as multiple-choice, open-ended questions, and performance assessments, and the relationship between these formats and what the assessments is measuring. The most recent research shows that there is not a one-to-one correspondence between assessment format and constructs beings assessed, yet there is consensus among researchers that the format does affect what is assessed by the test (Ercikan, 2006). The international mathematics assessment example I have been using contains both multiple-choice and constructed-response questions. For example, the TIMSS 2003 grade 8 mathematics assessment is comprised of a combination of both multiple-choice (MC) and constructed-response (CR) items, and has a total of 194 items. About one-third of the items were in the CR format, requiring students to generate and write their answers.

Five mathematics content areas were assessed at the eighth-grade level: numbers, algebra (patterns and relationships at the fourth grade), measurement, geometry, and data. The items assessing these content areas were grouped into 14-item blocks, which were distributed across 12 booklets, each containing six blocks of items. Only one booklet was administered to any given student. To what extent the item formats used in the assessments measure intended constructs is an empirical question. The operationalization of the mathematics outcomes are at the core of making claims about these learning outcomes and whether these operationalizations reflect the targeted constructs is another factor that needs to be considered in making claims about population learning outcomes.

Settings

To what extent is the performance on the assessment an indicator of the learning outcomes and not of other setting or context related factors such as language, familiarity with test and test formats and importance given to the test?

The fourth key factor that needs to be taken into account is the setting of assessments. Examinees' knowledge and competencies are among many other factors that may affect their responses to test questions and their performance on the test. Student performance is affected by their familiarity with test format and content, the context in which test items are presented in, additional cognitive demands such as language competency for English language learners (on this point see also chapter 3), the perceived importance of the assessment and therefore student motivation. Previous research has shown that context and the language in which test items are presented in can impact examinee performance even when all necessary information for responding to the question is presented to students.

There are psychological and cognitive factors that are associated with examinee cultural background that have been shown by previous research to impact examinee performance on tests. This research has focused on sensitivity of student performance to item contexts that are not directly relevant to the construct intended to be assessed. In a review, O'Neill and McPeek (1993) summarized the results of empirical research on the relation between characteristics of test items and how they are demonstrated to be related to examinee performance from different groups. For example, this research found that males perform better compared to a matched sample of females on reading passages with science-related content and antonyms and analogies classified as "science" or "world of practical affairs." This difference is found despite the fact that all of the information necessary to answer the reading comprehension questions is present in the reading passage.

This research is clarifying and reminding us that individuals from different cultural backgrounds may use different cognitive processes in learning, they may use different strategies in responding to test questions, their differential familiarity with contexts, and formats may affect how they understand and respond to test questions. Therefore, there is plenty of evidence that shows that examinees' responses to test questions are not just a function of what they know and what they can do but also their cultural background.

Results from such research demonstrate the sensitivity of examinee performance to their cultural and language background and the interaction of this background with performance on tests. Considerations of the generalizability of performance results need to take into account to what extent the cultural factors and assessment settings may affect performance on the assessments and how these factors affect generalizability of performance results within countries and across countries.

Applicability of Findings to Practice and Policy

Even when all possible factors affecting sample-to-population generalization of research findings are considered this generalizability does not include to what extent research findings inform education practice either within the context of research conducted or beyond the research context. Given the purposes of most educational research to inform education practice, the use and value of educational research needs to be defined in terms of its function to inform education pedagogy, policy, and social theory. Howe and Eisenhart (1990) emphasize this function of education research and its relationship to education research questions and methodology "it is incumbent upon educational researchers to give careful attention to the value their research questions have for informing educational practice, whether it be at the level of pedagogy, policy, or social theory, and then to ground their methodology in the nature of these questions" (p. 7).

In sample-to-population generalizations, most commonly used statistical tools are intended to make claims about groups. The claim regarding a group mean may not hold for any particular individual in the sample. In fact, when the data scale is continuous interval the probability of an individual having the same variable value as the mean is 0. Similarly, claims about group mean provide very little information about how subgroups of students are performing.

Education practice and policy are targeted to groups of individuals rather than to the "population" and whether the research provides useful direction for practice and policy depends on the degree to which findings apply to the relevant sub-group of individuals. Sample-to-population generalizability is an indicator of the degree to which total sample findings generalize to the total population. This generalizability does not address whether the findings are meaningful for individuals or groups of individuals. Applicability of research findings to sub-groups is at the core of potential for research to inform pedagogy, policy or social theory. Inferences targeted to overall group comparisons have significant limitations in their applicability to understanding or making decisions regarding sub-groups such as gender, ethnic, and ability groups of students. My colleague Wolff-Michael Roth and I (Ercikan & Roth, 2006) discuss this point as follows: "To make educational decisions based on research findings, we need to look closer at which groups of girls are performing different than boys and what it is about being girls that may lead to differential performance in mathematics" (Walkerdine, 1988, p. 21). We go on to further emphasize the need for research that focuses on sub-groups for research to inform policy and practice: "Research that examines representative groups for purposes of generalizability, as well as the individual and groups of individuals with certain characteristics, is expected to provide a more complete picture of the nature of and sources of differences and to provide better guidance for education decision makers and policy makers" (p. 21).

There are limitations of group level statistics in informing particular cases in program evaluation research as follows:

> The summary statistics on the sample, or the estimates for UTOS (population of Units, Treatments, Observing Operations and Settings) or a sub-UTOS (subset of instances in UTOS), are usually not an adequate base for inference about *UTOS (situation or class about which a conclusion is wanted). Insofar as there is diversity in the data, the consumer should be told about that diversity and any factors associated with it.... An interpreter is likely to work back and forth between the gross statistical analysis and the differentiated, select cases, taking one level of analysis as background for the other. (Cronbach, 1982, p. 167)

As an example of group level statistics, let us take a look at a claim such as "boys are performing better than girls" based on group level statistics. Such a statement is statistically supported when between gender group variability is greater than within gender group variability and the distribution of scores for boys has a higher mean. However, the distributions of scores often overlap. This overlap of distributions means that there are "some girls" who are outperforming "some boys." If such a claim is not true for some portion of girls, how can that statement be useful in guiding education practice that focuses on the gap between boys and girls in mathematics learning? Figure 10.1 displays hypothetical mathematics score distributions for girls and boys. On this diagram,

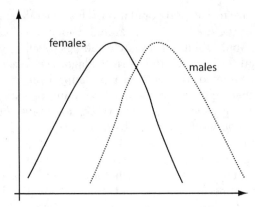

Figure 10.1 Mathematics score distributions for females and males.

the mean of the mathematics score distribution for boys is greater than that for the girls. However, as can be seen on the diagram, there are large groups of girls who score higher than a group of boys. Therefore, making claims at the overall group level that "boys are scoring higher than girls" is not generalizable to large groups of girls and boys in this sample.

Similarly in correlation research, a correlation between two variables such as teacher classroom practices and learning outcomes based on nationally representative sample of data is an approximation of degree and type of association between the two variables across sub-groups such as rural and urban communities, small versus large-schools, experienced versus non-experienced teachers, among many others. The correlation within each of these sub-groups may vary and indicate different direction and strength of associations. Figure 10.2 displays some of the possible patterns of relationships between teacher practices and achievement test scores. The overall correlation for the total group (across these three hypothetical patterns) is expected to indicate a weak to no relationship between teacher practices and achievement scores. This overall

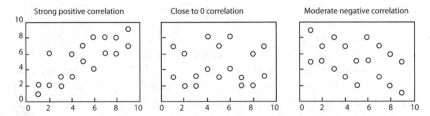

Figure 10.2 Different patterns of relationships between teacher practices and learning outcomes.

sample level correlation cannot provide meaningful direction to education research and practice.

The generalizability arguments need to take into account to what extent a claim such as "boys are performing higher than girls" is meaningful and for which groups of boys and girls. Similarly correlational claims such as "there is no association between classroom assessment practices and learning outcomes" need to be examined and demonstrated for sub-groups that are relevant for policy decisions.

Examples of Research Demonstrating Limitations in Sample-to-Population Generalizing

The sub-sections below elaborate on the limitations in generalizing in two research projects—one correlational research and the other focused on group comparisons—I conducted during the last three years. Correlational research is based on a nationally representative data collected at the pan-Canadian level on student learning outcomes, teacher practices and school contexts and focused on correlational research and focuses on limitations in making generalizations when outcome, measurement and settings are not taken into account. The group comparison research is based on international assessment data comparing gender differences in mathematics in 40 countries. These examples are intended to elaborate on the two limitations in sample-to-population generalizing considerations of all possible factors affecting generalizability and applicability of research findings to sub-groups of the sample.

Limitations in Generalizing in Correlational Research

This sub-section describes and discusses research to elaborate on two key limitations in sample-to-population generalizing: (a) multiple factors in addition to sampling of students (outcome, measurement, settings) that affect generalizing; and (b) applicability of overall group level findings to sub-groups, which I refer to as variation across sub-groups. Three years ago, I was awarded a grant funded jointly by the Canadian Education Statistics Council (CESC), Statistics Canada, and the Social Sciences Humanities Research Council (SSHRC) to conduct research using Canada's national survey of achievement, the School Achievement Indicators Program (SAIP). The purpose of the funding program was to support research that may inform policy and practice in education using one of many large-scale data sets available in Canada. The purpose of the research I proposed was to examine classroom practices that are associated with higher learning outcomes in schools with high levels of resources, and in schools with low levels of resources. The rationale was that policies for improving resource allocation and student learning critically depend on how teacher classroom practices are associated with learning outcomes and whether there are differences between effective teaching practices when school resources are high versus when they are low. The research focused on the relationship between each of the learning outcomes in the areas of reading, writing, mathematics, and science on the one hand and teacher classroom practices on the other hand.

Correlational analyses using large-scale databases such as the ones I had access to are the most common and inexpensive ways of identifying potential teacher practices to target and possibly investigate further. A nationally representative database on students' learning outcomes, teachers' classroom practices and school context variables would seem like an ideal data source to investigate the research questions I set out to investigate. Such a database would be expected to lend itself to make claims about education practices, outcomes, and contexts in the country.

Previous research mostly from small-scale studies identified that effective teachers planned carefully, used appropriate materials, made the goals clear to students, and checked student work regularly. More effective teachers used class time well and had coherent strategies for instruction. They believed that their students could learn and that they had a large responsibility to help (Cohen, Raudenbush, & Ball, 2003). These practices were used to identify variables to focus on in the database.

Similar to other national surveys of achievement such as the National Assessment of Educational Progress (NAEP), the SAIP data provide information about student learning outcomes, teachers' classroom practices, school resources and school climate. A sample of schools that are representative of Canada and each of the jurisdictions (provinces and territories) are randomly drawn for each assessment. My research used data sets for writing, mathematics, science, and reading assessments administered in 2002, 2001, 1999, and 1998, respectively, for representative samples of 13- and 16-year-old students. In addition to the overall assessment scores for students, data from teacher and school surveys were also used. After examining the SAIP teacher survey questions, we determined that these surveys provide information about all of the effective teacher classroom practices identified in previous research except for the pace of instruction in classrooms and whether teachers taught material again when students had trouble understanding it. Therefore, all of the previously identified effective teacher practices except for the two that are not included in the surveys were included in the analyses.

The first step in our research was to conduct correlational analyses between SAIP scores and each of the teacher practice variables. All the correlations were close to 0 but statistically significant (see Table 10.1).

If we had ignored these correlations and pursued regression analyses, we would have ended up with these instructional practices as statistically significant predictors of learning outcomes and a regression model

Table 10.1 Correlations between Teacher Practice Variables and SAIP Science Scores

	Mathematics	Writing	Science
Planning On average, how many hours per week do you spend on planning and preparation outside of formal school hours?	<0.1	<0.1	<0.1
Use of appropriate materials When planning lessons, to what extent do you use student textbooks?	<0.1	<0.1	<0.1
Classroom assessment practices In assessing the work of students in your courses, how much weight do you give each of the following (standardized tests, homework assignments, peer evaluation, etc.)?	<0.1	<0.1	<0.1
Use of class time On average, how many minutes of each class period would you say are lost because of disruption?	<0.1	<0.1	<0.1

accounting for 20%–30% of the variance in SAIP scores. Even though such a regression model would be considered weak, it is quite common for education research to result in such regression models. Researchers often acknowledge the weakness of such models but nevertheless continue to try to interpret what the regression model would imply. When the results indicate no meaningful association between these teacher practices and learning outcomes how can we interpret these findings? Typical claims based on these findings and challenges to such claims regarding three of the teacher practices (planning, use of appropriate materials, classroom assessment practices) are discussed below Challenges are presented as questions about the meaningfulness of such a claim and the factors affecting the generalizability of findings related to outcome, measurement, and variation across sub-groups are identified.

How Is Planning Related to Learning Outcomes?

Reasonable Claim

There is no association between the number of hours teachers spend on planning and learning in classrooms. After all, the analyses were conducted to determine if such a claim could be rejected (whether the null hypothesis could be rejected). The statistical significance would indicate that such a claim could be rejected, the effect size (correlations less than 0.1) indicate that even though there may be some systematic association, it is too weak to be meaningful.

Challenges to Such a Claim

There are many reasons why a correlation of 0 may not indicate lack of association between planning and science learning outcomes. Some questions about the meaningfulness of such a claim and the factors affecting the generalizability of findings are presented below:

Are there different types of associations for different sub-groups? (Variation across sub-groups)

- Does this teacher survey question tell us how many hours teachers spend on planning? Is it possible teachers in some systems do their planning mostly during formal school hours? Since the question focuses on hours spent on planning outside of formal school hours, teachers are in fact not reporting the total number of hours they spend on planning. (Measurement)
- Is the number of hours spent on planning confounded with teacher experience, and therefore, teachers who spend long hours planning are the newer teachers? In fact, this was the case in the SAIP data analyses. (Outcome/measurement)
- Are the SAIP scores capturing science learning in schools adequately? (Outcome/measurement)

Is Textbook Use Associated with Higher Learning Outcomes?

Reasonable Claim

There is no meaningful association between textbook use and higher learning outcomes.

Challenges to Such a Claim

First, association of textbook use with science scores varied across jurisdictions. At the pan-Canadian level, use of textbook was not associated with learning outcomes but in some provinces, some use of textbooks were associated with somewhat higher learning outcomes. The lack of association indicated by the correlation is questionable:

- What information do the teacher responses tell us about appropriate material use? Could the teachers who are not using textbooks be using other, perhaps richer, learning materials? The question is limited to the extent to which teachers use textbooks. Since the textbooks and their quality and appropriateness vary across schools and jurisdictions, responses to this question have very limited value. In the best-case scenario where text books may be well targeted to school curricula, how well is SAIP aligned with such curricula? (Outcome/measurement)

- Could the use of different textbooks in different systems account for the lack of consistent patterns across jurisdictions? (Variation across sub-groups)
- How is SAIP Science Assessment related to "textbook curricula"? (Outcome)

How Is Use of Standardized Tests in Assigning Grades Associated with Learning Outcomes?

Reasonable Claim

There is no meaningful association between use of standardized tests in assigning grades and learning.

Challenges to Such a Claim

The association of use of standardized tests in assigning grades with learning outcomes varied across jurisdictions (variation across sub-groups). In most jurisdictions and across the nation little to no association was identified. The meaningfulness of lack of association is questionable:

- Do the responses to this question tell us about the quality of classroom assessment practices? (Outcome/measurement)
- Without knowing which standardized tests how can we make meaningful interpretations? (Outcome/measurement)

This narrow question does not lend itself to understanding what teacher responses may imply about their assessment practices.

Discussion of Limitations of Correlational Research

National surveys of achievement are intended to provide data to conduct research that would be expected to have the greatest level of generalizability, from a nationally representative sample of students to all students in Canada. This is the typical generalization done in sample-to-population generalizations in SAIP and other national surveys of achievement such as NAEP. The randomization and the selection of the sample focus on obtaining a nationally representative sample of schools. Classes are randomly selected from within the selected schools and their teachers of the students assessed are included in the teacher sample. In this case, generalizability of findings regarding students, teachers, and schools depend on whether the sample of these units are representative of their respective populations. In SAIP, since the sampling is done at the school level and students are cluster sampled, the student and teacher data deviate from national representativeness. Researchers are often aware of such limitations of sampling of units on generalizability of findings. However, researchers and consumers of research are much less aware of the representativeness of outcomes, measurements, and settings and their effects on generalizability in research. They are much less aware of the effects of variation across subgroups on making generalizations. The challenges to the research claims discussed above were not due to non-representativeness of the units. Instead, all of the challenges were related to outcome, measurement, and setting representativeness and the limitations due to overall group level statistics.

In the SAIP example, outcomes may be broadly defined as learning outcomes in science. There are many components of science learning that the assessment may or may not focus on. In SAIP, attempts are made to assess a wide spectrum of science learning outcomes by considering science curricula throughout the country as the content domain for the assessment. One of the key factors that affects the meaningfulness of the findings regarding the relationship between teacher practices and learning outcomes is whether SAIP scores are related to learning in schools. National surveys of achievement are based on curricula that are common across jurisdictions and are not closely tied to school curricula. The lack of a strong connection between learning at school and performance on assessments limit meaningfulness of research targeted to understanding factors affecting learning outcomes.

The measurement of the targeted outcomes is done by having multiple forms of the assessment given to randomly equivalent groups of students. Each school or district curriculum on the other hand is not targeted to all of these learning outcomes, but only covers a subset of these outcomes. Therefore, students in a particular school are exposed to only a subset of the sample content domain. This results in assessments that capture competence, knowledge, and skills that are not part of the school curriculum and therefore have a very weak association between teaching practices teachers use in schools. The low correlations observed in the SAIP research discussed above would be expected to be affected by the varying degree of overlap between school curricula and the assessment content.

The generalizability of measurements of outcomes is critical to the data constructed for research in SAIP research we conducted. A few examples of possible measurement generalizability related problems were raised with respect to the low correlations. These problems were related to whether test questions provide generalizable scores representing learning outcomes in science and whether teacher survey questions provide generalizable measurement of teacher practices.

In SAIP, measurement of teacher instructional practices are done by posing teachers a single question related to a particular practice. For example, a single question is presented on each of planning, numbers of hours spent on planning outside of school hours. A single question is expected to capture very narrow aspects of planning practices and on its own may not provide sufficient information about teacher planning practices. In addition, reporting existence or degree of existence of a particular practice does not tell us what teachers may do instead of that practice and how they implement it. For example, the question about the use of a textbook in teaching, does not provide any information about the quality and appropriateness of the textbook or what other instructional materials the teachers may be when they were not using a textbook.

Limitations of Group Level Inferences: Gender Differences in PISA 2003

This sub-section describes and discusses limitations of generalizing from overall group level statistics to sub-groups. International assessments such as PISA are intended to provide nationally representative sample data to allow countries to conduct research the results from which generalize to the country. In addition to within-country analyses, international assessment data are used to make comparisons across countries. To discuss the limitations of generalizing group level statistics to inform policy and practice, I focus on research that compared differences between gender groups in their performance on the PISA 2003 mathematics assessment within each country and compare gender differences across countries. On this mathematics assessment, there were small but consistent differences in favor of boys in 38 out of 40 participating countries; and in only two countries, Iceland and Thailand, the differences were in favor of girls. These very small mean differences between gender groups may suggest to practitioners and policy makers that there is not an alarming gap between boys and girls, and there is not a need to close the gap between gender groups since the gap is so small. The subsections below describe and discuss some findings that demonstrate that if the gender differences were examined by sub-groups, the findings may imply a different direction for policy and practice.

Gender Differences in Mathematics in PISA 2003

These limitations are elaborated on by demonstrating the variation of findings for the following: (a) low versus high achieving students; and (b) enrolment in high, medium, or basic mathematics classes.

Gender Differences for Low-achieving and High-achieving Groups

For research on gender differences in mathematics to inform policy and practice requires examining patterns in and potential sources of these differences. One question that may help guide education practice and policy is how consistent these differences are for different groups of students. Are the gender difference patterns the same for students who are performing at different levels? These patterns can be examined by comparing the percentage of girls and boys in each of the mathematics literacy proficiency levels. Figure 10.3 shows the differences in the

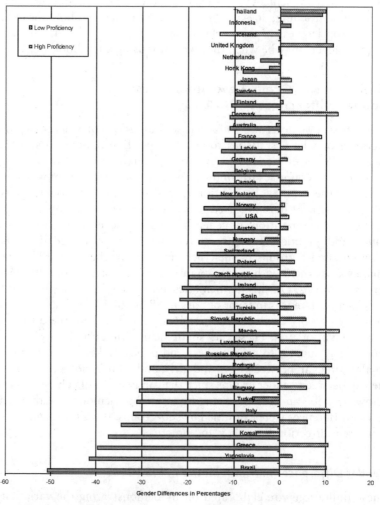

Figure 10.3 Composition of the high and low performance levels by country: differences between percent of girls and boys in each category.

percentages of boys and girls between gender groups in the high and low proficiency levels for each country. The length of the low proficiency bar for each country on the graph shows the difference between the percentages of girls and boys among the low performing students for that country. The length of the high proficiency bar for each country shows the differences between the percentages of girls and boys among the high performing students for that country. Differences were calculated (girls minus boys) so that a positive difference indicates that a higher percentage of girls was represented in that performance level group. In making the graph, the countries were first rank ordered according to the size of their overall gender differences among the high performing students.

An example may help interpret the meaning of the graph. In Thailand, for example, the makeup of the low performance level was 55% girls and 45% boys. This 10-percentage-point difference in favor of girls is indicated by the crosshatched bar shown on the graph for Thailand. The high performance level in Thailand was made up of 54% girls and 46% boys; and this is indicated by the shaded bar that extends to +9 on the graph. These differences provide information about the similarity of the distributions of scores on the mathematics scale for the two gender groups. Having a higher percentage of girls or boys in the low proficiency level in a given country indicates that a larger percentage of students of that gender were in the low proficiency level; and this proportional difference in the distribution of scores may be the source of the overall gender difference. Differences in the high proficiency level indicate, in a similar fashion, that the two groups did not have similar representation at the high proficiency level. The differences tended to be positive (i.e., higher percentage of girls) among the low proficiency students and negative (i.e., higher percentage of boys) among the high proficiency students, as would be expected since the gender differences were in favor of boys in most countries. For example, in Brazil there was a 10-percentage-point difference between the proportions of girls and boys in the low proficiency level, with girls having the larger proportion; and there was about a 50-percentage-point difference between the proportions of girls and boys in the high proficiency level, with boys making up the larger group.

Differences in the distribution of gender differences in scores for girls and boys varied across countries. Whereas some countries had large percentages of girls performing at the low proficiency level, resulting in an overall gender gap favoring boys, other countries had similar percentages of students performing at the low proficiency level and the differences were distributed across the proficiency levels. Most countries had fewer girls performing at the high proficiency level, the differences being greater than 10 percentage points in 33 countries.

This finding highlights the significance of gender differences in mathematics to a greater degree. Even though, overall gender differences may be small in most countries, there are large differences in the percentages of girls and boys who attain high scores in mathematics. This graph tells a different story about gender differences than would be inferred based on overall math scores for the whole sample. Figure 10.3 points to a more serious difference between boys and girls in most countries.

Summary of Limitations of Inferences Based on Total Sample

On the PISA 2003 mathematics assessment, in most countries, fewer girls performed at the high proficiency levels. The differences at the high proficiency levels were high with gender differences greater than 10% for 33 countries and in some countries 50% fewer girls reaching the high performance levels. This difference in distribution of scores for the gender groups highlights the significance of gender differences in mathematics to a greater degree than would be understood from the overall gender differences. Even though overall gender differences were small in most countries, there were large differences in attainment of high scores in mathematics in many countries.

The analyses of gender differences for students taking high-, medium-, and basic-level mathematics classes provided some evidence that the overall gender differences against girls were not due to self-selection of girls out of high-level mathematics classes. In fact, greater degrees of difference in performance were observed against girls who were taking the same high-level mathematics classes as boys. These findings, combined with the higher degrees of gender difference among high-performing students, have significant implications for how gender groups are formed or selected to go into mathematics-related studies and careers and, therefore, for the representation of females in professions that involve mathematics.

Gender Differences for Students Enrolled in High, Medium, or Basic Mathematics Classes

The main issue that may help education policy and practice regarding gender differences is finding the source of those differences. In other words, we must ask the question, "Why and how do girls and boys start developing increasing levels of differences in their performance in mathematics?" One possible factor is whether they are exposed to similar mathematics curricula as a result of self-selection into different kinds of mathematics classes at the secondary school level. To explore whether gender differences varied across different types of mathematics classes, and whether gender differences were greater in one type of mathematics class than the others, three levels of mathematics classes—high, medium, and basic—were plotted against gender differences in mathematics literacy scale scores for all countries with the needed data available. These mathematics class levels were based on students' responses to the question, "What type of mathematics class are you taking?" with the options given as high, medium, and basic.

The patterns of gender differences varied across countries. In four countries (Australia, Greece, Korea, and the Slovak Republic) gender differences in favor of boys were largest among students who were taking high level mathematics classes. In two of these countries, Australia and the Slovak Republic, gender differences were in favor of girls for students who were taking basic level mathematics classes. In Germany, gender differences against girls were smaller for students in high level mathematics classes than for those who were taking basic level mathematics classes. Similarly, in Great Britain, gender differences were larger and in favor of girls among the students who were taking high levels of mathematics classes. In Iceland, where gender differences were in favor of girls for all three groups of students taking different levels of mathematics classes, with the differences being smallest among the students taking high level mathematics classes.

A somewhat differential pattern of gender differences for students taking different levels of mathematics classes across countries is not surprising, given that students are likely placed in a particular level through different mechanisms in each country. Yet, a pattern that applies across four out of seven countries does emerge. In these countries, gender differences in mathematics literacy are larger against girls who are in high levels of mathematics. This means that, in these countries, the overall gender differences against girls are not due to self-selection of girls out of high levels of mathematics classes. In fact, greater degrees of differences in performance are observed against girls who are taking the same high levels of mathematics classes as boys. Overall closer examination of gender differences lead to different conclusions than would be expected from overall mean differences.

Implications

I used two examples to illustrate and discuss limitations in the arguments used in sample-to-population generalizing. First, I highlighted possible misleading interpretations if all factors affecting generalizability (outcome, measurement, settings) are not considered. Second, using nationally representative data, I demonstrated that statistics at the national level have little value in guiding policy and practice. In fact, I demonstrated that the requirement of "representativeness of the sample" is not an adequate criterion for evaluating generalizability as a degree of value of research to inform policy and practice. The misleading aspects of total group-level findings have critical implications for practice and policy.

The examples presented in this chapter demonstrated that focusing only on random representation of units such as students and schools in national surveys of achievement has great implications on the value of research based on such data to inform policy and practice. For research findings to inform policy and practice, the findings need to be applicable to the settings that are being considered for policy decisions. For findings to be generalizable to different settings such as urban or rural schools, the randomization need to include these setting factors as well.

Even though some of the settings that are relevant for policy and practice may be thought of ahead of time, randomization may not take all possible settings into account and all relevant setting factors may not be known to the developers of national surveys of achievement. For example, gender differences research identified differential patterns of gender differences for students who were taking different levels of mathematics courses. Such patterns were discovered after the data were collected and importance of mathematics course levels as a factor may not have been anticipated. Therefore, sampling design could not have used mathematics course level as a randomization variable (or stratification variable). Even more difficult is to include in randomization are outcome and measurement factors. Assessing multiple definitions of a construct or multiple ways of measuring a construct are not expected to be feasible in a national survey of achievement. As Cronbach (1982) argued, true representativeness of a sample may never be achieved. Researchers can create greater degrees of generalizability by taking into consideration as many factors as possible. Equally important is that researchers who use data from national surveys of achievement to conduct research need to be aware of and be explicit about limitations in generalizability of their research findings. Researchers need to be explicit about the variation of research findings for key sub-groups in order for consumers of research to be able to judge the applicability of findings to different settings. Variation in findings such as different correlations between variables for different settings such as urban versus rural schools should not be considered as a weakness of research. Rather, it is an indication that generalizing across these settings may not be meaningful.

Some of the limitations in sample-to-population generalizing apply to analytic and case-to-case generalization as well. Analytic generalizations that are aiming at developing a theory, such as how students learn, are different than other kinds of analytic generalizing that use experimental design to examine causal effects. In research methods discussions, typically experimental designs are argued to be the only way for establishing causal relationships. In experimental design research, the established causal inferences are at the group level and in typical experimental design research, almost always, there are exceptions to the causal link across individuals. Ignoring these exceptions may have detrimental effects. Imagine an educational intervention that targets improving student mental concentration by giving students a pack of peanuts a day at school. Given the current beliefs about protein, fat, and carbohydrate combinations, these interventions may very well result in better student concentration and learning, as may be established by test or observational data. The causal inference may be stated as "peanuts as snacks improve student concentration and learning." Even though such a claim may be true for 98% of students, it can have detrimental effects on 2% of school population who have peanut allergies. The example—perhaps an exaggerated one to highlight the point that group-level research findings in analytic generalization—shows how research may provide highly problematic directions for policy and practice. Similarly in case-to-case generalizing argumentation, if the findings from research are summarized by overall group level statistics, similar limitations in "transferability" from one case to another are expected.

Final Note

Upon revisiting the chapter, I noted that some readers may think that I am very pessimistic about education research informing policy and practice. However, by highlighting limitations in the most highly regarded type of generalizing, sample to population generalizing, my intention is not to bring a pessimistic perspective to educational research or the value of educational research. In fact, by expanding the considerations to include outcome, measurement, and context into generalizations based on educational assessments and focusing not just on group level statistics but also other levels such as individual and sub-group, I hope to open up our view of what generalizing means and improve the potential for educational research to provide meaningful guidance to practice and policy.

References

Cohen, D. K., Raudenbush, S. W., & Ball, D. L. (2003). Resources, instruction, and research. *Educational Evaluation and Policy Analysis, 25*, 119–142.

Cronbach, L. J. (1982). *Designing evaluations of educational and social programs.* San Francisco: Jossey-Bass.

Ercikan, K. (2006). Developments in assessment of student learning and achievement. In P. A. Alexander & P. H. Winne (Eds.), *American Psychological Association, Division 15, Handbook of educational psychology* (2nd ed., pp. 929–951). Mahwah, NJ: Erlbaum.

Ercikan, K., & Roth, W-M. (2006). What good is polarizing research into qualitative and quantitative? *Educational Researcher, 35*(5), 14–23.

Erickson, F. (1986). Qualitative methods. In M. Wittrock (Ed.), *Handbook of research on teaching* (pp. 199–161). New York: Macmillan.

Gall, M. D., Borg, W. R., & Gall, J. P. (1996). *Educational research: An introduction* (6th ed.). London: Longman.

Howe, K. R., & Eisenhart, M. A. (1990). Standards in qualitative (and quantitative) research: A prolegomenon. *Educational Researcher, 19*(4), 2–9.

O'Neill, K. A., & McPeek, W. M. (1993). Item and test characteristics that are associated with differential item functioning. In E. W. Holland & H. Wainer (Eds.), *Differential item functioning* (pp. 255–276). Hillsdale, NJ: Erlbaum.

Walkerdine, V. (1988). *The mastery of reason*. London: Routledge.

Chapter 11

Phenomenological and Dialectical Perspectives on the Relation between the General and the Particular

Wolff-Michael Roth

In much of the debate on the value of educational research, we find a polarization in which generalizability, generally associated with large-scale studies, is pitted against contingency, generally associated with ethnography and case study research. There are, however, forms of scholarly inquiry in which the general and particular, abstract and concrete, universal and specific, and collective and individual are completely integrated and are used in complementary ways. In this chapter, I articulate two such approaches: phenomenology and materialist dialectics. I exemplify how educational researchers can find and articulate the general in the particular in non-dualistic approaches. The outcomes of research studies designed accordingly offer researchers the best of both worlds—general knowledge of interest to academic researchers and situated knowledge of interest to educational practitioners.

Introduction

In education, as in human sciences generally, different forms of research—often dichotomously captured in the terms *quantitative* and *qualitative*—are used not only to understand and explain phenomena of interest but also to design interventions and research at multiple levels. From an epistemic perspective, those explanations are favored that are more parsimonious; from an intervention perspective, those understandings that have most practical relevance weigh into decision-making processes. The key question therefore is whether something researchers learn studying one sample (individual, group) can inform scientists and users about the phenomenon in another sample specifically and in the population from which the sample has been taken more generally. A central concept (and practice) in educational research is that of generalization and generalizability. To generalize—derived from the old Latin term *general*, class, kind, and the Latin/Greek form *genus* (γένος), birth, race, stock, kind—literally means forming a class or reduce to general laws. The general is opposed to the partial and particular. In the following subsections, I articulate the perspectives of different forms of research on the question of the general and the particular.

Generalization Based on Statistical Inference

In "quantitative" research the assumption is that the information was collected from a small sample of a larger population. The researcher is interested in making statements about the entire population based on limited information. This comes with uncertainty. Statistics provides an apparatus allowing researchers to evaluate the possibility of making incorrect statements about the population (i.e., Type I and Type II errors). The so-called "quantitative" research has as its goal to make claims about an entire population of cases on the basis of a subset of this population—the population most often consists of people ("grade eight students," "African Americans") but may also consist of events. One can characterize this class of research, therefore, as making inferences of a certain type, from observations in a sample of specimens to the probability to making the same observations in the entire population. The statistical apparatus provides a set of procedures to assess such issues as probability of making an erroneous inference or the power of an analysis. Thus, if a statistical comparison in a study suggests a difference between Francophone and Anglophone students on some test is associated with a $p < 0.01$, it means—all other things being equal, normal, controlled, e.g., independence of measures, total number of analyses conducted—that there is possibility of less than 1 percent that the difference has arisen by chance. In other words, there is a possibility of less than 1 percent for being wrong in saying that Francophones and Anglophones are different, for whatever reason that might be.

For the purposes of the present discussion, there are two major forms of weakness in generalization through statistical inference. First, generalizations in covariation studies are made on the basis of *attributes* and, second, generalizations in experimental (cause–effect) research presuppose human behavior to be determined (S–R type) rather than based on grounds/reasons. The first problem arises from the fact that attributes, which are *external* aspects of being, are correlated and used as basis for making inferences. Being external, attributes are indifferent towards each other and lack the necessity for one another that ought to lie in their relation (Hegel, 1806/1977). For example, educational sociologists frequently relate socioeconomic status and achievement on some test, using the former as independent variable that "causes," "affects," or "influences" the latter. The problem is that both variables have nothing to do with the conscious decisions made by students while taking the test. Both variables are external to the life of the person, which leads to the fact that for *quite different reasons* students may give *the same* answers on a multiple choice test.

The problem with generalizing from attributes can be formulated in terms of family resemblances (Wittgenstein, 1958). Thus, given the family name Roth, we may find that the individuals Roth-A and Roth-B have the attributes a, c, and d in common; Roth-B shares with Roth-C the attributes b, c, and e; Roth-D and Roth-A share attribute b; and Roth-E and Roth-A have no observable attribute in common but their name. There is therefore no single attribute that *all* Roths share, though any sub-sample of Roth may have one or more attributes in common. (As educational examples, any set of attributes can be inserted for the letters a through e, including "high-SES," "race" [white, métis], "culture" [Anglo-, Franco-, Eurasian], high/low IQ, and "learning disabled.") Yet despite the lack of a common attribute, all the Roths in our sample may still be related in a more fundamental way: for example, Roth-A may be a parent of Roth-B, Roth-C, and Roth-D, and a grandparent to Roth E. Roth-A therefore embodies the (genetic) possibilities for certain attributes that are concretely realized in the filial generation; but each offspring realizes these possibilities in very different ways.

Concerning the second weakness, inferences from controlled experiments or quasi-experiments correlate independent (observation, treatment) and dependent variables (observation). A typical experiment comparing a treatment group to a no treatment

$$\frac{O_1 \ X \ O_2}{O_1 \quad O_2}.$$

Where the line indexes the comparison process, O_1 and O_2 refer to pre- and posttest (observations), and X indicates the treatment. Here, the differences in the dependent variables in the two groups are ascribed to the treatment, and the statistical apparatus provides the probability that the differences are due to the treatment or, alternatively, that these differences would be observed with certainty if the treatment groups were infinitely large. The key problem with this form of research, apart from its correlation of observations (attributes) is the absence of the mediation of human behavior by meaning and grounds/reasons for actions. Variations are ascribed to error variance rather than to systematic deviation that arises from the fact that human beings make sense of their situations and have specific grounds and reasons for acting in one rather than in another way. This form of research, therefore, does not consider the specifically human nature to concretize collectively available and subjectively grounded/reasoned possibilities for acting; that is, it fails to acknowledge the specifically human capacity to *consciously* relate to the objectively given historical situation as reflected in the personal life-world. For example, Holzkamp (1983a) tells the story of a 16-year-old who has been expelled from a school for the fourth time, each requiring the father to find a new school to which he had to accompany his son. Each time, the two enter physical fights at home. Expulsion and low achievement, however, do not have to be causally related to low-SES or working-class nature of the family—though in this situation this may have turned out to be the case. Rather, the mutual actions of father and son in and outside their home (school, work) result from the tension that they mutually held each other responsible for experienced miseries in their lives. Once they recognized the societally mediated nature of their problem, the son finished high school without further problems. The point here is that any (external) attributes would not have captured the grounds on which their everyday decisions were made. In fact, the "quantitative" approach focusing on causal variation would have had little to contribute to counseling sessions, as in its models low-SES and low achievement are correlated. Engaging with the special case and helping father and son become critical of their situation and previous grounds of action allowed the situation to change.

Transferability of Observations

In "qualitative" research many researchers contend with describing some phenomenon in the tradition of ethnography concerned with one culture, subculture, group, village, and so on. Others seek to create parsimonious descriptions generally using some form of method to generate "grounded theory." Whether descriptions or structures are applicable in or to other settings than those observed is a question of *transferability* (Guba & Lincoln, 1989). The individual researcher or research group is not interested in making judgments about the transferability based on their study, but rather assumes that the degree of transferability is an empirical matter, which is shown after a second, third,... nth study has been completed. The *confirmability criterion* of qualitative research, "concerned with assuring that data, interpretations, and outcomes of inquiries are rooted in contexts and persons apart from the evaluator" (p. 243) maps onto the goals of intra-sample statistical analysis concerned with assessing the viability of *these* observations within a larger hypothetical set of observations in the same setting. "Would other observations in *this* sample confirm or disconfirm the patterns reported?" The problem of this type of research lies in the fact that it usually concerns the sampling of experiences without asking and answering questions concerning the source of variations. Why does one student living in poverty succeed in science and later goes on to college whereas her sibling does poorly and ends up leaving high school and makes a living dealing drugs? How can understandings derived from a study involving this student be generalized to inform our understanding of her sibling? More so, how can what we learn about the student and her sibling in Philadelphia inform us about families living under similar conditions in New York? The failure of this kind of research to go beyond the case—the educational literature provides ample evidence for the existence of large numbers of qualitative studies that are seemingly unrelated despite many common traits and there are few efforts in making inferences from sets of qualitative studies made under similar conditions—has led many policy makers and researchers to question the usefulness of this kind of research.

Beyond the Qualitative-Quantitative Divide

Not all research that would fall into the currently used qualitative category restricts itself to describing a population and finding (sets of) patterns *within* the description, that is, generating a grounded theory. For example, in the phenomenological tradition, some scholars are not interested in describing the experiences of merely one or more (small group of) people but rather attempt to make an inference about what makes the different experiences possible in the first place. Thus, when Edmund Husserl investigated the experience of time, he was not interested in describing *his* experience (consciousness) of time but in describing what makes a variety of time experiences possible, not only his own but experience in general. Critical psychologists practice a type of qualitative research in which generalization is handled very differently. Grounded in Russian psychology of the Vygotsky-Leont'ev lineage, critical psychologists conceive of cultural-historical phenomena (including knowing and learning) in terms of the unity of quantity and quality, which leads to the notion of the concrete universal. Thus, each observation (case) is understood to constitute a concrete realization of a possibility that exists at the collective level (population). Each observation therefore is simultaneously particular and universal, concrete and abstract, or specific and general. In the following two sections, I articulate the two approaches to producing generalizations based on a small number of research participants, which, in any concrete situation, may be one person (traditionally conceived of as $N = 1$) though there are large number of instances ($n \gg 1$) taken into consideration by means of, for example, within person variation.

Generalization in Phenomenology: A Practical Example

In true phenomenological research, the purpose is not to provide (potentially infinite) descriptions of how something or some event can be seen and understood; rather, the purpose is to derive the conditions for having a diversity of experiences given some common underlying processes. To understand human cognition, researchers seek variability by including a range of research participants—the sample size depending on the research paradigm and the particular sampling process chosen (e.g., maximum variation). In phenomenological studies, however, variation in experience is generated within individuals, generally the investigator, with the purpose of understanding, for example, the cognitive processes and conditions that lead to the different (perceptual, cognitive) experiences. It should be evident that all other differences that inherently exist between any two individuals—because of the singular nature of any and all being—does not operate in research that only involves one individual ($N = 1$).

The phenomenological method requires two steps: bracketing of experience—also referred to as phenomenological reduction or *epoché*—and expression and validation. In the following, I focus on *epoché*, the cornerstone of the phenomenological method, because expression and validation are little different from those in other sciences. *Epoché* (from Gr. ἐποχή [epoché], suspension of judgment) is a systematic method for suspending judgment, a process of stepping outside our usual, preconceived notions about how the world works to gain greater insights and better understanding. There are three stages of *epoché*, which consist of an initial phase, during which experiences are systematically produced all the while suspending one's beliefs about them, a conversion phase during which attention is changed from the content of experience to the process of experience, and a phase of accepting experience (no-attention). The first stage requires an unprejudiced openness to the details of experience, whereas the second stage requires analysis of the processes that make experience possible in the first place. The third stage constitutes a systematic approach to a phenomenon many scientists have experienced: after wrestling long and hard with difficult problems, the solutions come to them while engaging in very different activities (sleeping, exercising). To allow readers a better appreciation of a research method that often is placed in disrepute—frequently justified because of the abusive labeling as *phenomenological* of woe-me-type of research, which shares little with the method of serious philosophers and practitioners of the phenomenological method from other fields—I use the following practical example. By following the descriptions through inspecting the figure provided, readers normally should experience for themselves the method at work.

Praxis of Method

To experience stage 1, take Figure 11.1, which represents the type of images researched by the Gestalt psychologist Edgar Rubin. What do you see? Take a look at it now and prior to proceeding. Most people perceive the image as a cross that is oriented along the diagonals rather

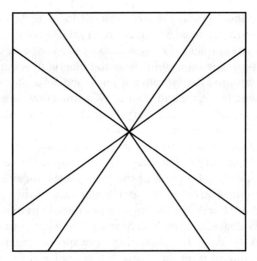

Figure 11.1 Maltese Crosses have been used in Gestalt psychology to study perceptual processes.

than a broad-leafed Maltese cross. That is, although we have one material configuration (the ink dots on the page), there are at least two figure-
ground configurations that can easily be seen in consecutive fashion.
Gestalt theorists explain the phenomenon in terms of the law of proxim-
ity, according to which items that are closer together in physical space are
grouped preferentially. In the present situation, the cross that is oriented
along the diagonals is perceived preferentially rather than the upright,
broad-leafed Maltese cross. Can you see the second cross stand against
a more diffuse ground?

With some practice, you notice the upright, *broad*-leafed Maltese
cross as a figure with the remainder of the square as diffuse ground.
You do not attend to the ground, which precisely makes it ground; if you
attend to *that* aspect of the graphic then *it* will be figure against everything else as ground. Therefore, figure and ground mutually constitute
each other, which for me is the reason to write the pair dialectically as
figure|ground, a notation meant to portray that each term is the negation
of the other.

Can you gaze at the image and make it switch back and forth between
the two configurations? Once you can easily switch between the two
figure|ground configurations, try to understand *what* makes you see
the broad-leafed cross in one instance and the narrow-leafed cross at
another? What are you doing that brings about the switch between the
two ways of perceiving?

Your inquiry will show that the figure|ground reversal, which here is a
figure to ground and ground to figure transformation, is associated with

a shift of your focal point. Prepare yourself to focus on a point about one-third the distance between center and boundary of the image. If you now focus on a point near the vertical axis, the broad-leafed cross will be figure; if you focus on a point near the diagonal, the narrow-leafed cross will be figure. That is, moving back and forth between the two focal points switches figure and ground. We now know more about what makes something a figure and everything else the ground; and we can use this knowledge intentionally to reverse figure and ground.

In stage 2 of the *epoché*, the perceptual experiences of stage 1 become the raw data for reflection. For example, you may realize that figure and ground are not only a function of the locus of the focal point but also of the eye movement itself, in this particular case of the eye itself when head and body are fixed. Try staring at a point without moving your eyeballs: This is not easy, because you have to stop what your eye naturally and unconsciously does. (Psychologists have special apparatus to fix an image on the same spot on the retina, which makes it easier to produce the phenomenon we are after here.) That is, you likely notice how the eye saccades between figure and ground, staying longer on the figure, which becomes the distinct figure against an indistinct ground. (Notice, the boundary is always part of the foreground figure.)

The third stage commences when, after intense reflection on the processes, the phenomenological researcher engages in times of non-attention to the phenomena. (Absorption in a sport, for example, can lead to moments of non-attention to cognitive content.) You may want to walk away from this task and do and think about other things or, more habitual for phenomenological philosophers and Zen Buddhists alike, engage in meditation to produce moments of no-thought. It is during this time of non-attention that the researcher accepts new understandings to emerge in his or her consciousness. It is during such moments of non-attention that I developed the insights about perception described here.

So far, I presented the process of *epoché* in a linear fashion through the three different stages. In fact, phenomenology recurrently cycles through these stages. For example, we can further extended our research into perceptive experiences through systematic inquiry and variation. Taking another look at Figure 11.1, we might move our focal point from within the figure toward the intersection of the four lines, which provokes a constant flipping back and forth between the two figure|ground configurations. The analysis of the process reveals that this flipping is still due to the generally unnoticed, rapid movement of the eye—for when, after some training, you arrive at holding the focal point constant (not easy because the eye normal saccades three to five times a second), first the individual lines themselves become figure and then begin to disappear.

From such inquiry I come to understand that perception is not merely a passive process of recognition of features in the visual input but that a continuously developing perception creates the perceived world in a constructive or generative process. What I perceive is a function of what I do (locus focus, movement of focus). That is, what I experience perceptually is a matter of sensorimotor contingency. What is experienced as visual information from the environment is a function of the relative movement within the *person-in-situation* unit. More so, we infer that attention is needed to see anything specific, which arises from access to and control over one's perceptual activity. Any particular figurelground configuration is therefore dependent not only on the specific focal point, but also on the relation of particulars of the local features in the global context. An assessment of these features requires the movement of the entire body or relevant parts (eyes, head). The body therefore comes to be the (always latently present) third term that mediates the figurelground structure. My visual experience does not arise in my brain alone but from the motivated transactions involving my whole person and the situation I find myself in. My perceptual experience is related to my knowing of what will happen when I engage in some action such as shifting the focus of attention—the experience is contingent on my sensorimotor competencies.

This example shows how the phenomenological method begins with (perceptual) experience but then engages in systematic inquiries (variation of experience that leads to variation in sensations) and descriptions thereof so that these can be repeated and validated by other researchers. If other researchers were unable to validate some descriptions and experiences, we would return to solipsism (a constructivist mind stuck within itself). What I am describing, therefore, is a form of analysis that acknowledges subjectivity but investigates it in ways that can be shared among researchers generally. After creating experiences and after engaging in careful observation that goes beyond preconceived notions about cognition, I focus on the processes associated with the experiences—here the normally unnoticeable eye movement. These processes, ordinarily invisible in everyday life affairs, constitute the central object of the recursive and reflexive side of phenomenology. In the final step, after intensive analysis, I deliberately abandon all reflection to permit new insights to arise. This abandonment of conscious thought is actively and intensely practiced as part of meditation. Novice researchers can provoke inattention by becoming absorbed in some other activity that does not require thought, for example, working out on a treadmill, going for a walk, or pulling weeds.

This example shows how the phenomenological method begins with (perceptual) experience in stage 1 but then engages, in a second stage of the process, in systematic inquiries (variation of experience that leads to variation in sensations) and descriptions thereof so that these can be repeated and validated by other researchers. After creating experiences and after engaging in careful observation that goes beyond preconceived notions about cognition, the analyst focuses on the processes associated with the experiences, here the normally unnoticeable eye movement. These processes, normally transparent in everyday life, constitute the central object of the recursive, reflexive side of phenomenology. In this situation, generalizations are about the possibility of experiences not about specific experiences as such. These generalizations, even if based on the experiences of one person, pertain to the experiences of many if not all persons in a culture or humankind in most general terms. The power of this method became evident when recent neuroscientific research acknowledged that its own result confirmed the findings concerning perception that Maurice Merleau-Ponty had arrived at half a century earlier using the phenomenological method.

Experiential Generalization (Abstraction)

A second aspect of generalization from a phenomenological perspective can be gleaned from the study of how human beings form concepts in the process and as outcome of engaging with objects and phenomena. In the classical approach—predominant, for example, in mathematics education—learners (students, researchers) are said to generalize when they form a class containing the objects of experience; the class is defined by one or more (mathematical) property common to all objects. For example, if we think about the red color of a cylindrical object only, then we abstract it *from* the object. If we also abstract from the red color to think about materiality in general, then we abstract from several determinations, and our resulting concept is even more abstract. Abstract concepts therefore should be called "abstracting concepts," that is, concepts that contain several abstractions simultaneously. In cognition, the class has become a transcendental category that is independent of the actual objects in which it is realized. Theorizing knowledge in this way is problematic, as one may think individuals (students, teachers, researchers) are knowledgeable when they know the name of the class/category—a rather familiar form of discourse blames individuals for being unable to *apply* a concept that they have been taught. Fundamentally, this theoretical approach to generalization is problematic, as there is a gap between knowing a word and knowing one's way around (being knowledgeable in) the world.

Generalization (abstraction) from experience is described and conceptualized very differently from a phenomenological perspective. Here, all knowing is related to concrete experiences. For example, the ability to see some entity as a sphere (ball) is based on repeated experiences of seeing spherical objects and moving (body, eyes) with respect to it. Knowing something therefore means being able to anticipate what will happen if I move with respect to the object, touch or handle it, or somehow involve it in my actions in some other way. Any one of these experiences, including words and sentences related to the perception and use of an object (material, conceptual entity), for example, serves as an index for the class of related experiences. Any one experience allows the activation of all other experiences. In this approach, therefore, the concept exists in and of the totality (class) of experiences related to the object, the different experiences as a function of the relative viewpoints one has taken with respect to it (Merleau-Ponty, 1945). The following episode from a study of mathematical learning exemplifies these aspects of generalization (abstraction).

In a second-grade mathematics class recorded on videotape, children are asked to engage in practical classification tasks to learn geometrical shape-related categories. In a whole-class session, each student draws an object from a bag and then associates it with an existing set of objects— each located on a separately colored paper associated with a label a child has generated—or to begin a new category. As exemplified in Figure 11.2, the children use vision and touch to explore the objects, orient themselves differently with respect to the target and other reference objects, and compare existing with new objects. For example, Kendra initially grabs the cylinder she has drawn with both hands around its curved surface (Figure 11.2a); later, she folds the fingers of both hands over the

a   b   c   d   e

Figure 11.2 From a phenomenological perspective, a concept consists of the interconnection of forms of experience, each of which in a metonymical way concretely realizes the concept.

circles at the end of the object (Figure 11.2b); she holds her object over the object in the existing class labeled "tube" in such a way that the circular surfaces perceptibly come to face each other (Figure 11.2c); Kendra folds both hands around the curved surface in the way she also may hold a post (Figure 11.2d); and she moves her hands back and forth thereby exhibiting its "roll-ability" (Figure 11.2e), a characteristic that the object does not when rotated 90 degrees (e.g., Figure 11.2b).

All of these experiences come to be associated with and define a particular class of objects, where these and other possible forms of experience define the class (Figure 11.3a). This class is open—has no boundaries—so that any new experience can become part of it. One possible form of experience is constituted by recurrent sounds (heard as "tube" or "cylinder"), that is, words and sentences that denote or describe the object at hand. The point then is that children have formed and know the concept when the different experiences come to be related in the form of a network (Figure 11.3b). Knowing a concept then means that any one of these experiences can activate any or all other possible experiences (Figure 11.3c). One may know a concept word (e.g., "tube") but if it does not yet (as children taught color words to name a set of objects but who do not group same-colored objects) or no longer (as in amnesia) vectorially link together the set of experiences, it does not constitute knowledge of the concept. In other words, the person is able to "apply" the concept and brings it to bear even when the activation has been by means other than the concept word (Figure 11.3c). This approach differs from the one Kant specifically and all idealists generally are taking, as the class here is defined in terms of the actual sense experiences rather than of one or more properties that they have in common.

The concept therefore exists only in and of the set of physical or linguistic experiences and their relations to one another—the set is a plurality of singularities. Generalization here means that any one (singular) experience has come to synecdochically (metonymically) stand for the set (plurality) of experiences and leads to the activation of any other singular experience.[1] In the context of a concept, therefore, the belonging-

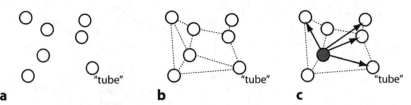

a   b   c

Figure 11.3 a. In the course of acting in the world, human beings cumulate experiences. b. When the experiences related to one object or phenomenon come to be interconnected. c. A concept is understood when any one of its associated experiences can activate any or all the others.

ness of any singular experience to the set is defined by its context, which consists in all the other experiences. As such, a concept no longer is transcendental, beyond the senses and experience: as a result of a generalization it is as concrete as all the specific experiences that constitute it.

General|Particular Dialectic (in Cultural-Historical Activity Theory)

Culture in general and language in particular constitutes generalized possibilities, but is available only through the ways in which it is actually realized. Both possibilities and realizations are concrete, though the former are general and the latter specific. Therefore, some cultural possibilities are not realized at a given moment although they do exist and are recognized as possibilities by individual subjects. Each observation in a culture, for example, concerning a single subject, therefore provides us insights not only about the particular but also of the general. In this section, I begin by articulating individual and collective as moments of a dialectical unit and then provide conversation as a paradigmatic example exposing this dialectic. I then show how those psychologists concerned with establishing a "science of the subject" (Ger. *Subjektwissenschaft*) conduct two forms of analysis concerned with (a) the concrete cultural-historical possibilities for acting at a given time and (b) identifying the conditions that mediate individuals' participation in society and thereby lead to different concrete realizations of the collective possibilities.

Culture and the Individual|Collective Dialectic

In the statistical approach to psychology, there is no inherent link between the individual and the collective. Generalization establishes an external link between measured properties, which themselves are one-sided, external expression of the entity under investigation (Hegel, 1806/1977). The latter merely constitutes an ensemble of singularities, each of which has properties that vary around some central (mean) value (e.g., IQ). This completely obscures the inner connections that exist between an individual and the society (culture) of which the former is a *constitutive* part; it also obscures the fact that people do not act randomly but rather in ways that make sense not only to themselves but also to others; and it obscures the fact that human beings act in ways that anticipate the possible responses. Thus, individual human beings are not independent and do not act independently. Rather, "each [human being] is for itself, and for the other, an immediate being on its own account, which at the same time is such only through this mediation. They *recognize* themselves as *mutually recognizing* one another" (p. 112). The results of recent neurophysiological research on mirror neurons precisely support this fact that others recognize actions only when their mirror neurons are activated, the same neurons that are activated in the observer's own actions.

From a cultural-historical perspective, the individual human being is not even the proper unit of analysis, as it society that reproduces itself in and through the concrete individuals all contributing to—though in various ways because of a division of labor—to the collective. The essence of human nature consists of a well-developed and articulated system of possibilities, realized in the diverse abilities of mathematicians, researchers, and teachers: "Thus, the real *universal* basis of everything that is human in man is production of instruments of production. It is from this basis that other diverse qualities of the human being developed, including consciousness and will, speech and thinking, erect walk and all the rest of it" (Il'enkov, 1982, p. 74, my emphasis). Therefore there exists a deeper connection between individual and collective, a connection explicitly made thematic, for example, in cultural-historical activity theory, a theory grounded in materialist dialectics.

Culture consists of more than a collection of (cultural) artifacts and observable (cultural) practices; it in fact consists of possibilities for acting, some of which are realized at any given point in time, others are realized for a first time. But because concrete action possibilities exist at the collective level, *any* person may concretely realize them. That is, collective culture comes about through the actions of individuals, but individuals realize collectively available possibilities—individual and collective mutually presuppose each other. I came to understand this aspect of the human condition a few years ago, just as the Google search engine became available. My wife and I began to switch from the other search engines we had used thus far and, whenever we had a question, at any moment of the day, were using this new search engine to find what we needed. One day I jokingly said that I would "google for..." whatever we wanted to know. From this day on, and without ever having heard it before, we used the company name as a verb similar to the way that the company name Xerox is used as a verb. Months later we found out that other people, too, were using the verb "to google." This anecdote exemplifies two important aspects: (a) collectively available possibilities are a function of cultural history, requiring a historic genetic approach to understand their existence and (b) particular conditions enable/constrain any one individual to perceive and concretely realize these possibilities in and through their actions.

In materialist dialectics, the relationship between the general and particular, universal and specific, or abstract and concrete is thought in a way that radically differs from the idealism that is embodied in the work of the philosopher Immanuel Kant and even in the work of the dialectical philosopher Georg W. F. Hegel. Fundamentally—and relative to our problematic of generalizing (abstracting) from individual experiences and phenomena to arrive at statements describing a collective—culture is thought in terms of an individual|collective dialectic. This means that each term presupposes the other, includes it in its determinations, so that neither one can be thought without the other. This has serious methodological consequences in the sense that whenever we collect some data at the level of the individual, we obtain something that has the collective written all over it. In the physical sciences, it is possible to deconvolve the true signal from a measured function when the instrument function is known; it is also possible to decompose, for example, the movement of an object in two different types of movements, as long as they do not affect each other (e.g., translational, rotational movement). Such deconvolution and uncoupling are not possible, however, when two (cognitive) entities or two properties presuppose one another, because the differential equations describing the two are irreducible and have to be solved together. Human phenomena generally and cognition specifically has this property in that the individual cannot be uncoupled from the larger system in which it is a constitutive part. Taking a more positive stance, such a situation provides us with the opportunity to understand collective phenomena in each and every concrete case under consideration.

From Individual to Collective

The principle of empirical generalization and the conditions under which statements about *my* forms of experience and power to act can be used to make statements about *someone else's* forms of experiences and power to act. This generalization may occur in the sense that our respective experiences and power to act constitute different concretizations of general (collective, cultural) action possibilities. The different concretizations are subjectively necessary variants of general action possibilities that arise from the different (biographically situated) premises and functional patterns of grounding/reasoning actions (Holzkamp, 1983b). The general action possibilities are derived through a historical-genetic analysis that reconstructs, from the beginning, the system or category of interest. This perspective is powerful as it allows me to understand why, for example, locking up criminals does not inherently diminish the number of crimes in a society: The United States has the highest crime rate in the world and the highest percentage of its population imprisoned; and Britain has the highest imprisonment rate in Europe and the highest crime rate. Why would it be the case that higher imprisonment rates are associated with higher crime rates? Should not locking up criminals decrease their numbers in the streets? On the other hand, if criminal acts are viewed through the lens of cultural possibilities, then it is obvious that locking up criminals does not by necessity get rid of the collective possibilities of such acts. What *individual* acts therefore reveal are *general* possibilities for acting, and in this recognition we have made a generalization.

The most famous and celebrated analysis of this kind consists in Karl Marx's analysis of political economy, which begins with the earliest forms of barter and then shows how, through a series of transformation, the capitalist economy has emerged. In social psychology, the Berlin-based Critical Psychologists around Klaus Holzkamp reconstructed in this way, for example, the categories of emotion, motive, intention, and motivation beginning with the first correlation of sensory signals with availability of food of one-cellular organisms. This type of analysis also illustrates the different conception of the universal, which is viewed in a historic-genetic manner. Thus, the first commodity exchanges and the first orientations of one-cellular organisms already contain possibilities that subsequently concretize themselves in more differentiated and variegated forms that nevertheless are as concrete as the original form (think of the parental relationship between Roth-A and all the other Roths in my earlier example). This precisely is the way in which Vygotsky (1986) presents the evolution of thought both on historical, ontogenetic, and on micro-genetic scales. Because the possibilities are inherent in the original form, it is considered the universal, general but also un- and underdeveloped, which as it concretizes and particularizes itself in the course of evolutionary processes, develops and matures.

In this approach, the analysis of the personally relevant conditions that mediate the concretization of general action possibilities are not abstracted—as in statistical approaches where these are part of error variance—but are explicitly described and theorized. Resembling in this aspect the above-described phenomenological approach, the cultural-historical method seeks to understand the conditions under which different forms of experience arise that exist in some objectively given historical situation of society and culture. Generalization here has the sense not of abstracting (taking away context) but of understanding context and experiential differences as different realizations of the same action possibilities.

The question one may legitimately ask at this point is how to get at the action possibilities available in a collective (culture, society, community) and how to explain the different possibilities in different communities that nevertheless have some common origin or that are built on the same model (pursue the same object/motive). For example, why do individuals having come through the same teacher education program with its focus on constructivist epistemology nevertheless come to teach in very different ways? Or why do schools in different school boards following the same national (provincial) curriculum and the same instructional principles nevertheless have very different school climates, learning outcomes, etc.? A categorical reconstruction, that is, an historical-genetic one, takes us a step further. Here, too, we begin with the general/universal, which subsequently is concretized in different ways by different systems/individuals.

Conversation as Model for the Individual|Collective Dialectic

One of the worries that can be found in the research community with respect to the nature of studies and generalizability has to do with going from the level of the individual to the level of the collective. If it is the case, however, that we can think the individual only in and through the collective—i.e., if individual and collective are dialectically related—then we can in fact find collective phenomena right in each encounter of two or more individuals. Even individuals acting in privacy do so in ways that are soci(et)al through and through, but because they do not articulate it for someone else in the situation, the onus is on the researcher to explicate what is happening, whereas in everyday situations, interaction participants make available to each other whatever they need to produce not merely talk but talk that reproduces the *type of* soci(et)al situation. They do so not based on independently functioning schema but right at the heart of the interaction itself: In talking, participants do not merely exchange information—in fact, this is not what they do at all—but they produce the interaction itself and provide one another with the resources to make the event not just any event but the recognizable event it turns out to be. The following analysis articulates these issues in an exemplary way. I return to the classroom in which second-grade children learned geometrical concepts; more specifically, I precisely return to the moment—depicted in Figure 11.2—when Kendra was engaging in the task of picking and then categorizing some object.

The episode begins with the teacher articulating for everyone present that it is Kendra's turn; her pitch descends toward the end of the utterance, as it is usual for end of statements. Just as the teacher begins uttering Kendra's name, she turns her gaze toward Jonathan. There is a pause, followed by her articulation of Jonathan's name (turn 03) and then another statement that after the fact can be heard as a continuation of the description of the current activity (turn 01). In this situation, the teacher utters the first syllables of Kendra's and Jonathan's names with two-and-one-half and four times the energy per unit time (power) than the surrounding speech. We can see that Jonathan turns away from the neighbor he was talking to and reorients to the teacher just as she pronounces the "tch" sound. Any adult outside observer (researcher, teacher) will hear the situation as one where the teacher called the attention of students to the fact that now it is Kendra's turn and, when during the developing pause there were still students speaking, among them Jonathan, she utters his name. The energy distribution allows us to hear that it is Kendra's turn rather than that of others, and we can hear that she "admonishes" Jonathan in particular. This is an ordinary, mundane situation of the kind that we might find in any classroom on any given day. But what makes it possible for us to orient and hear in this way?

```
01  T:   now remember it is [kENdras turn.
                             [((Begins looking toward Jonathan, talking
         to his neighbor, very low voice))
02       (1.03) ((Jonathan points to some objects; side talk))
03       J[ONathan, (0.13) to explain] her thinking.
         [((Jonathan turns body, gazes at teacher))]
                                      ((Teacher returns gaze to black
         bag where Kendra reaches to get her object.))
04       (3.26) ((Kendra digs for an object in the black garbage bag))
05  Ss1: OO::::[:::]    ((Fig. 11.2a))
06  Ss2:      [yea]
07  S:   aoo that
08  T:   kay; look around, ((Fig. 11.2b)) does it get its own (1.16)
         <<p>how many werent out there?>
         [(0.49)                           ]
         [((places new colored sheet))] 'does it get its own spot?
         (0.51) or is it like another one.
09  K:   [(5.39)                                              ]
         [((Kendra looks, holds object; nods; then places it on the sheet
         with those on the sheet labeled "tube"))]
10  T:   and tell us your thinking.
11       (0.33)
12  K:   its because o hm; (1.13 its shorter bu um ((Fig. 11.2c)) (1.18)
         theyr sort of ((Fig. 11.2d)) (0.43) round; (0.49) like this one and
         this one ((points to each of two other "tubes")) becau (0.95)
         because um; ((takes taller "tube" holds it next to her object))
         (4.07) ((Fig. 11.2e)) when i was- (0.99) when i got it=it felt (0.52)
         like (0.96) smooth (0.52) and=um (2.33) it had (1.76) round
         sides (0.53) <<dim>but flat top.>
13       (0.59)
14  T:   okay, (0.37) we called that group the tube, do you think that fits
         in with (0.26) the tube?
15       (0.44)
16  K:   ^yep.
```

It is particular that Jonathan is beginning to turn his body and gaze toward the teacher at the very instant that she utters his name, thereby singling him out. But when she has finished pronouncing his name—the admonishing nature coming from the increased speech energy—he has already turned, that is, he has acted much faster than it would have taken if he has had to interpret the utterance of his name. He was called to order specifically. That is, he has understood and begun to act based on what has been available to him auditorially (being oriented to his left, he could not see the teacher) before that. The teacher then goes on as if no further action pertaining Jonathan was necessary. That is, he has exhibited the behavior that she has intended. But how could he have understood what she has wanted to say if she has not told him so? This can be so only if there already exists intersubjectivity, that is, a *collective* understanding of *this* situation, which reproduces *such* situations. That is, Jonathan, his peers, and the observers act as if they knew what the teacher intends—draw attention to Kendra and her public thinking ("explain her thinking" [turn 03])—even though she has not specifically articulated such an intention. More so, the teacher enacts her intention knowing that others (here, the students) understand it as such. That is, the understanding of the intention already is collective, intersubjective, and therefore shared. In the high-energy utterance of the onset of Kendra's name and the subsequently developing pause that is interrupted by the naming of Jonathan's, everyone present can hear that it is he in particular who is not attending to the fact that it is Kendra's turn to speak. But in going on immediately after saying his name, stating that what is to come is Kendra's explanation of her thinking, the teacher also signals that at this precise moment, the order she intends has been re-established. If it had not been in this way, we know from experience that the teacher likely would have enacted other measures to ensure that what she intends to happen in fact does happen.

The collective nature of the actions is written all over this episode, but for exemplary purposes I articulate the collective nature of individual actions. As the episode unfolds, Kendra holds and feels the object, looks over the existing groups of objects, then places her object with another group containing two objects and labeled "tube." By the time she has placed the object (turn 09), she has not yet uttered a word despite the teacher's previous description that it was the girl's turn to "explain her thinking" (turn 03). The teacher then utters "and tell us your thinking" (turn 10), which Kendra, after a brief pause, follows with a punctuated—notice the conversationally long pauses in turn 12—utterance. Although the pause following the utterance of "top" is shorter than six of the pauses in Kendra's speech, the teacher now utters an "okay" followed by the statement that the group of objects to which the girl added her own has been called "tube" and then utters, "Do you think that fits in with the tube?" (turn 14). After a brief pause, Kendra utters "yep." Here, too, the collective is written all over what the participants make available to one another, so that looking at the transcript provides us much more than information about individuals. It provides us with description of transactional patterns characteristic of collectives, and therefore, a form of knowledge that generalizes to other situations as well.

We can hear this part of the episode as beginning with the teacher's invitation or request to Kendra to "tell her thinking." Kendra then speaks at length and, at a certain point, the teacher says "okay" (turn 14). Kendra uses the word "because," which is a conjunctive used in causal reasoning. That is, in uttering this word she lets her audience know that what it articulates are reasons. That is, she places her object with the group labeled "tube" *because* ... and then utters "it felt like smooth ... had round sides ... but flat top" (turn 12). In saying "okay," the teacher in fact reifies Kendra's utterances as having done what she earlier requested, "tell us your thinking." That is, whereas Kendra's initial actions—looking about and then placing her object has not satisfied the desired and requested description ("it is Kendra's turn ... to explain her thinking")—have not satisfactorily responded to the task, her present actions have. This is made available to those present not only in the fact that the teacher utters "okay," but also in the fact that she does so rather quickly after the Kendra utters the word "top."

How can the teacher know that Kendra is done now rather than, for example, during the long 4.07-second pause and how does Kendra show to the teacher that she is finished? That is, Kendra at least implicitly knows how to signal that she is done and the teacher hears Kendra as finishing off or as having finished. One way in which this happens is by means of trailing off—decreasing speech intensity (see "diminuendo" in description)—and by allowing the pitch to fall from "but" to "top," which therefore is produced as the end. Similarly, Kendra produces markers that allow everyone present to recognize that she is not done even though there are long or longish pauses. For example, preceding the 4.07-second pause, Kendra has uttered "because um" with a slightly falling pitch. Grammatically, the utterance is unfinished, for "because" is a conjunctive, and without something following it, nothing has actually been conjoined. Prosodically, the slightly falling pitch signals the coming of a clause or pause but not the end of a unit, only at the end of which someone else could take a turn. Not only the teacher and Kendra know this, but also the other students, the other teacher in the classroom, and the observers, including myself. That is, Kendra and the teacher do not just express their subjectivity—e.g., intentions, thinking—but they do so in ways that inherently are intelligible by the other, and, therefore, they fundamentally express intersubjectivity, both in the content and in the process.

Finally, the teacher and her students produce an event that recognizably is a mathematics lesson. But if it is recognizable as such—both teachers, observers, students, analysts—then the event itself is not merely singular, which it is because it happened only once, but also the inherently different repetition of a mathematics lesson particularly and schooling more generally. Again, this shows that the event we witness goes beyond mere singularity and that the fact that all participants in the event and we, readers and analysts, can see the event for what it is share forms of knowledgeability which inherently is shared, therefore collective, and generalizable not only to this school but far beyond it to readers of this analysis around the world. More so, if we, observers and researchers, were not already having this knowledge in *com*mon *with* these interaction participants, then we would not be able to conduct any form of an analysis such as the one I exhibit here. Thus, our (observer, researcher, analyst) own competence of understanding conversations specifically and societal activities generally already transgresses our individuality toward the collective.

In summary, therefore, this episode exemplifies the dialectic relation that ties general action (talk) possibilities and their concrete realizations in actual classrooms. Each individual—the teacher and students—uses a language that is not their own to express her or his thoughts, which is a condition for the intersubjectivity that it takes for others to understand even novel utterances. The children in particular, about seven years of age at the moment the episode was recorded, have not learned words via dictionary definitions. They use language as they have found it in the settings that they have frequented so far in their lives, including home and school. The language is not their own, but something that has come to them from the generalized other. That is, at the very moment that Kendra realizes in a concrete way what her teacher intends and expects her to do—i.e., explain *her* thinking—she does so in and with a language that not only is from the other specifically but also from and for the other generally. In a sense, therefore, it is through Kendra, her teacher, and her peers that *the English language* concretely realizes itself and its possibilities; it also reproduces itself and produces new possibilities for subsequent speakers and generations of speakers. Therefore, the proper unit of analysis to understand the episode is not the individual—Kendra and the teacher and Jonathan—but language and culture (society), which concretely realize and thereby reproduce themselves. This reproduction never is identical, which explains both (a) linguistic drifts at the historical levels of language and cultures and (b) drifts in ways of talking at the scale of lessons and units.

Historical-Genetic Approach to Language

In a previous section I provided the example of the impossibility of deriving the causal connections between the different Roths based on a study of the attributes that each individual Roth exhibits. The underlying parental relationship between the different Roths, despite the apparent differences, calls for a (cultural) historical, that is, genetic explanation. A historical approach allows us to understand how the action possibilities in some collective entity (e.g., a classroom) unfold and how new action possibilities are created in and through the concretization of previously existing possibilities. In this approach we are enabled to *explain* concrete human behavior in terms of the generalized action possibilities— people do this or that *because* they have a reason, even if they leave a decision to others or to chance "*because* they don't care." Formally, we are dealing with a genetic explanation when a certain fact is not derived from antecedent conditions and laws (deduction) or observations and antecedents (induction) but when the fact is shown to be the endpoint of a longer development the individual stages (phases) of which can be followed. In *causal genetic* explanations, the antecedents B of a step (B → C) coincide with the outcome B (philosophically, the *explanandum*) of the previous step (A → B). In historical genetic explanation, the antecedents B_2 of one step (B_2 → C) do not coincide with the explanandum B_1 of the previous step (A → B_1), requiring new pieces of information (X) to be added (i.e., $B_2 = B_1 + X$). To concretize the implications of the historic-genetic approach, I return to Kendra's classroom.

In the section on phenomenology, I describe how generalization in learning can be understood as a process of the formation of a network of concrete experiences, any single one of which may serve as metonymic constituent, that is, as index (activator) of the network as a whole. In fact, when we study the actions of individuals in this classroom over time, the possibilities for expressing themselves mathematically and about mathematical objects change as the second-grade children engage with the successive tasks. What individual students do at any one point in time is a function of the action possibilities in the classroom (e.g., availability of particular forms of talk), but any action possibility is itself a function of what individuals contribute. As we study the classroom, we see an expansion of (material, discursive) action possibilities as an initially more constraint set of possibilities is partially realized and in its concrete production gives rise to further possibilities. What Kendra does in the episode featured cannot be understood outside the historical context of the collective development. For example, if Kendra had been the first student to pull a cylinder from the black plastic bag, then the action of holding the object next to other cylinders for making a perceptual comparison would not have existed. Thus, we can say very little about Kendra's actions and change in action possibilities (learning) unless we study the concrete possibilities in the collective as a whole. But in making the comparison, Kendra exhibits a form of action the reproduction ("copying") of which becomes immediately available to others. Thus, when the first student who pulled a cylinder created a category that he then named "tube," he created the possibility for other students, such as Kendra, to make new forms of comparisons.

By studying the interface of individual|collective learning in *this* classroom, we can learn something about the ways in which action possibilities generally expand and how some subset of them comes to be concretized and, in so doing, realizes the development of a collective entity. The process of learning through the concretization of action possibilities that are changed in the course is a realization of a process not just in *this* classroom but also of a form of process enabled by the nature of the culture itself. *This* process is a concrete realization of possible processes, and by studying *it* we learn something about culture more generally.

An important aspect of generalization relates to the use of language and the possibility for constructing tests in multiple languages for the purpose of making international comparisons. To understand the sense that interaction participants expose to each other, it is necessary to know both the cultural-historical possibilities generally and the concrete history of the interaction itself. In Kendra's classroom, the children initially named the type of objects she had categorized a "tube"; the teacher did not insist on the mathematical term "cylinder." A few remarks from the perspective I articulate in this chapter are in order. First, etymologically, the word cylinder entered the English language from the French *cylindre* (~14th century), adapted from the Latin *cylindrus*, roller, itself adapted from the ancient Greek *kulindros* (κύλινδοσ), "roller." The experience recorded in this word is precisely the one Kendra made when she rolled her object between two hands (Figure 11.2e). This experience, however, no longer is available through the descriptive name to non-speakers of Greek; the word tube, known to children from settings outside this classroom, however, allows them to use a familiar name associated with iconically (perceptually) similar objects already within the range of experiences (some) children have made.

Second, in the construction of tests across languages, there is a need to study the semantic fields that are associated with particular words because the sense of a word is a function of its semantic field—similar to the nature of a concept, which is a function of experiences (Figure 11.3). The word *tube* the children use in the mathematics lesson has its origins in the Indo-Germanic root *tu-*, meaning tubular, hollow. The English word *tube*—taken over from the old French term *le tube* during the 15th century—is used to signify, among others, (a) long hollow bodies often used to convey liquids, pipe; (b) glass containers used in chemistry labs; (c) collapsible containers of oil colors and tooth paste; (d) television sets (historically from the fact that cathode ray tubes are used); and (e) inner tubes for bicycles. Some of the different senses are equivalent in the French *(le) tube*, but other senses are not shared. For example, in French *le tube* also has the sense of a musical hit but cannot be used to refer to an inner tube (*chambre à air*) and is not used to refer to the a English slang term for cigarette or the penis (also "tube steak"). In English it may denote the Fallopian tubes; in Australia it has the sense of a bottle of beer; and "The Tube" is a teen show broadcast on Television Northern Canada but in the UK, it is the London Underground. But in both countries the term may refer to the telephone. In French there are none of these equivalents.

In German—as in the French language from which the Germans copied it during the early part of the 19th century—the word (die) *Tube* refers to containers such as for toothpaste, but not for any other of the senses outlined so far (for which the word *[das] Rohr* has to be used) with the exception that the French *à pleins tubes* means at the full power of a car engine and *auf die Tube drücken* means quickly accelerating in German. That is, although the three languages share the mathematical term derived from the Greek *kulindros*, French and English share a number of significations related to the term *tube*, but German has only the compressible container as its denotation. The common forms of sense are due to the common root, but since the adoption of the word into English, it has developed differently than it has in French.

A study of language in a classroom has to take into account the different senses in which words are used and how these senses unfold in time (see also the perspective on linguistic differences within groups outlined by Solano-Flores, chapter 3, and the diachronic perspective articulated by Gee in the Mislevy et al. chapter 5). Because of the different semantic fields even within a culture, the terms constitute different cultural possibilities for classroom conversations to unfold. Similarly, any transnational test has to consider the semantic fields and how they change even over the course of a few years. Thus, the different forms of sense available to a researcher may no longer be available for a student, and vice versa, the different forms of sense in which the students in a particular classroom employ words may differ from those that educational researchers use. More so, certain ways of speaking may come with negative consequences for students from their peers, so that, drawing on my experience of doing research in inner-city schools in Philadelphia, an African American high school student may refer to the penis of a frog as "tube" or "tube steak" (familiar navy expressions) in lieu of the more common "dick," or refuse talking about the organ as such, because employing the word *penis* would signify "acting White." It therefore should not surprise if a researcher notes a lot of laughter, giggling, and other "off-task" behavior if the word "the tubes" were to be used in a junior high school class where the students might connote it with Fallopian tubes.

Coda

In this chapter, I describe, exemplify, and explicate two approaches to research in which the study of individual cases gives us access to knowledge that goes beyond the partial and particular often associated with case studies, ethnography, and other types of interpretive research. Both forms of research, the phenomenological and materialist dialectical, seek to identify that which is general *in* the particular. In the former approach, this is achieved through a variation of experiences, for example, on the part of one person for the purpose of identifying the general laws and conditions that allow us to have the experiences under investigation in the first place. The second approach theorizes the relation between individual and collective (particular and general, specific and universal) as a dialectical one, which means that the two no longer are diametrically opposed elements standing in an external relation but are moments of an overarching unit that mutually presuppose each other but which cannot be reduced to (explained by) one another. The question arises, why would two seemingly different approaches, having developed from very different origins, arrive at similar characterizations of generalization from the experience (actions) of individuals to experiences (actions) possible within a collective?

The answer to this question has been set up in and through the work of the German philosopher Edmund Husserl, who pushed Kant's constructivism to its limit in the attempt to explicate how knowledge and the world could be constructed departing from the individual knower (cogito). Without taking the ultimate consequences—abandoning the intent to establish an *egology*, a science of the "I" or ego—he realized that I cannot identify the behavior of an other person as quick-tempered and irascible without first adopting over my own affects an external perspective, that is, the point of view of the other person: "it is only on this condition that I can understand such a bodily manifestation of others as irascibility" (Franck, 1981, p. 157). At its very heart, the "I" is not really subjective but intersubjective; the other, and therefore the general, is at the very heart of being an individual and particular. In the analysis of the episode featuring Jonathan, Kendra, and their teacher, I also show that researchers can only understand what is said when they are in cahoots with the interaction participants under study, who not only expose the sense of the situation but also make available what it takes to align and realign one another with respect to this sense. All of this requires that the sense is already intelligible and therefore available both to the participants and the researchers; this sense and the resources for aligning one another therefore transgress individual subjectivity toward intersubjectivity. The two approaches I outline here are ideal methods for articulating, making foreground, and theorizing all those aspects of human activities and experiences that are common; the common is shared together (Latin *co[m]-*) with others, the general. It is the researchers' task to enact rigorous forms of research to isolate in an unambiguous way precisely those common features that are shared *within* the relevant *com*munity.

In the limit, the two approaches merge, as phenomenological studies show: there is not nor cannot there be anything like thinking and consciousness without the body, which therefore mediates not only between the material and ideal moments of life but also between the individual and the social. Recent formulations of a philosophy of difference, first philosophy, and hermeneutic phenomenology converge in recognizing the multiple and mutually constitutive dialectics involving the material body, flesh, Self, Other, individual, collective, and so forth. Precisely because of these dialectics it is possible to identify the general in the particular, the collective in the individual, or the universal in the specific.

Note

1. A figure by which a part of some phenomenon is used to denote the phenomenon as a whole, such as when waitresses use the term "the ham sandwich" to refer to a person eating a ham sandwich. See also Lyle Bachman's (chapter 7 of this volume) use of semiotics to characterize similar relations.

References

Franck, D. (1981). *Chair et corps: Sur la phénoménologie de Husserl*. Paris: Les Éditions de Minuit.
Guba, E., & Lincoln, Y. (1989). *Fourth generation evaluation*. Beverly Hills, CA: Sage.
Hegel, G. W. F. (1977). *Phenomenology of spirit* (A. V. Miller, Trans.). Oxford, UK: Oxford University Press. (Original work published 1806)
Holzkamp, K. (1983a). Der Mensch als Subjekt wissenschaftlicher Methodik. In K.-H. Braun, Hollitscher, W., Holzkamp, K. & Wetzel, K. (Eds.), *Karl Marx und die Wissenschaft vom Individuum* (pp. 120–166). Marburg, Germany: Verlag Arbeiterbewegung und Gesellschaftswissenschaften.
Holzkamp, K. (1983b). *Grundlegung der Psychologie*. Frankfurt/M.: Campus.
Il'enkov, E. (1982). *Dialectics of the abstract and the concrete in Marx's Capital* (Trans. Sergei Kuzyakov). Moscow: Progress.
Merleau-Ponty, M. (1945). *Phénoménologie de la perception*. Paris: Gallimard.
Vygotsky, L. S. (1986). *Thought and language*. Cambridge, MA: MIT Press.
Wittgenstein, L. (1958). *Philosophical investigations* (3rd ed.). New York: Macmillan.

Section IV

Highlights

A scientific practice that fails to question itself does not, properly speaking, know what it does. Embedded in, or taken by, the object that it takes as its object, it reveals something of the object, but something which is not really objectivized since it consists of the very principles of apprehension of the object.

Bourdieu, 1992, p. 236

The two chapters in this section constitute attempts at critiquing and rethinking concepts from the inside and outside of educational research, and thereby working toward a discipline that does not fail to question itself. Not doing what they do is a charge more theoretically inclined researchers around the world launch at very pragmatically oriented (North American) researchers in education. There are perhaps too many in our field who administer some quick assessment tool prior to articulating and theorizing some of the presupposition and antecedents of the research before actually launching into it.

Following Lee Cronbach (1982), Ercikan identifies at least four sets of factors to be considered in generalizing from a sample to a population: the units affected, the treatments, the outcomes, and the settings. Her chapter highlights how data may be misinterpreted if the different sets of factors mediating generalizability are left unconsidered. Her chapter also demonstrates that statistics at the national level have little value in guiding policy and practice, especially as these relate to the local levels. Therefore, the requirement of the degree to which a sample is representative may not be the best or even an adequate criterion for evaluating generalizability.

A very different approach to the question of generalizing from educational research is proposed in chapter 11, an approach based on dialectical materialism, which takes a developmental approach to the question of the general and particular, abstract and concrete. Accordingly, the less developed unit under study is the more general, because it constitutes many possibilities that are differently realized like parental genes are differently concretized in their children. Much like a germ cell in different context, the unit concretizes itself in development and thereby becomes concrete and particular. But in the same way as a germ cell, the general (abstract) unit is also concrete. The old distinction between the general and particular, the universal and the specific, the abstract and the concrete thereby is done away with and replaced by the dialectical unit of which the polar opposites are but one-sided expressions.

As we have been rereading the chapters in this book repeatedly, it has become clearer to us that a rethinking of the relationship between the general and the particular brings with it opportunities for dealing with the gap often experienced, discovered, and actively located between theory and practice. Such an approach is articulated in chapter 11, "Phenomenological and Dialectical Perspectives on the Relation between the General and the Particular" (Roth). Accordingly, each practical action is understood as the realization of a general possibility, which, because it does not determine action, constitutes an abstract form. Possibilities are enacted in this or that way, always taking into account the specifics of the singular case, but also always accounting for the intelligibility in and accountability to culture more broadly. Understanding this relationship brings with it a realization of constraints on current actions and offers opportunities to rethink the extension of cultural possibilities more broadly.

There may also be a need for being more critical with our own concepts and methods, much in the way that chapter "Limitations in Sample-to-Population Generalization" questions the assumptions made within your own discipline. It points the way for educational research to become a more reflexive science, one in which ideologies, presuppositions, concepts, and methods are questioned, deconstructed, and further developed.

The problematic may be framed in a dialectical way. On the one hand, an over-concern with method will lead us down the wrong path, to scientificity—methodology, Bourdieu (1992) suggests, like spelling, is a "science of the jackasses" (p. 244), consisting of a compendium of errors that one must be too dumb to commit most of them. On the other hand, an over-concern with method allows us to institute a reflexive science that does not simply apply method but interrogates the research enterprise as a whole, including its objects, methods, and results. It is only within this inner contradiction of the over-concern that educational science can move forward and truly lead to the change and improvement of the extant material and social relations toward greater equity and (social and environmental) justice.

References

Bourdieu, P. (1992). The practice of reflexive sociology (The Paris workshop). In P. Bourdieu & L. J. D. Wacquant, *An invitation to reflexive sociology* (pp. 216–260). Chicago: University of Chicago Press.
Cronbach, L. J. (1982). *Designing evaluations of educational and social programs*. San Francisco: Jossey-Bass.

Chapter 12

Discussion of Key Issues in Generalizing in Educational Research

*Edited by Kadriye Ercikan and Wolff-Michael Roth
with Contributions from Lyle F. Bachman, Margaret
Eisenhart, Robert J. Mislevy, Pamela A. Moss,
Guillermo Solano-Flores, and Kenneth Tobin*

To provide an opportunity to address issues in a way that cuts across sections and thereby provides opportunities for moving to new levels of understanding, we (the editors) invited contributors attending the 2008 Annual Meeting of the American Educational Research Association to this volume to address three sets of questions. In this chapter, we reproduce the edited responses to the three sets of questions as these were presented during a Division D-sponsored session. Wolff-Michael Roth had the task to provide some overarching comments, followed by rejoinders by other panel members. The time available for the session allowed panel members to respond to one question from the audience.

How do you define "generalization" and "generalizing"? What is the relationship between audiences of generalizations and the users? Who are the generalizations for? For what purpose? Are there different forms and processes of generalization? Is it possible to generalize from small-scale studies?

Lyle Bachman

What I hope to discuss is how I see generalization as a series of inferential links from the phenomenon to the consequences of the research. I will also talk about some of the purposes or uses of educational research and what I call a research use argument. Then, I will summarize with some concluding remarks.

When we do educational research, empirical research in education involves going out and looking at things. There is some phenomenon that a researcher may be interested in. In my field that may be something like a conversation between two individuals, it might be a speech event involving a classroom interchange between teachers and students. It might be a performance on a language test. From that phenomenon, the researcher has some perceptions and there may be several researchers involved; and each researcher may have a different perception of those phenomena. Or the same researcher may have different perceptions at different points in time.

Those perceptions are filtered. They are filtered by the researcher's own research interests, by his or her particular epistemological stance, by his or her own individual characteristics, and so on. On the basis of those perceptions, the researcher prepares a report, and that report might be a conversation analysis; it might be an ethnography of the speech event; or it might be a test score. It might be a pre-post test of a quasi-experimental design. And those reports again are filtered by the method, that the researcher has used to observe the phenomenon or used to record it. So if the choice is conversation analysis, then there would be a very particular method for transcribing and analyzing the conversations, or if it is a test score there would be a particular test, a procedure of designing the test, and so on. From those perceptional reports then, from the scores, from the conversation analysis, or from the ethnography, we arrive at an interpretation. In other words, we make some sense of those reports and again, those interpretations are filtered by the way we define the construct that we are trying to under-stand, defined again by the purpose of the research, by the research perspectives, and so on.

On the basis of that interpretation then, researchers make a deci-sion or several decisions. The researcher may choose to move on to the next point in the research agenda. (The best research always generates more questions than it answers so the decision may be made to go in one direction or another.) The decision may be to publish the report. Decisions by other stakeholders may also be made. The researcher may use that research publication to get tenure or to get promoted. Or a practitioner may look at the research and believe that it applies to his or her situation and make educational decisions about instruction or curriculum design or so forth on the basis of that research. And again, those decisions will be filtered. They will be filtered by the kinds of con-sequences that the stakeholders intend to promote on those decisions. They will be filtered by the context, by the stakeholders' perceptions and so on.

Finally, those decisions have consequences. The decisions have con-sequences for the researcher, for the whole research team. They may have consequences for a school, for a university, an educational setting that actually makes some decisions on the basis of the research. So if somebody finds out in a second language acquisition, for example, that a particular activity type or task is useful for helping students learn a language, they may build a syllabus around that research and they may decide to use that as an instructional intervention. In this case the instructional intervention will have consequences for the teacher, the students, the school, etc.

So all of these levels can be considered to be aspects of generalization. In other words, I see generalization as a process of inferring. When we generalize we want to have some qualities; and one quality that we want to have is consistency across those perceptions. Consistency is going to take a lot of different shapes. In measurement it takes the form of reliability. In ethnography it may be trustworthiness. We want the interpretation to be meaningful. In other words, we want that interpretation to have some meaning on the basis of the way the researcher has defined the abilities, the way the researcher has defined the construct that he intends to look at. And we want those decisions to be equitable for all stakeholders, and finally, we want the consequences to be beneficial. Those are the qualities that we hope, I believe, that we will find in our research.

What are the consequences of doing the research and the decisions made? I have talked about some of the kinds of decisions that are made on the basis of research: decisions about the researcher's own professional career, decisions about whether some particular view in the field is supported or rejected, and decisions about children in schools. And all of these have consequences. So we need to ask these questions. We need to ask who the stakeholders are. The stakeholders are more than just the researcher and his or her research team. The stakeholders include anybody who is going to be affected by those decisions. It might be as widespread as a whole school district or a whole state.

The last question is, of course, what is the researcher's responsibility for the consequences of the research. If I do some research and I do a language test and I place people in a language class on the basis of those tests, suppose somebody gets misplaced. Am I responsible for that misplacement? That is not something that I am going to attempt to answer, but I think it is something that researchers will always need to consider; and our responsibility for the consequences of the research need to be taken into consideration from the very beginning as we design the research.

The question poses itself, for which consequences can the research be held accountable? We may not be responsible for all the consequences, but for those consequences for which we are responsible how can we be held accountable to stakeholders? I am just going to go very quickly over this, what I call a research-use argument that explicitly states the interpretations and uses that are to be based on the observations. These are up front, these are the consequences, these are the decisions, these are the interpretations, and so on. And it provides an over-arching inferential framework to guide both the conceptualization, design, and implementation of research and the interpretation and use of research results.

The structure of the research argument I am talking about basically consists of a data-claim pair based on Toulmin's argument structure. A claim is a conclusion that we seek to establish. Thus, we might typically say that we claim that these results mean this. That is a claim. And we base these claims on data. Data consists of the information on which the claim is based. So what we have is a series of steps to an argument. We start with some sort of phenomenon that is observed in some setting. On the basis of that we infer a report and so the data upon which we based the claim. That report in turn becomes the data upon which we make the interpretation. The interpretation becomes the data upon which we base decisions. Those decisions are the data on which the consequences occur.

In conclusion, I see generalization as a series of inferential links from observations to report to interpretation to decisions and consequences. Educational research has consequences for a wide range of stakeholders. In designing and implementing educational research, the educational researcher should consider these consequences and their potential for benefiting stakeholders along with the extent of the researchers' responsibilities for these consequences. The research-use argument provides an over-arching framework for doing this and what I argue that we should cultivate a research milieu of argumentation that moves educational research away from the competing epistemologies and approaches that seem to be driven more by a preoccupation with or differences toward one which admits a wide range of empirical methods and stances. Cultivating such a milieu would enable researchers in education to break away from attempts to emulate scientific research in the natural sciences, on the one hand, and from the never-ending paradigm debate between so-called quantitative and qualitative approaches to research, on the other hand.

Ken Tobin

I pick up where Lyle left off. I think we need to transcend more than the two dichotomies that Lyle mentions. There is an empirical/non-empirical dichotomy that we need to transcend as well. And so perhaps what we are thinking about is transcending all dichotomies. How do we do that, and what would it mean if we did that? When we look at research and we ask a question about generalizability and about what it means to us. As a consumer of research, the first question that comes to me is how do I access research? I get 10-minute looks at it at AERA, I read the journals, I keep up in a variety of other ways doing my own research, and so forth. As a consequence, I come away with a sense of the game. The question that I ask about research is, to what extent is this research meaningful to me? Does it address the curiosities that I have or any of the problems that I need to resolve? And, is it repeatable? Can I make this work in similar circumstances? Based on the research that I do (which is in science classes), the key question that I have as a researcher as I tell others about my research is this: "Will they be able to repeat this and get results that have a family resemblance to mine if they work in the same circumstances?" There are a lot of "ïfs," a lot of contingencies. But I think this is the game that we are in if we think about generalizability more in terms of repetition. We have an issue of substitution.

When I was doing research many years ago, one of the ideas that we had was that we would have samples, and the samples consisted of objects that were in some ways the same as one another, the same as those in a larger population. But as we know as educators, humans have agency, and according to the structures of the time they'll do what they're going to do. If you take some ideas that you have for your research and as the teacher you try to make them work, the first thing that you find is that the objects that you are working with are actually people and that they have agency. As well as wanting to learn some physics, if you are lucky, they are engaging in multiple activities at the same time. So classrooms are replete with contradictions. When we try to make this work, to make it repeatable, we come up against structures and so you come up against this agency | structure kind of thing and I think that it is important to factor that in.

I am a teacher educator. I was doing my teacher education at the University of Pennsylvania some years ago and talking to a group of students in a masters-of-teaching program each of whom had paid $35,000 to be there. We had them teaching in urban settings. They were taking what we had learned from the research and they were enacting it in their classrooms. One day McKenzie Smith said to me, "Hey Tobin, does any of this work?" And I said, "Sure it works, and if it isn't working for you it is an enactment problem." So he said, "would you come and show me how this works?" Well, I groaned a little, but I went to the school and I tried to make it work. It was a humbling experience. It didn't work the way I thought it was going to work. I thought I was a pretty good teacher and I probably was when I taught 30 years ago in Australia. But teaching in West Philadelphia was a little bit different. The research that we had read, the research that was in our methods course didn't work at all. I needed a different knowledge base to try and make it work. I needed to structure the places, the fields in which this was going to work such that they were similar to the structures in the field in which the research was done. And I think that is a key point for researchers to keep in mind. If we are going to have repeatability, we need to create structures that are similar, that have a family resemblance to those situations in which the claims were made in the first place.

The second thing I learned from doing my research was the inadvisability of separating the theoretical claims that we make from research from the practices that produced those claims. In other words, there is a kind of a connection between practices and the schema that come from those practices. Now as a teacher in West Philadelphia, it was very important to me that the knowledge that I had would produce a change in practices. In fact, it is those changes in practices that enable researchers to look and see patterns, in other words to do the empirical work. As a person who was involved in the research, it was important to me to acknowledge the inability to separate, sensibly, the schema from the practices. And this leads me to a different type of position with research: when we do research we have the obligation to our participants that the research benefit them. So the issue of beneficence can be applied to those who participate in research.

The idea of beneficence gives us a different set of criteria to start looking at what we take away from this that might be repeatable. If we want to have repetition, it is not just the claims that need to be repeated but in fact the change in practices. This has lead us to think a lot more about how we spread and how we disseminate what we have learned from research. We have this notion or this idea of ripple effects, namely that people learn from one another by being with one another. Thus, if you set up some research in a school and things start to happen. We do work on cogenerative dialogue with kids and the teachers work together in the same classroom sharing the responsibility for the teaching and learning. What you find is that in one classroom good things start to happen. But the kids do not just stay in one classroom, nor do the teachers. They go to other classrooms. What you find is the ripple effects are going through the school to produce desirable changes. And that is what we want when we think about repetition. We want to see the good effects of research making a positive difference within the sites in which the research is being undertaken.

Kadriye Ercikan

Lyle and Ken presented very different notions of generalizing in educational research that is particularly representative of the context, for example, the schools, the samples, and the teachers involved are to the populations that we are generalizing. They introduced the idea that consistency is very similar to the notion of generalizability; but they also introduced the notion of beneficial usefulness. Ken talked about repeatability and consistency; and repeatability pertained not just to the research outcomes and the claims that we make, but to the processes as well. The core of generalizing is the arguments that we make to support those generalizations.

What types of validity arguments are needed for generalizing in educational research? Are these forms of arguments different for different forms of generalization? Can there be a common ground for different generalizability arguments?

Pamela Moss

My remarks are drawn from a chapter that reflects a dialogue, or a trialogue, among Bob Mislevy, Jim Gee, and me. We chose to take up Kadriye and Michael's questions about generalizability in the context of educational assessment. This dialogue actually grew out of a larger collaboration funded by the Spencer Foundation that focused on exploring the potential synergy between psychometrics and sociocultural studies and the theory and practice of assessment.

Our work evolved to focus on the relationship between assessment and opportunity to learn. The focus on opportunity to learn allowed us to explore our differences in a way that brought them to bear productively on a common problem. Our chapter reflects some of the sidebar conversations that Jim, Bob, and I had about validity. Our three-way dialogue in the chapter for this book focused initially on validity of interpretations, models, and theories that are intended to have some broader relevance in multiple educational contexts. Or they are intended to contribute to understanding in a field, in our case focused initially on interpretations associated with scores on standardized tests that always entail generalizations, theories, and models in which those scores are or should be grounded. I believe Bob is going to speak to you about that level of our dialogue.

Of particular interest that I brought to the dialogue was this: "How are those arguably generalizable interpretations, models, and theories taken up in local contexts by the actors who use them to address their own questions and make their own interpretations, decisions and actions?" I am going to speak to that validity issue first and use it to illustrate some of the general agreements that Bob, Jim, and I reached from our different perspectives.

Generalizable interpretations—like the presumptive meanings associated with standardized test scores—are always put to work in particular situations by particular people. How they are put to work depends on the sense people can make of them including whether they attend to them at all, the resources people use to interpret them, the locally relevant questions that they provoke or provide evidence for, the other evidence brought to bear, local values, and commitments and the local supports or constraints for making meaningful interpretations, and so on. A robust theory of validity needs to be able to take situated and dynamic interpretations into account. The interpretations made when generalizable interpretations are put to work in the local context. This is not to diminish the importance of validity issues involved in developing generalizable interpretations that can and should provide a crucial piece of the background against which educator interpretations on the ground are made. It is simply to argue that it tells only one important part of the story that a comprehensive theory of validity for generalizations needs to address. My thinking about validity in educational assessment has been deeply informed by reading accounts of accomplished educational practice about how evidence is used to monitor and support learning. To provide a concrete example in our chapter, I drew on Magdalene Lampert's (2001) book Teaching Problems and the Problems of Teaching, and I consider the questions or problems that she needs to address, the kinds of evidence that she attends to, and the nature of interpretations she draws in teaching mathematics to fifth graders.

In conceptualizing the problems she faced, Lampert uses the metaphor of a camera lens shifting focus and zooming in and out, and this allows her to represent the problems in practice that a teacher needs to work on in a particular moment, along with the problems of practice that are addressed in teaching a lesson or a unit or a year-long curriculum. Throughout her text we see how she uses evidence to address different sorts of problems on different time scales to make decisions about what to do next in interactions with students, to select and sequence mathematical problems, to support students in becoming the kinds of learners inclined to collaborate, and to reason about mathematical ideas and take stock of their accomplishments. For instance, Lampert describes her questions about students' capacities while preparing for a series of lessons in late September on how and when to use multiplication and division in solving problems, and I am quoting here: "It would help me to know whether any of my students could already multiply large numbers using a conventional procedure. It would help me to know if anyone understood that multiplication is about groups of groups no matter how big the numbers. It would help me to know if anyone would be disposed to work independently in ways that were reasonable and if anyone would be likely to focus on more than simply producing the answers" (p. 108). So her interpretation of students' standardized tests at the beginning of the year takes on meaning only in light of how it works to address questions like these. We see her attend to student strategies for solving problems, from a standardized test, from their notebooks, from their talks with her and each other. We see her attend to how students interact with her, with the material, and with one another. This sort of information along with what she knew—the generalizable knowledge of her coursework, her own work with the problems and previous knowledge and experience with fifth graders—helped her make decisions about what problems to select and about how to support students' dispositions to reason and collaborate.

Her attention to evidence and teaching a problem was routinely situated in the ongoing interaction of which it was a part. It was cumulative in the sense of drawing on other available evidence, fitting this piece of evidence, a test score for instance, into her evolving understanding of students' learning, and anticipatory in a sense that she was always considering how her next move was likely to affect student's learning. Her interpretations and actions were also, of course, informed by a robust theory about teaching mathematics to children.

While the focus of the example has been on the teacher as an interpreter, an analogy may be easily drawn in the problems or issues facing professionals in other contexts. So consider how test scores might be used to inform questions that school and district leaders might ask about allocating resources, planning professional development, selecting and refining curricula, developing local policies, evaluating the impact of those policies, and so on. And for educators up to the federal level, I could address similar kinds of questions about how they use test-based information. Many of the problems are of the what-do-we-do-next variety although at quite different levels of scale. They therefore require evidence about students' learning and the factors that shape it.

What does this suggest about what a theory of validity needs to accomplish? What is needed is a flexible approach about validity that begins with the questions that are being asked that can develop, analyze and integrate multiple kinds of evidence at different levels of scale. The approach has to be dynamic in the sense that the questions, available evidence, and interpretations can evolve dialectically as enquirers learn from their enquiry and that allows attention to the antecedents and to the anticipated and actual consequences of their interpretations, decisions, and actions.

And how does this illustrate the sorts of agreement that Jim, Bob, and I reached? We found considerable complementarities in our approaches to validity. Bob's in psychometrics, mine in hermeneutics, and Jim's in critical discourse analysis. We also agreed that valuable inferences about students' learning occurred at various levels or grain sizes of reality and take into account the relationship between learners and their environment. That as Bob said, "different kinds of phenomena can be conceived of, become manifest and explored at different levels of analysis with different methods that suit their respective levels, that the validity of inferences at any particular level can and should be challenged by inferences at other levels, and that validity enquiry is best treated as a dynamic process that seeks corroboration and challenge for evolving inferences or models from multiple perspectives and sources of evidence." I have been working out a theory of validity to attempt to deal with the always partially unique circumstances that occur on the ground, in particular classrooms, schools, and so on. Bob is considering how psychometrics and probability-based reasoning can function in a way that is consistent with these agreements.

Willy Solano-Flores

One of the questions is, "What types of validity arguments can we use to provide evidence of generalizability in educational research?" My chapter is on the evidence that you use in the assessment of English language learners (ELLs). Essentially, the basic claim in the chapter is a view that the system does not work as we want to think that it works. We have this notion that students are identified and classified according to their level of proficiency, and then they are given tests that have met basic minimum requirements, and that based on those tests we make generalizations to the general population of English language learners. This is a deterministic model. Everything works fine. Everything works as planned. I claim that ELL testing is actually a stochastic process, it is probabilistic. There is a lot of uncertainty and a lack of fidelity to implementation. Many processes in life are probabilistic so the best approach for a probabilistic process is to have a probabilistic view.

What we try to do is question what the assumptions are that we make about the students that we test? Are we really obtaining accurate measures of language proficiency? Will we ever be able to obtain accurate measures of language proficiency? What are the characteristics of our tests, how good are they, and should we focus not only on the tests but also on the process of the testing, the processes in which we adapt or translate those tests or make accommodations that we provide for English language learners?

Then there is the context to which we generalize evidence from our research. As we all know, English language learner populations are very heterogeneous, so everything that we come up with might not apply entirely to different contexts. I am essentially trying to define the process of ELL testing as a communication process, a communication process in which we ask ELL students questions: in a test, they give us answers and we interpret those answers. When we approach the process of ELL testing with this kind of mind set we realize that we as an assessment system might not be very proficient in the kinds of actions we are taking to obtain accurate measures of academic achievement for these students. This is the idea of the situation, and this is how we would like things to be working.

If we think about all these three basic stages, we have to deal with the population specification, then we have to deal with the developing and administering and interpreting of the tests, then making generalizations or designing testing policy what we have is three threats to validity. One is population misspecification, a typical case and false positive and false negative cases of classification. This includes the ELL who is not actually an ELL, or the student who is ELL and is not identified by us as an ELL; and it includes the student who is identified as an ELL based on oral proficiency but actually that ELL is very good at reading and writing in English and probably would do much better if he or she were tested in English than in the native language.

Then we have measurement error, but this is not the measurement error as we think about it when we examine a report with coefficients. We are thinking not only about the measurement error—which we see with that little lower case e that we see in reports of generalizability studies—but also we are thinking about the error as the thing that we want to dissect. This is not only unexplained or unaccounted for error; it is only the structure of the error that we see throughout the process of testing.

Then we have overgeneralization. Usually the editors of the journals or policy makers want us to say this is what works, this is what does not work. We obtain this kind of dependability coefficients, but that is not going to generalize to everybody in the same way. And we have evidence that the moment you move from one context to another, even within the same broad linguistic group, your dependability coefficients may be different. Therefore, regardless of the language in which you are testing English language learners you might need a certain number of items to obtain dependable scores for, let's say, Spanish speakers in certain schools or school districts. But you may need a different number of items to obtain dependable scores for another group of Spanish speakers in another context. Everything has to do with variation, variation about the fact that each ELL is unique, variation in terms of all the things that may happen throughout the process of testing, and the variety of contexts to which we are generalizing.

Just to give you a flavor, think about language variation—we have the student's native language, and we have the student's second language. Even if we just use a simple conceptual framework, we will have listening, speaking, reading, and writing modes in each language, and we will have issues of dialect and register in each language for the students. Now think about these also in the context of academic language. Think about this in the context of the linguistic proficiencies of those individuals who provide accommodations for English language learners. So as I mention more and more factors you may be thinking, "This is a chaos." And, yes, this is a chaos. This is a stochastic process, and we need to develop stochastic models to address them. That is essentially my claim.

My conclusion therefore is that if you think about test score variation with a generalizability theory approach, we have rater, occasion, item, and method of assessment as the typical facets that are investigated, but essentially we could also include facets like the test development procedures, approaches to adapt or translate a test or provide accommodations, the proficiencies of test developers and translators, and so on. There are all these facets that have not been investigated and should be investigated in order for us to have a good idea of how this is working or how this is not working, how there is context variation with broad linguistic groups, communities, school districts, locals, socio-economic status, and so on.

Noreen Webb

My presentation builds very well on Willy's. There is a lot of common ground across these, which is nice to see. I am going to talk about using generalizability theory in a little bit more detail to think about validity issues. When designing and carrying out empirical studies researchers make decisions about who to study, what to study, what data to collect, and how data will be collected and analyzed. All of these decisions have implications for the generalizability of research findings. We often discuss these as aspects of validity. Generalizability theory was developed as a comprehensive approach to assessing measurement consistency that is reliability. But G-theory also gives us a way to think about validity issues and provides a means of systematically investigating the extent to which these factors might limit generalization. So, in a nutshell, G-theory proposes reliability as an index of how consistently we can generalize from a sample of measurements in hand to some universe that we might be interested in. For example, if we are going to measure social studies knowledge, we might consider a variety of test forms, different occasions of testing and a set of raters and might be interested in any score that arises from some combination of that. We therefore might design a G-study with students crossed with test forms crossed with occasions crossed with raters. It will show us how variable performance is across these measurement facets. Then the results will show how well we can generalize from the scores in hand to this broader universe we might be interested in.

G-theory also helps us move beyond these typical types of reliability questions to the validity concerns that have already been discussed in my chapter. In particular, the sources of variability that might otherwise be hidden from view but which do limit our ability to generalize. It is helpful to start as a launching point to consider a concrete study and this is one that actually was done in Australia by Ashman and Gillies (1997).

It was an experimental study or quasi-experimental study comparing a cooperative learning program, actually two variations, one with and one without special training in interpersonal skills. I am giving a few of these details for a reason. It was based in a 12-week social studies unit on the British exploration of Australia. It took place in 8 public schools in Brisbane, Australia, a metropolitan area. The particular instantiation of the treatment was in heterogeneous small groups, and results yielded higher achievement and more cooperation in the experimental treatment with the special preparation.

In such situations there are typical reliability issues we might consider. How many test forms or raters or occasions do you need for a dependable measurement? There are important issues about defining these sources of variability. What are the possible items that might comprise each test form? What are the characteristics of raters you might want to consider? How will occasions be considered? How will you sample these levels of the different facets, and are the test forms, raters and occasions exchangeable with or representative of any forms, raters or occasions that might be selected? We can move beyond the bounds of reliability to consider validity issues. Content validity issues can be generalized from responses about English exploration of Australia to another content area or to social studies critical thinking skills. Or we may pose a convergent validity question: can we generalize from one test item format to another, short answer, or an essay? Can we generalize from one observation method to another, such as from a behavioral checklist versus analyzing transcripts from videotapes? Or we may have a predictive question: "Can we generalize from something we have in hand to something months or even years away?"

We can also ask questions about the population. We have already seen and heard a number of issues that would relate to this. Any particular study uses a sample from a population and we could ask questions like can we generalize from a lower SES urban population to a middle class suburban population? Can we generalize from Caucasian students to other racial or ethnic or cultural backgrounds or other language backgrounds as Willy was talking about? Or we may ask, "Can we generalize from heterogeneous achievement schools like the one in Ashman and Gillies' study to classrooms that are more homogeneous to schools that are more homogeneous?" "Can we generalize from schools with many opportunities for professional development for teachers to schools with few opportunities?" I would add to this list something from what we heard from Ken Tobin and Pam Moss: "Can we generalize to other school contexts, from science classes in Australia to Philadelphia, or considering other kinds of fifth grade mathematics classrooms?"

We can also talk about generalizations made from the particular way the treatment is implemented, so we might call this ecological validity. In the context of the Ashman and Gillies study, we may ask, "Can we generalize from heterogeneous groups that are used in this particular treatment to homogeneous cooperative groups, or some other kind of grouping arrangement?" "Can we generalize from four person groups to other group sizes?" Or, "Can we generalize from open-ended activities to more structured tasks and activities?" These are questions that are usually not considered in the context of reporting results from any particular study.

In conclusion, we have seen just a little bit about how generalizability helps us make the sampling framework explicit both for reliability and validity related concerns. It helps us pay attention to and hopefully address such questions as how the sampling is performed, what the universes of possibilities are, what the desired generalizations are and, very importantly, what the limits are on the generalizations that we want to make?

Kadriye Ercikan

One of the things I struggled with, and which I saw throughout the chapters, is this: Here we are trying to break the boundaries of and polarization between what is called qualitative or quantitative research. Yet it is quite challenging to move away from this terminology that often has inaccurate meaning attached to them. In other words, by qualitative research we do not really quite understand what the research is about and that does not mean that it does not have any statistics or numbers involved in them.

Given that qualitative researchers may count objects, and numbers in categories and even use descriptive statistics, do quantitative and qualitative labels serve a useful function for education researchers? Should we continue to use these labels? Do you have suggestions for alternatives including not having dichotomous label possibilities?

Margaret Eisenhart

The comments that I make in my chapter and the ones that I am going to make here are addressed primarily to an audience unlike the one that we have been sort of assuming. I think we have been assuming that generalization or generalizability is a good thing, and there are certainly people in the so-called qualitative community who have challenged that, criticized that, and do not believe that. My remarks are aimed at that community more so than the community that is already convinced that generalization or generalizability is a good thing. So let me start by saying that the labels quantitative and qualitative have been very convenient shorthand notions for identifying methodological expertise or preference, for developing methods courses and requirements for students, for marketing research texts and handbooks, and even for making a few careers here and there.

The distinction between quantitative and qualitative research certainly has been useful in opening up space for non-experimental and non-survey research methods in education. Arguably, the distinction has contributed to the development of post-positivist and post-interpretivist approaches to educational research. Now the problem with the distinction is that it has been constructed and enforced to create this artificial boundary. As Kadriye and others have already said, the two terms are misleading in their basic connotations in that both quantitative and qualitative work is both, and there is an element in every kind of research of deciding what is relevant, that is the qualitative side, and what needs to be counted, that is the quantitative side. Dichotomizing the distinctions encourages educational researchers—and I think unfortunately it encourages novices particularly—to think in terms of one or the other of these and not both. So people decide that they want to learn one or the other, or that they are suited for one or the other, or they are more competent in one or the other. Worst of all they come to believe or act as if one is superior to the other in a general way. Each type has come to be known in terms of these kinds of essentialist hegemonic categories that I think many of us would object to in our theoretical work where we get one thing is for positivist, another is for interpretivist; one is for measurement, the other is for interpretation; one is for prediction, the other is for diagnosis; one is to test hypotheses, the other is to generate hypotheses; and so on.

It has been more than 15 years ago that my colleague Ken Howe and other people have said (e.g., Howe & Eisenhart, 1990) that we should get over this qualitative/quantitative debate. But we do not seem to get over it, and I think that is crazy. The concept of generalization is one casualty of a forced choice between quantitative and qualitative research. Boundary setting between quantitative and qualitative research has included the proposition that quantitative research is generalizable and qualitative research is not. Even if you look at very recent textbooks in which qualitative research is discussed, many of them say that qualitative research can not be generalized, does not want to be generalized, should not be generalized, and so on.

On the other side, I should say that most quantitative textbooks claim that quantitative research is generalizable and go on to explain what that means and how you do that. Interestingly, I would say that survey research is probably the best tool we have for generalization. It clearly straddles the line between qualitative and quantitative, but that is another story. So in my chapter I argue that differentiating qualitative and quantitative research is wrong-headed, and it has contributed to some very unfortunate tendencies particularly, I think, in the qualitative community because we are convincing ourselves somehow that it is reasonable to say that we do not want to generalize when we do qualitative research.

I submit that there are at least seven very legitimate, well-used strategies by which qualitative researchers do generalize their findings and that we, I think it is too bad that we are ignoring these in having such attention on the conversation about whether it is qualitative or quantitative and how you divide up that pie. I do not have time to give you details of these seven. But I do want to say briefly that probabilistic ways of generalizing, transferable ways of generalizing, user-oriented, grounded, synthetic, meta-analytic, and theoretical are seven ways in which researchers have consistently, historically generalized.

- Probabilistic would be when a case or a set of cases has been chosen according to probabilistic sampling criteria.
- Transferable would be when a good argument can be made that findings in one site because of the characteristics of the site are likely transferable to another site.
- User-oriented generalizability is when potential users of the information provide evidence of the utility of the information.
- Grounded would be when the findings have been developed through a process of analytic induction such that any negative cases are subsumed or explained in some way.
- Synthesis and meta-analysis across multiple cases is a very underexplored area among qualitative researchers.
- And theoretical, which to me is the most important, is when a theory can be extended to new cases or refined in light of them.

So I have to ask what would happen if we stopped dividing up the educational research world into qualitative and quantitative parts. First of all, I would be missing a lot of words in this talk that I just gave you. We have that problem; and it is not a trivial one. But it is very important to try to overcome this distinction. One way that I can imagine doing it is to focus on research traditions in the forms that they are actually practiced. So let us talk about experimentation or ethnography or regression analysis or critical analysis and those kinds of things rather than trying to categorize them as one thing or another. We practice our craft, our research, in much more specific ways than labeling ourselves as qualitative or quantitative researchers. We would be well-advised to talk in those terms rather than these larger global terms. I submit that we would think differently about the methodological possibilities and productive combinations of methods needed to answer complex research questions if we were not burdened with the limitations of this dichotomy. We would think differently and more productively about the research skills that our graduate students need to have and the methodological possibilities in their work and for their work if we were not handicapped by this distinction that we make not only in the way we talk about research but also in the way we structure our graduate programs for training and research.

Doing away with the qualitative/quantitative distinction would remove at least some of the barriers to mixed-methods research. I know in my own program that my students tell me that we never talk about mixed-methods research, and I feel like we talk about it all the time. But somehow they get the impression that if I am talking, then it must be qualitative; if Willy is talking, it must be quantitative or something like that. Doing away with the quantitative/qualitative distinction is something that I hope that the so-called qualitative researchers will take up as a challenge for them in their work. I do not think that we have to be embarrassed about the way we do generalization or whether we can do it or not. I think there is plenty of ways to do it and I really cannot imagine that we do research solely for the purpose of having one particular case. I really do not believe that that is why we are involved in this profession.

Bob Mislevy

I was trained as a statistician. Jim Gee was trained as a linguist in discourse analysis and Pamela Moss thinks in both of those ways. In our NSF-sponsored project, I think at the first meeting, she could talk to Jim and she could talk to me, but Jim and I could not talk to each other yet. So we had to learn how to do that. And it was a lot of fun.

One of the most important things that we learned was that despite very different appearances in the sorts of things that the three of us did, there are some deep underlying similarities. So those are some of the things that I would like to mention here. There are three main points. The first is that there is no such thing as quantitative analysis without a qualitative frame underlying it. To have a strict dichotomy would mean that the quantitative analysis does not really mean anything. The second bullet point is that analyses by Hans-Georg Gadamer and John Tukey have more in common than might meet the eye at first blush. Gadamer might do a hermeneutic analysis on the meaning of a philosophical track. John Tukey might use statistical models to analyze the impact of a volcano in Japan on the waves washing up on the shore of British Columbia.

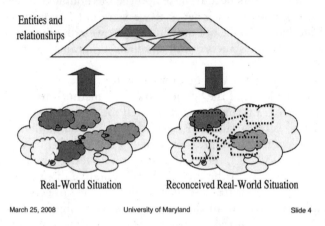

Figure 12.1 Entities and relationships in educational research.

They look pretty different on the surface but it turns out that they are not. And third is a project that needs to be done: there is no quantitative analysis without a qualitative frame. All the quantitative models that we talk about are overlaid over some substantive model that concerns the concepts, the entities, the relationships, and the events that they are supposed to be about. They are tools to help us understand patterns in these terms. In Figure 12.1, I feature a diagram that sometimes we use in our classes to talk about this.

We have real-world situations down in the lower left. There are clouds there. Everything is a little bit fuzzy compared to what is up in that middle layer, the layer of entities and relationships—which is much more crisply defined but that is what we use to understand the real world situation. In the lower right is our reconception of that real-world situation and you see that some of the clouds are still there. They have dotted rectangles around them, and those are our reconceptions. They are not quite perfect; they do not totally fit. There are some other dotted rectangles in the lower right that did not even show up in the lower left. Those are the generalizations. You see the dotted lines connecting those rectangles. Those are relationships that are suggested by our substantive understanding of that situation. So what is down in the lower right is by necessity a generalization coming through that substantive plane.

Now in some problems it is possible to gainfully employ mathematical quantitative relationships to help us understand things that are happening in the conceptual plane and also to help us analyze how well that conceptual plane accords with what is happening in the real-world situation. In the lower right there is an empty box with the dotted rectangle. That is something that we did not see in the situation that we would be led to expect to some degree based on our model, based on our quantitative model overlaid on our substantive understanding. We do a study. We go out and we find out what really happened in that situation. Does it look anything like what was expected given that box or not? How much variation is there? How often do we get surprised? Generalizability analysis is part of how we answer questions like that.

Another thing that was noted in Pamela's talk was that there are many different levels and aspects that we might be addressing with quantitative models in real world situations. And it is important to mention that the quantitative/qualitative distinction is much too stark.

In educational research, here in the secondary bullets, there are three really distinct things. One is using quantitative reasoning to think about the nature of the real world counterparts. For example, Joel Mitchell talks about whether things like mathematical ability are quantitative properties of humans. That is quite debatable, and you may come one way or another but that is a very distinct way of thinking about quantitative reasoning. When you look at relationships among variables, and the variables that you have might include mathematics scores, you do not think that those are anything like extant measures of common properties among people. They are summaries of behaviors that have quite different ways of understanding where they come from. There is also the third bullet: probability model for the knowledge of the analyst. This means that we think about using quantitative methods to talk about what your evidentiary base is and how strongly that makes you believe something quite aside from how quantitative or qualitative the substance. And these can be involved in any combination in given studies. This is one source of confusion of qualitative and quantitative.

One thing the quantitative does is a disservice to understanding the nature of the arguments that are being made; and here is a point why I like Wyle's discussion about this being about arguments. What are the warrants for the arguments? What are the kinds of backing? Different arguments at different levels have different kinds of backing, some of which are qualitative and some of which are quantitative; and the quantitative ones can be addressing different aspects. On the point about the relationship between Gadamer and Tukey: they have in common that they are coming to some situation, some interpretation with concepts and models based on past experience. They are bringing these as frames to understand what is happening. Gadamer talks about the hermeneutic circle, where you are looking at the interplay between details of situations and the larger picture, the larger understanding. At a given point in time your provisional understanding helps you understand the details better. How do they fit in? Where do they not fit in? What does that tell you?

It turns out that if you look at Fred Mosteller and John Tukey's (1977) book Data Analysis and Regression, this is exactly the same kind of reasoning that they use to describe successive fitting of regression models. You fit a model to the situation with data, which helps you understand some of the patterns. You look at the residuals. What funny is going on? How does that improve your understanding? What is the next model? It is the same sort of circle going back and forth toward better coherence, toward better understanding, or toward better fit. That led us to our taxonomy of statisticians. And this is where some of the problems with quantitative/qualitative dichotomy come in. A bad statistician would be somebody who takes the data and the interpretations as given, takes them as extant, does not question where those numbers come, and looks at relationships as a purely statistical exercise. The mistake in this is when the statisticians and the policy makers they advise mistake that model for the real world and then base policy on that. That problem was discussed in Scott's interesting book Seeing like a State. A good statistician carries out the analyses but understands that interpretive interplay between the levels, what is happening on the ground, the interactions between kids and the teachers in the classrooms. The numbers are summaries. They are filtered summaries of that. Your understanding of these relations helps you come back and understand the ground level as well. So a good statistician does not accept, but, in a sense, problematizes, takes into account that level of filtering. And great statisticians—and I include people here like John Tukey, Edward Jenning, and Lee Cronbach—do work at the level of the models. Their insights in this circular going back, cycling to the data, what makes sense, what does not, lead to new insights and new ways of thinking at the lower levels. Sometimes they lead to insights that people working only at one level might miss. Here is the project that needs to be done.

In summary then, what I would like to see would be a larger frame for understanding research in terms of arguments, in educational research the kinds of warrants we have, the kinds of generalizations we make, a larger taxonomy so we can understand what are the various types of generalizations, what are the kinds of backing, which kinds of them and where and which types of research do use quantitative reasoning and in what ways. This is the way forward, for going beyond the unhelpful quantitative versus qualitative dichotomization. This I think is a good idea. I do not have the time or the money to do it. But I put it out there for the next generation.

Commentary: Dialectics, Contradictions, and Dialogicity

Wolff-Michael Roth

I am in an odd situation here right now in that I am asked to provide an overview and do that in a monologue when the whole intent of the book was to bring together people who do different kinds of research. In the book, we attempt to bring this more dialogic aspect into parts of the book. Rather than an overview going over the same terrain, I decided to take another step back and make a few comments with the intent to ratchet up: much like Gregory Bateson (1972) does with his metalogues, I talk about previous talk—i.e., the present speakers—to take us to a new level of understanding.

My first comment is based on my reading of Pierre Bourdieu (1992) and his project of a reflexive sociology. About thinking about what we are doing: one of Bourdieu's comments that has stuck in my mind for a long time is about how many in our community have become mono-maniacs of method. What happens is that the methods come to drive the research rather than the interesting questions that we have, which are the things we really want to answer independent of the method. Bourdieu suggests that people sometimes feel very good about them-selves when they combine things like ethnomethodology and discourse analysis or ethnography with some quantitative work. But they really have not made progress because they have not asked, "What is the object of the research?" and then engaged critically with the object, even redefining and critically analyzing the object before using this or that method.

Second, more than 100 years ago Émile Durkheim stated an apho-rism and the aphorism deals with the objectivity of social facts that we encounter in everyday life. And this objectivity of social facts is sociol-ogy's fundamental phenomenon. Now, where do we find this objectiv-ity of social facts? The answer depends on the grain size that we take. Imagine looking at a river. You are standing far away and all you see is a laminar flow, but when you come closer you will note that there are actually some back currents, that there is detail that an ethnographer might identify. When you go even closer you will find—within what we thought was laminar flow and laminar back currents—a lot of eddies. When you ask, "Is the river an assembly of eddies or is it laminar flow?," then the answer depends on how close we go to the river. Similar with our research: our research identifies social facts but it does so at various grain sizes. Which grain size you have to or want to choose depends on the phenomenon that you are interested in; and I want to come back to that in my second point from here when I address the use issue that Lyle began with.

One of the questions that we can ask is "What more?" and for the last few weeks Ken Tobin and I have had this discussion. "What more?" Well, there are a number of levels that we can ask, "What more?" For example, to someone who is interested in policy analysis or in patterns of large populations and does some quantitative research or experimental research, we can ask, "What more?" And if this person worked together with someone like Margaret Eisenhart, then Margaret might say, well when you look at that there is meaning and there is difference within this larger picture that you have designed. And the converse is also true. If Margaret does some research, or Ken, then we could also ask "What more?" A policy analyst or someone who does research that looks at marginal populations might answer that there are patterns that you can identify that are very similar in Los Angeles and in New York and in Miami or Philadelphia.

But on a second level, you can also ask, "What more?" When you take the second level, then you will see that both what we used to call quantitative and qualitative research make certain assumptions about patterns and investigate these independent of articulating the processes or methods that produce the patterns. In any event, what both forms of analyses leave in the background is doing the work of structure, explaining the work required for us to identify the structures that Durkheim outlined as constituting the objectivity of social facts. Harold Garfinkel (e.g., 2002), in his ethnomethodological project, attempts to specify that "What more?," namely the *work* that a quantitative or qualitative or mixed methods person engages in and draws on without being aware of. For example, a researcher studying line ups—i.e., queues—requires the same competencies that allows us to form line ups and that allows us to recognize that something is wrong with the line up or that someone has not obeyed the implicit rules in line ups (e.g., jumped a queue). This is Garfinkel's answer to the "What more?," that is, specifying the underlying knowledge that researchers have to share with the research participants to be able to identify any useful pattern in the behavior of the participants.

We have another comment here that is especially salient because there are people who do design experiments to answer salient research questions independent of whether these ask for quantitative statistical work or qualitative work to be completed. In fact, it is a combination of the two because as soon as you have these tools available you can ask questions independent of the grain size and whatever grain size is important at the moment you pursue with appropriate method.

The next question of course is, "What for?" "What is this research for?" And Lyle Bachman articulated this question quite eloquently in his chapter; and he did so again this morning. Ken Tobin also makes a research-use argument by looking at urban classrooms and what they, teachers and students, need to know to be able to transform their everyday life and to make it better. That is, Ken is interested in the kind of knowledge required for these stakeholders to make their everyday life better for everyone so that they can come out of it with more. And Allen Luke, who is not here today, also asks a question about research use, but he asks a question at a different level: "What kind of knowledge does a policy maker need to make policy decisions?" These decisions are not the same as those that a class of students and their teacher have to make. The kind of decisions that Ken Tobin pursues with the students and teachers he works with and the ones that Allen Luke being associated with the Minister of Education in Queensland has to pursue are very different in scale and grain size. When you look around yourself in the world, you will see that there is a polyphony of inferences and uses; so you do not have to want to overcome the dichotomy if you accept that there is a polyphony of inference questions and uses. You have to accept that people choose the methods that they need.

How do we overcome dichotomies? Well, if you look at the history of thought, you will come across the idea that Hegel sort of turned into a science: dialectics. And dialectics is not really about having opposites and playing them out against one another in a "from-thesis-to-antithesis-to-yield-synthesis" manner. Georg Wilhelm Friedrich Hegel and Karl Marx suggested that we actually need to think in terms of higher-order, all encompassing units and what seem to be diametrical opposites are really one-sided reflections of the whole, just like wave and particle character are one-sided depictions of the phenomenon of light. Hegel, Marx, and, especially relevant to education, the Russian psychologist Lev Semenovich Vygotsky, view that we search for a higher-order unit. All the dichotomies that we can identify are one-sided or partial reflections of this whole and therefore cannot represent the whole in and by themselves. For example, for Vygotsky "word meaning" was a whole, which is only one-sidedly expressed in and by speech and thought. These one-sided expressions can be thought as inner contradictions in and of the higher unit.

And my final comment therefore concerns the question, "How do we overcome these unavoidable inner contradictions in an irreducible unit?" Here I point to Mikhail Bakhtin (e.g., 1986), who also works with materialist dialectics. Actually, he says that "mine is not a dialectical approach" because he sees in dialectics a formalism. In Bakhtin, you will find an alternate term: dialogics. And dialogics means talking, talking together, communicating. We do not understand a conversation when we thinking about two independent people speaking. Rather, because each person speaks for the other, using the words that came from the other, and that in speaking return to the other, only the encompassing unit of dialogicity provides for the inherent connections between consecutive utterances. It is between speakers so we can only understand meaning if we look at the speaker and the listener at the same time—which then comes back to our theme for this book, namely bringing people who have done different kinds of approach back together to speak to and with one another.

Now if we want to speak together, we have to be both good speakers and good listeners because the speaker speaks to the listener and the listener pays respect in attending to the speaker. We look at what we are trying to do through dialogics—which is not a dialogue, a dialogue is just talking. If two or more individuals have an argument and each person is only talking and not listening to the other, then we are no step further with our conversation. To get any further with this debate about quantitative and qualitative research and the level of generalization we can make, we need to engage in the kind of dialogic approach that Bakhtin talks about. That is, meaning is there and that the kind of meaning that we make wherever we come from, whatever position we have been taking before that we open up and become speakers for other people and listeners to other people. It is only in that way, in this transaction of speaking/listening, that we will be able to move further and step out of the dichotomization in the pursuit of a greater goal. And the ultimate goal that we have, as a society, is this: taking control of our conditions and to improve them so that our lives as educators, the lives of society as a whole, the lives of the students and teachers that we are working with, that all these lives are improved. And that is what really matters, rather than the quibbling about matters of quantitative or qualitative research.

Comments

Lyle Bachman

I just want to respond to Michael's question "What more?" I think it is an excellent question. For me, the whole point of doing research is to try to convince people, other researchers, teachers, practitioners, that what we found is meaningful, has beneficial consequences and so on. So "What more?" can be answered by who it is we are trying to convince. Who are the stakeholders? So that other researchers who are doing the same kind of research that we are doing and published in the same journals may be perfectly satisfied with the kind of evidence that we present. But if we want to convince or persuade educators or practitioners that these results might actually have applications in the real world, that it might generalize to the real world, then we might need to provide more evidence. That could be either what we used to call quantitative or qualitative.

Pamela Moss

I don't know if I'm going to be able to say this very well because it feels a little abstract, but I am completely in support of what Margaret Eisenhart and others are saying about the problems with the qualitative/quantitative dichotomy. I am also completely in support of finding a way to move beyond that. I am worried about the notion that we need to do then is move beyond our differences. One of the points that Margaret made is this: We all work in our own research communities that have their own sense of concepts, issues, and problems that they deal with. Understanding those differences is really useful. So take hermeneutics, the thing that I have been working with. The hermeneutic circle is the cartoon version of hermeneutics. Bob Mislevy always talks about the cartoon version of psychometrics. There are many, and I cannot even name them all because I have not studied them enough, eddies and flows within hermeneutics that really raise instructive questions. Do we believe that there is a correct interpretation that resides in the intention of the author? Or do we believe that the interpretation is always shaped by the preconceptions, the situativity of the interpreter who is making the interpretations? If you take one or another of these issues, you are going to practice research somewhat differently, and I think the issues are interesting. Say, moving to the issue that Michael raised, I think it is sometimes useful to say that it is the question that should guide our choice of methods but the fact is that we are brought up in different traditions and the way we are brought up, the kinds of methods we study, shape the kinds of questions we can ask. So I am someone who was brought up in educational measurement but I have been hanging out with sociocultural theorists. I am starting to ask questions about students' identities and how they are positioned by certain practices in education. It would never have occurred to me to ask that question given the way that I was brought up. So I think certain dichotomies are really not very useful. I think difference is tremendously useful and I am frightened about a notion that expects us move to the grand synthesis. I think what we really need to do, picking up on what Michael said, is respect the differences that we have, listen really carefully to what we hear to see how those differences challenge our own perspective. And what we aim to do is collaborate. But I do not know that we aim to move toward an overall conception of what educational research is because our differences are resources.

Ken Tobin

Just a quick comment. Lyle said to me earlier on that perhaps one of the issues here is epistemological, and maybe he said ontological, and I think you could throw in axiological. So the way that people look at the world makes a difference in all of this. We had an issue in our journal, Cultural Studies of Science Education, with the idea of methodology. Everybody wanted to write about methodology and actually what they seemed to mean was method. When Pam was talking earlier, she finished up with a fairly provocative comment to me because I thought to myself, I wonder if she means methodology as she said, or whether she really means method, which I think she meant. And then I thought maybe she means methodology, which makes it a really profound comment. Speaking of dichotomies there is a dialectical relationship between methodology and method; and it is really very important. If we can think about that dialectical relationship as we think about these issues of research—and when you get into this if we are going to have these conversations that Pam speaks about, conversations over difference—then what is that going to look like? Is it going to be some sort of colonization where we convince others to be like us and we build coalitions around sameness? Or can we build coalitions around difference? (Which I think she is advocating which is much tougher to do but maybe it contains the seeds for production.) I think one of the things that happens is that people speak and you cannot find listeners. The reason you do not find listeners is because of these axiological, epistemological, and ontological commitments. So the act of not listening makes your position incommensurable.

Bob Mislevy

I would want to mention that where you have different grain sizes or different methodologies that lead to different policy implications those are both particularly fruitful places to investigate and are particularly important things. For example, different ways of thinking about assessment that lead to contradictory policies. Differences are great. Studying how different approaches lead to these differences, I think Pamela's point of looking at how people are conceptualizing situations can make you aware of what you are leaving out of your own models and your own theories. And that has a very productive effect of saying, "What does my model not tell me? What are some hidden assumptions that are going on here? Just what might be going on that leads us to different policies here?" And I think a very nice goal would be analyses across different levels or different grain sizes that aren't the same, they are not going to be, but you would like them to have a certain consistency rather than contradictory results. Contradictory results are important ones to pay attention to partly for us as researchers because they are fun and they are productive but partly also because this is where real people are spending real money in teaching real kids.

Lyle Bachman

Both Margaret and Pamela mentioned this whole idea of how we have been brought up as researchers as part of our education. I just want to share an anecdote from our department of applied linguistics. We have people like myself who do measurement and statistics, we have people who do conversational analysis, and we have people who do ethnography and a whole range of things. We admit students into our department to work with individual people, and that is the way I think it is in a lot of places. So we end up with students who are brought up to do this with so-and-so and that with another person. And we saw this sort of thing happening in our students, that they were being brought up to do one thing. They were never questioning why they were doing that but they always questioned why those assessment people over there just want to crunch numbers? Or how come those CA [conversation analysis] people just want to do this fuzzy stuff. So we decided to eliminate all the course requirements except for one and we designed a course that is basically epistemology for applied linguistics. The whole point of the course is to raise these issues beyond method, beyond methodology, epistemology, ontology, how do we know what we know, and how do we know when we are done as researchers. The whole idea is then when they do work with their individual mentors hopefully they will have a little broader perspective on how to relate what they do to other methodologies and other approaches in our field.

Kadriye Ercikan

As I hear Pamela talk about how we are brought up and the culture we grow up in, I come to think about something happening at my university, where we are in the midst of discussing courses about research methodology. Perhaps a subsequent book should be about how we raise graduate students to break the boundaries between the so-called quantitative and qualitative distinctions. At the same time, to do this in an informed way, I am an advocate of learning methodology but in terms of how the different methods fit together. To fit them together, we have some work to do. So I appreciate Bob's comment about the project, about understanding how we make generalizations, bringing it back to the issue about generalizing and generalizability in educational research, at least in a descriptive way. I appreciate his comment about how we all make different generalizations from different perspectives, and from a socio-linguistic perspective what we leave out in a model that is so popularly used in one way or another. So I think there is some work to be done to describe, if not make any attempt, to bring things together but to understand the similarities, the differences, and the usefulness of differences.

Question from the Audience: Those who are supporting the unification of these two fossilized dichotomies, functionally how do you go about doing that? I'll give an example, which I think is very appropriate. Almost 10 years ago we had this chat about validity and doing away with terminology but it is still being used today. So short of an Orwellian "you speak" kind of thing how do we functionally make this work?

Bob Mislevy

Rather than thinking about unifying these, I think a broader and more synthetic framework that encompasses them is more productive. Especially work that draws upon that framework shows how there are some things that were formerly called qualitative and some that are using quantitative methods to fit into the argument. So what I see is how you structure arguments, what tools you make, why those tools are justified by the goals you have, certain kinds of observations, certain kinds of purposes and leaving quantitative/qualitative distinctions in the dust but backing up arguments. And if that is the way people talk and the way they think, eventually the people who want to argue about it will not find anyone who wants to argue with them.

Ken Tobin

I would argue that the best way to learn about research is to do research. I like what Michael said about focusing on the object. I think that you need to attract graduate students with research squads, where people love to do research by working with others. In my physics days, things were as Lyle articulated them for his department: If you wanted to do astrophysics, you worked with John Galeda; if you wanted to do something else, you worked with someone else. In education we need to move in a direction where we learn the methods and the methodologies that go with what you want to learn about.

Wolff-Michael Roth

You probably heard from Pamela's and my comments that the point is not to create a mish-mash. The point is to admit difference, specialties, and expertise. We need to open up the dialogue so that people with very different expertise can decide to work together rather than saying, "This doesn't make sense" or "that doesn't make sense."

Lyle Bachman

I would like to use an analogy from building. If you need a screw, you use a screw and not a nail. If you need a nail, you don't use a screwdriver. And if you want to saw a board, you don't use a wrench. But if you want to build a house, you need all of these things.

Margaret Eisenhart

I would just add that Lyle made the comment that they had done away with some the research courses in his department and, instead, offered just one course. I would say that I think the idea of that course is really good. But I also think that it would be worthwhile for those of us who are committed to these different kinds of research traditions to teach at a more microlevel "What is ethnography?," "What is a case study?," "What is an experiment?," "What is a quasi-experiment?," and those kinds of things that have been with us a long time. We have a very rich and robust tradition in these methods. We senior faculty ought to take more responsibility for insisting that students take courses in those things whether it is in our department or someplace else so that they really learn. Not that everybody has to learn everything: that is not going to work. But I would say that students could learn two or three of these methods in some detail so that they could understand what is being privileged and what is being closed off in these various things. It would give them a much broader, more informed way of talking about what needs to be done next and about interacting with each other because they would have a more expansive sense of what is involved in each particular one.

Pamela Moss

Just to add that I do not have a solution, but I think there is also political work to be done. I do not want to go too far with that, but I think there is this notion of academic capital and some of us have more of it than others. There are some of us who are closer to the field of power with the language you use. So it is easier to get funding for certain kinds of research and, if you are someone who tends to get funding for that kind of research, your ideas get into the prominence. Or you get appointed to a panel on the National Academy of Sciences and get to participate in the writing of a white paper that makes certain statements. Or you get appointed to the Testing Standards and you get to say what validity is, at least you know for 10 years, and then it is going to be somebody else's turn to say what validity is. I think we really need to take those kinds of political aspects of our professional work into account. And I do not know how to do that. I am incredibly naïve. I do not know the extent to which one should do that. But they are there, they are operating, and attending to them is more useful than not attending.

Willy Solano-Flores

Here is a practical suggestion. I propose that at the end of this session we write some work for AERA and push for a Division D and a Division G joint symposium for the next AERA meeting. Essentially the idea for this came up when I realized that whenever I propose an AERA paper for Division D with the word "culture" in the title, it will be rejected and it will be forwarded to Division G in spite of the fact that what I was writing about was measuring and cultural issues. So it was like that the word "cultural" did not belong in Division D. Somehow we have to change the mentality not only of our students but also our own, and I think that we should start pressure to have those joint sessions next year.

References

Ashman, A. F., & Gillies, R. M. (1997). Children's cooperative behavior and interactions in trained and untrained work groups in regular classrooms. *Journal of School Psychology, 35*, 261–279.

Bakhtin, M. M. (1986). *Speech genres and other late essays*. Austin: University of Texas Press.

Bateson, G. (1972). *Steps to an ecology of mind*. New York: Ballantine.

Bourdieu, P. (1992). The practice of reflexive sociology (The Paris workshop). In P. Bourdieu & L. J. D. Wacquant (Eds.), *An invitation to reflexive sociology* (pp. 216–260). Chicago: University of Chicago Press.

Garfinkel, H. (2002). *Ethnomethodology's program: Working out Durkheim's aphorism*. Lanham, MD: Rowman & Littlefield.

Howe, K. R., & Eisenhart, M. A. (1990). Standards in qualitative (and quantitative) research: A prolegomenon. *Educational Researcher, 19*(4), 2–9.

Lampert, M. (2001). *Teaching problems and the problems of teaching*. New Haven, CT: Yale University Press.

Mosteller, F., & Tukey, J. W. (1977). *Data analysis and regression: A second course in statistics*. Reading, MA: Addison-Wesley.

Contributors

Lyle F. Bachman is Professor and Chair, Department of Applied Linguistics and TESL, University of California, Los Angeles. His current research interests include validation theory, issues in assessing the academic achievement and English proficiency of English language learners in schools, the interface between language testing research and second language acquisition research, the dialectic of abilities and contexts in language testing and educational performance assessment, and epistemological issues in applied linguistics research.

Betsy J. Becker is a professor of measurement and statistics in the Department of Educational Psychology and Learning Systems, College of Education, Florida State University, Tallahassee. Her primary research interest is in methodology for quantitative research synthesis, or meta-analysis, and she is currently developing and studying methods for summarizing series of correlation matrices and regression models.

Margaret Eisenhart is University Distinguished Professor and Charles Professor of Education at the University of Colorado, Boulder. Her research focuses on the understandings of gender, race, and academic knowledge that young people construct inside and outside of school and on applications of ethnographic methodology in educational research. In recent years, much her research has focused on the experiences of girls and women in science and technology, and much of her writing and speaking has focused standards for qualitative research in education.

Kadriye Ercikan is an associate professor of measurement and research methods in the department of Educational and Counseling Psychology and Special Education, at the University of British Columbia, Canada. Her research focuses on design, validity, and fairness issues in large-scale assessments and the links between validity of interpretations and research methods. In recent years her research focused on constructing data as a measurement activity, validity and comparability issues in multi-lingual assessments, assessment accountability and links among research questions, data and research inferences.

James P. Gee is the Tashia Morgridge Professor of Reading at the University of Wisconsin-Madison. His book *Sociolinguistics and Literacies* (1990) was one of the founding documents in the formation of the "New Literacies Studies," an interdisciplinary field devoted to studying language, learning, and literacy in an integrated way in the full range of their cognitive, social, and cultural contexts. His book *An Introduction to Discourse Analysis* (1999) brings together his work on a method for studying communication in its cultural settings, an approach that has been widely influential over the last two decades.

Allan Luke is professor of education at Queensland University of Technology, Brisbane, Queensland. He is author and editor of numerous volumes, chapters, articles, Australian state government curriculum reforms and policies. *Struggles over Difference: Curriculum, Texts and Pedagogy in the Asia-Pacific* (with Yoshiko Nozaki and Roger Openshaw, SUNY Press) received the 2005 AERA Curriculum Studies Book Award.

Robert J. Mislevy is a professor of measurement and statistics at the University of Maryland, College Park. His work has included a multiple-imputation approach to integrate sampling and psychometric models in the National Assessment of Educational Progress (NAEP), simulation-based assessment of design and troubleshooting in computer networks with Cisco Systems. His honors include the Raymond B. Cattell Early Career Award for Programmatic Research and the National Council of Measurement in Education's Award for Technical Contributions to Educational Measurement.

Pamela A. Moss is a professor in the University of Michigan's School of Education. Her research agenda focuses on validity theory, educational assessment as a social practice, and the assessment of teaching. She is co-founder and co-editor (with Mark Wilson and Paul DeBoeck) of the journal, *Measurement: Interdisciplinary Research and Perspectives,* and is editing a 2007 NSSE Yearbook entitled *Evidence and Decision Making.*

Wolff-Michael Roth is Lansdowne Professor of Applied Cognitive Science at the University of Victoria, British Columbia, Canada. After graduate training in physics and statistics in the social sciences, he taught statistics and interpretive research methods for the past 15 years. His research crosses disciplinary boundaries and is published in education and its subfields science, mathematics, and curriculum studies; qualitative research methods; sociology; applied linguistics; and epistemology. He has authored and edited over 20 books, more than 270 peer-reviewed articles, and over 100 book chapters.

Richard J. Shavelson is the Margaret Jacks Professor of Education, Professor of Psychology, Senior Fellow in the Stanford Institute for the Environment, and former I. James Quillen Dean of the School of Education at Stanford University, Palo Alto, California. Before joining Stanford, he was dean of the Graduate School of Education and professor of statistics at the University of California, Santa Barbara. His publications include *Statistical Reasoning for the Behavioral Sciences, Generalizability Theory: A Primer* (with Noreen Webb), and *Scientific Research in Education* (edited with Lisa Towne).

Guillermo Solano-Flores is associate professor of bilingual education and English as a second language at the University of Colorado, Boulder. He specializes in educational measurement and the linguistic and cultural aspects of testing. His research examines ways in which linguistics and psychometrics can be used in combination to develop improved models for both the testing of linguistically diverse populations in international test comparisons and the testing of linguistic minorities.

Kenneth Tobin is Presidential Professor at the Graduate Center of the City University of New York. In 2004 he was recognized by the National Science Foundation as a *Distinguished Teaching Scholar* and by the Association for the Education of Teachers of Science as *Outstanding Science Teacher Educator of the Year*. Prior to commencing a career as a teacher educator, Ken taught high school science and mathematics in Australia and was involved in curriculum design. His research focuses on the teaching and learning of science in urban schools, which involve mainly African American students living in conditions of poverty.

Noreen M. Webb is a professor of social research methodology in the Graduate School of Education & Information Studies at the University of California in Los Angeles. Her research interests include classrooom processes related to learning outcomes, small-group problem solving, achievement testing in mathematics in science, aptitude-treatment interaction research and generalizability theory. Current research projects include (a) the effects of teacher practices and student participation on students' mathematics learning, (b) alignment of mathematics state-level standards and assessments, and (c) generalizability and validity.

Meng-Jia Wu is an assistant professor in the program in Research Methodology in the School of Education at Loyola University Chicago. She teaches introductory statistics and multivariate statistics. Her specialization is meta-analysis and she has conducted and consulted on different projects using meta-analytic techniques as well as other quantitative analyses in education and psychology fields. Her current interests focus on using missing data techniques to meta-analyze regression studies.

Index

A

Abstraction, 244–247, 248, 249

Academic capital, 293–294

Action, defined, 170

Activism, school-based research, 150, 164–168

  catalyzing educational improvements, 165–168

  student researchers, 164–165

  teacher researchers, 164–165

Agency, defined, 170

American Educational Research Association, 179, 180

Division D and Division G joint symposium, 294

Analogical reasoning, 5

Analytic generalization, 59–64

  sample-to-population generalization, 212

Analytic induction, 57–58

Argument structure, 143

Assessment use argument, 142

  structure, 143

Australia

  educational research, 183

  research and data-analytic capacity, 187

Australian Association for Research in Education, 183–184

Authenticity, forms, 126

Axiological commitments, 290

B

Bakhtin, Mikhail, 287–288

Behavioral measurements, generalizability theory, 14–15

  facet of measurement, 15

  universe of admissible observations, 15

Behaviorism, 177, 179, 180

Bourdieu, Pierre, 208, 285

Brazil, 162–164

C

Capital, defined, 170

Case-to-case generalization, 213

Catalytic authenticity, 126

Communication, cross-disciplinary project, 72–73

Conduct, defined, 171

Confirmability criterion, qualitative research, 238

Cooperative learning, generalizability theory

  dependability of measurements, 24–25

  example study, 22–27

  reliability, 23–24, 25–27

  reliability/validity relationship, 26–27

  validity, 23–24, 25–27

Core Research Program, Centre for Research in Pedagogy and Practice, Singapore, 189

Correlational research, sample-to-population generalization

  limitations in generalizing, 220–223, 225–227

Critical realism, educational research, 173–174, 186–199

  proposal, 196–198

  triangulating evidence, 194–195

Cross-disciplinary project, communication, 72–73

Crossed facet designs, 18–19

Cultural sociology, 151

Cultural theory, theoretical generalization, 62

Cultural-historical activity theory, 1, 123, 247–258

Culture
  defined, 151
  individual-collective dialectic, 247–249
  sample-to-population generalization,
    217–218
Curriculum, graduate students, 291, 293

D
Data collection, 105
Data evaluation, 106–108
Decision study, generalizability theory,
    17–18
  crossed facet designs, 18–19
  fixed facet designs, 20
  nested facet designs, 18–19
  object of measurement, 20–21
  principle of symmetry, 20–21
  random facet designs, 20
  study design, 18–21
  universe of generalization, 17
  universe score, 17–18
Decisions, generalizability, 13–14
Decontextualization, 191–192
Dependability of measurements, reliabil-
    ity, 24–25
Dialectics, 287
  defined, 171
  dialectical perspectives on general-par-
    ticular relationship, 247–258
Dialogic approach of Bakhtin, 287–288
Discourse analysis, validity, 73
Durkheim, Emile, 285

E
Education
  perceptions, 128–129
    entities of interest, 131–132
    factors affecting researcher's percep-
      tions, 129
    indices, 130
    phenomena representations, 129–130
    signs, 130
    symbolosphere, 131
    symbols, 130
  phenomena, 128–129
    entities of interest, 131–132
    factors affecting researcher's percep-
      tions, 129
    indices, 130
    phenomena representations, 129–130
    signs, 130
    symbolosphere, 131
    symbols, 130

Educational assessment
  evidence, 191
    evidentiary arguments, 69–74
      assessment design argument, 69–71
      assessment use argument, 69–71
      structure, 69–71, 70
    inferences, 69–74
      assessment design argument, 69–71
      assessment use argument, 69–71
      structure, 69–71
  psychological perspective, 71
Educational policy
  narrative function, 177
  pedagogical alignment, 178
  resource flow, 177
Educational progressivism, 183
Educational research
  Australia, 183
  beyond qualitative-quantitative divide,
    2–6, 239
  beyond research field, 161–162
  characterized, 180
  continuum vs. dichotomy of generaliza-
    tion, 2
  critical realism, 173–174, 186–199
    proposal, 196–198
    triangulating evidence, 194–195
  epistemological and methodological
    toolkits, 185–186
  generalization, 3–4
    characterized, 211–212
    naturalistic version, 208
    positivist version, 207
  improving praxis, 161
  normative reframings, 185–186
  parameters of design, 180
  polarizing into quantitative vs. qualita-
    tive categories, 2
  policy issues, 173–178
    history, 178–186
    neoliberal U.S. public policy dis-
      course, 175
    remaking policy, 176–178
  political debates, 4
  producing theory, 160–161
  quantitative vs. qualitative approaches,
    1–2
  research as culture, 151
  rising-up with, 168–169
  teacher wait time, 153–154, 155
  value, 153–154
Educative authenticity, 126
Effect sizes, meta-analysis, 101

Efficacy-oriented research, social life, 163–164
Empirical generalization, 59–64
Empirical research
　characterized, 127
　generalizability
　　decision consequences, 140–141
　　decisions, 140–141
　　in education, 137–142
　　interpretation meaningfulness, 138
　　observation consistency, 137–138
　　qualitative research meaningfulness, 139–140
　　quantitative research meaningfulness, 138–139
　　report consistency, 137–138
　　researcher responsibility, 141–142
　qualitative research, 128–133
　　commonalities across approaches, 132–133
　　generalization as inferential links, 133–137
　quantitative research, 128–133
　　commonalities across approaches, 132–133
　　generalization as inferential links, 133–137
　research use arguments, 142–143
　　characterized, 142–143
　　defined, 142
Encounter, defined, 171
English Language Learners, testing
　as stochastic process, 41–48
　cognition and language, 34, 35
　conceptual basis, 33
　context variation, 39–41
　evidence generalization, 41
　general assessment framework, 34–36
　generalizability theory, 36–37
　interpretation, 34, 35
　language variation, 39–41
　language-related sources of measurement error, 38–39
　multidisciplinary perspective, 33–34
　observation, 34, 35
　population specification, 39–41
　score generalizability, 40–41
　score variation, 39–41
　sociolinguistic perspective, 37–39
　stochastic model, 42–43, 44
Epistemological commitments, 290
Epistemology for applied linguistics, 291
Equity, 190–191

Ethical neutrality, 177
Ethnography, 59–64
　generalizing from, 53, 157
Eugenics, 179
Evidence, 81–83, 84
　educational assessment, 191
　epistemological limits, 191–194
　psychological survey instruments, 191
　technical limits, 191–194
　what constitutes, 186–187
Evidence generalization, 41
Evidence-based policy, 178–179
　triangulating evidence, 194–195
Evidentiary arguments
　educational assessment, 69–74
　assessment design argument, 69–71, 70
　assessment use argument, 69–71, 70
　structure, 69–71
　inferences, 79
Experiential generalization, 244–247, 248, 249
Experimental design, 3
External generalization, probabilistic generalization, 54
External validity, 10
　generalizability, 101

F
Factory model, 179
Field, defined, 171
Fixed facet designs, 20

G
Gender differences
　mathematics, 211
　sample-to-population generalization, 227–231
　　limitations, 227–231
General-particular dialectic, 247–258
　rethinking relationship, 207–209
Generalizability, 3–4, 149. See also Specific type
　autobiographical approach, 150–151, 153, 157–160, 164–165, 168
　changing theoretical frameworks, 150–151, 153, 157–160, 164–165, 168
　continuum vs. dichotomy, 5
　decisions, 13–14
　empirical research
　　decision consequences, 140–141
　　decisions, 140–141
　　in education, 137–142

Generalizability (*continued*)
  interpretation meaningfulness, 138
  observation consistency, 137–138
  qualitative research meaningfulness,
    139–140
  quantitative research meaningfulness,
    138–139
  report consistency, 137–138
  researcher responsibility, 141–142
  external validity, 101
  importance, 211
  levels, 4
  meta–analysis, 101–115
    conventional meta-analysis, 102–110
    data analysis, 108–109
    data collection, 105
    data evaluation, 106–108
    incorporating quantitative and quali-
      tative research, 110–111, 112
    interpretation, 109–110
    methodology bias, 107
    presentation, 109–110
    problem formulation, 102–104
    publication bias, 105
    qualitative studies, 110–115
    quantitative synthesis, 102–110
    randomized controlled trials, 106
  plausibility, contrasted, 158–159
  presence/absence of, 4
  quantitative research synthesis,
    101–115
  repetition, contrasted, 149–150
  research synthesis, 101–115
  research use arguments, 127–147
  sample size, 211
  validity, forms of arguments, 271–278
  value of, 4
Generalizability study, 15–17
  crossed designs, 18–19
  facets of measurement, 15, 16
  nested facet designs, 18–19
  object of measurement, 16, 20–21
  principle of symmetry, 20–21
  random facet designs, 20
  sources of score variation, 17
Generalizability theory, 13–32
  behavioral measurements, 14–15
    facet of measurement, 15, 16
    universe of admissible observations,
      15
  cooperative learning
    dependability of measurements,
      24–25

  example study, 22–27
  reliability, 23–24, 25–27
  reliability/validity relationship, 26–27
  validity, 23–24, 25–27
  decision study, 17–18
    crossed facet designs, 18–19
    fixed facet designs, 20
    nested facet designs, 18–19
    object of measurement, 20–21
    principle of symmetry, 20–21
    random facet designs, 20
    study design, 18–21
    universe of generalization, 17
    universe score, 17–18
  defined, 14
  English Language Learners testing,
    36–37
  generalizability study, 15–17, 16
    components of score variation, 16–17
    crossed designs, 18–19
    facets of measurement, 16
    fixed facet designs, 20
    nested facet designs, 18–19
    object of measurement, 16, 20–21
    principle of symmetry, 20–21
    random facet designs, 20
    sources of score variation, 17
    study design, 18–21
  peer-directed learning
    dependability of measurements,
      24–25
    example study, 22–27
  reliability, 23–24, 25–27
    reliability/validity relationship, 26–27
    validity, 23–24, 25–27
  research generalization implications,
    27–30
    population, 28–29
  treatment, 29–30
    research generalization, contribution,
      14–15
  validity, 21–22
Generalization
  analytic, 212
  as inferences, 68
  case-to-case, 213
  characterized, 265–270
  commonly understood notion, 10
  defined, 265–270
  educational research
    naturalistic version, 51, 208
    positivist version, 207
  ethnographic work, 53

grounded, 57–58
how research use mediates, 123–126
language, 257
    construction of tests across lan-
        guages, 257–258
meta–analysis, 58–59
nomological, 56–57
phenomenology, 239–247
    abstraction, 244–247, 248, 249
    experiential generalization, 244–247,
        248, 249
    expression and validation, 240
    person-in-situation unit, 243
    practical example, 239–247
    praxis of method, 240–244
    systematic inquiries and descriptions,
        243
population, 28–29
probabilistic, 52–55
qualitative inquiry, 51–66
statistical inference, 236–268
syntheses, 58–59
theoretical, 59–64
treatment, 29–30
types, 52–64
Generalizing
    characterized, 265–270
    defined, 265–270
    educational research, characterized,
        211–212
Graduate students, curriculum, 291, 293
Grain sizes
    policy issues, 290–291
    qualitative research, 286
    quantitative research, 286
    statistical modeling, 91
Grounded generalization, 57–58
Grupo Cultural AfroReggae, 162–164

H
Hegemony, defined, 171
Hermeneutics, 289
    policy issues, 190
    validity, 83–85

I
Icons, defined, 130
Idea of Testing Project, 67–68
Index, 130, 256
    defined, 130
Individual-collective dialectic
    conversation as model, 251–255
    culture, 247–249
        from individual to collective, 249–251
Inferences, 79–85
    educational assessment, 69–74
        assessment design argument, 69–71
        assessment use argument, 69–71
        structure, 69–71
    evidentiary arguments, 79
    validity, 93–98
Internal generalization, probabilistic
    generalization, 54
Interpretations, 34, 35, 81–83, 84
Interpretive inquiry, 1

K
Knowledge
    forms of knowledge, 123–124
    means of knowledge production,
        123–124
Kuhn, Thomas, 208

L
Labels
    qualitative research, 278–284
    quantitative research, 278–284
Language
    generalization, 257
    construction of tests across languages,
        257–258
    historical–genetic approach, 255–258
    sample-to-population generalization,
        217–218
Learning outcomes, pretest correlation,
    4–5
Learning sciences, 177

M
Macro, defined, 172
Marx, Karl, political economy, 250
Mathematics, gender differences, 211
    sample-to-population generalization,
        227–231
Meaning, 91–93
Means of production, 123–124
Measurements, 10
    sample-to-population generalization,
        216–217
Measures of outcomes, 193–194
Media, modal validity, 192
Mediation, 182
Medical models, 179
Meso, defined, 172
Meta-analysis, 102–110
    data analysis, 108–109

Meta-analysis (*continued*)
  data collection, 105
  data evaluation, 106–108
  defined, 101
  effect sizes, 101
  generalizability, 101–115
  incorporating quantitative and qualitative research, 110–111, 112
  interpretation, 109–110
  methodology bias, 107
  presentation, 109–110
  problem formulation, 102–104
  publication bias, 105
  qualitative studies, 110–115
  quantitative synthesis, 102–110
  randomized controlled trials, 106
    generalization, 58–59
    process, 101
    qualitative studies, 110–115
    quantitative studies, 102–110
Meta-ethnography, 58
Methodology
  method, distinguished, 290
  policy issues, 290–291
Metonymic constituent, 256
Micro, defined, 172
Miscontextualization, 191–192
Mixed methods research, 144–145
  typology, 145
Modal validity, media, 192

N
National Research Council's Foundations of Assessment Committee, 71
National Science Foundation, 71
Natural sciences
  perceptions
    entities of interest, 131–132
    factors affecting researcher's perceptions, 129
    indices, 130
    phenomena representations, 129–130
    signs, 130
    symbolosphere, 131
    symbols, 130
  phenomena, 128–129
    entities of interest, 131–132
    factors affecting researcher's perceptions, 129
    indices, 130
    phenomena representations, 129–130
    signs, 130
    symbolosphere, 131

  symbols, 130
Naturalistic inquiry, 3, 51
Neo-Marxian theory critiques, 179–180
Nested facet designs, 18–19
New Zealand Ministry of Education, Iterative Best Evidence Synthesis Programme, 187–188
Nomological generalization, 56–57
  reductionist conceit, 56
  social science, 56
  transferability, 56–57
Non-normative educational practice, 177

O
Object of measurement, 20–21
Objectivity of social facts, 285
Observations, 9, 34, 35
  transferability, 238–239
Ontological authenticity, 126
Ontological commitments, 290
Opportunity to learn, situative/sociocultural perspective, 73
Outcomes, sample-to-population generalization, 215–216
Overgeneralization, 275
  teacher wait time, 156–157

P
Particular, general, rethinking relationship, 207–209
Passivity, defined, 172
Patterns, statistical modeling, 91–93
Peer-directed learning, generalizability theory
  dependability of measurements, 24–25
  example study, 22–27
  reliability, 23–24, 25–27
  reliability/validity relationship, 26–27
  validity, 23–24, 25–27
Perceptions
  education, 128–129
    entities of interest, 131–132
    factors affecting researcher's perceptions, 129
    indices, 130
    phenomena representations, 129–130
    signs, 130
    symbolosphere, 131
    symbols, 130
  natural sciences, 128–129
    entities of interest, 131–132
    factors affecting researcher's perceptions, 129

indices, 130
phenomena representations, 129–130
signs, 130
symbolosphere, 131
symbols, 130
Phenomena
    education, 128–129
        entities of interest, 131–132
        factors affecting researcher's percep-
            tions, 129
        indices, 130
        phenomena representations, 129–130
        signs, 130
        symbolosphere, 131
        symbols, 130
    natural sciences, 128–129
        entities of interest, 131–132
        factors affecting researcher's percep-
            tions, 129
        indices, 130
        phenomena representations, 129–130
        signs, 130
        symbolosphere, 131
        symbols, 130
Phenomenology, generalization, 239–247
    epoch, 240, 242
        abstraction, 244–247, 248, 249
        experiential generalization, 244–247,
            248, 249
        expression and validation, 240
        person-in-situation unit, 243
        practical example, 239–247
        praxis of method, 240–244
        systematic inquiries and descriptions,
            243
Phronesis, 208
    defined, 208
Plausibility, generalizability, contrasted,
    158–159
Policy issues, 287
    educational research, 173–178
    history, 178–186
    neoliberal U.S. public policy discourse,
        175
    remaking policy, 176–178
    grain sizes, 290–291
    hermeneutics, 190
    methodology, 290–291
    policy relevance of current assessment,
        192–193
    quasi-experimental research, 178–179
    sample-to-population generalization,
        218–221

Political economy, Marx, Karl, 250
Population, 3
    generalizability theory, 28–29
    probabilistic generalization, 52–55
    specification, 39–41
Positivist paradigm, 3
Practical wisdom, 208
    defined, 208
Pre–post design, 180
Prescriptions, situated work of acting,
    125
Pretest, learning outcomes correlation,
    4–5
Principle of symmetry, 20–21
Probabilistic generalization, 52–55
    external generalization, 54
    internal generalization, 54
    population, 52–55
    study sample, 52–55
Problem formulation, 102–104
Problem space, 81–83, 84
Professional organizations, strategic shift,
    179
Psychological survey instruments, evi-
    dence, 191
Psychometrics, 1, 72, 74–79, 85–90
Publication bias, 105

Q
Qualitative research
    assumptions about patterns, 286
    confirmability criterion, 238
    empirical research, 128–133
        commonalities across approaches,
            132–133
    generalization, 51–66
        as inferential links, 133–137, 138
    grain size, 286
    history, 181
    labels, 278–284
    meta-analysis, 110–115
    quantitative research
        broader and more synthetic frame-
            work, 292
    unifying, 292
Quantitative research
    assumptions about patterns, 286
    empirical research, 128–133
        commonalities across approaches,
            132–133
    generalization, 101–115
        as inferential links, 133–137, 138
    grain size, 286

Quantitative research (*continued*)
  history, 179–182
  labels, 278–284
  meta-analysis, 102–110
  qualitative research
    broader and more synthetic frame-
      work, 292
    unifying, 292
Quasi-experimental research
  policy issues, 178–179
  variable processes and practices,
    188–189

R
Random facet designs, 20
Randomized controlled trials, 106
Reflexive sociology, 285
Reliability, 23–24, 25–27
  dependability of measurements, 24–25
Repetition, 149
  creating thought objects, 151–152
  generalizability, contrasted, 149–150
  perspectives on, 151–153
  research as culture, 151
  structure, 152–153
Representativeness, sample-to-population
    generalization, 214–215
Research courses, 291, 293
Research generalization, 14–15, 101–115
Research-use argument, 286–287
Ricoeur, Paul, 208

S
Sample size, generalizability, 211
Sample-to-population generalization
  analytic generalization, 212
  applicability of findings to practice and
    policy, 218–221
  characterized, 212
  correlational research
    limitations, 220–223, 225–227
  culture, 217–218
  factors affecting, 214–218
  gender differences, limitations, 227–231
  language, 217–218
  limitations, 211–233
    group level inferences, 227–231
  measurements, 216–217
  outcomes, 215–216
  planning and learning outcomes,
    223–224
  representativeness, 214–215
  sampling errors, 214

  sampling of students, 215
  settings, 217–218
  standardized tests in assigning grades
    and learning outcomes, 225
  statistical rationale, 213–214
  textbook use and learning outcomes,
    224–225
School ethnography, 62–63
School-based research, activism, 150,
    164–168
  catalyzing educational improvements,
    165–168
  student researchers, 164–165
  teacher researchers, 164–165
Scientific, myth underlying, 174
Score generalizability, 40–41
Signs, 130
Singapore, Core Research Program, Cen-
    tre for Research in Pedagogy and
    Practice, 189
Situated work of acting, prescriptions, 125
Situative/sociocultural perspective, 74–79
Social control theory critiques, 179–180
Social Darwinism, 179
Social historical school, 181
Social life
  efficacy-oriented research, 163–164
  improving, 162–164
Social reproduction, 183
Social science
  linguistic turn, 184
  nomological generalization, 56
Sociocultural studies, 74–85
  validity, 83–85
Statistical inference, generalization,
    236–268
Statistical modeling, 85–90
  grain sizes, 91
  patterns, 91–93
Structures
  defined, 172
  repetition, 152–153
Study sample, probabilistic generaliza-
    tion, 52–55
Symbolosphere, 131
Symbols, 130
  defined, 130
Syntheses, generalization, 58–59

T
Tactical authenticity, 126
Teacher wait time
  educational research, 153–154, 155

overgeneralization, 156–157
Test scores, validity of interpretations, 9
Testing, English Language Learners
  as stochastic process, 41–48
  cognition and language, 34, 35
  conceptual basis, 33
  context variation, 39–41, 40
  evidence generalization, 41
  general assessment framework, 34–36
  generalizability theory, 36–37
  interpretation, 34, 35
  language variation, 39–41, 40
  language-related sources of measure-
    ment error, 38–39
  multidisciplinary perspective, 33–34
  observation, 34, 35
  population specification, 39–41
  score generalizability, 40–41
  score variation, 39–41, 40
  sociolinguistic perspective, 37–39
  stochastic model, 42–43, 44
Theoretical generalization, 59–64
  cultural theory, 62
  defined, 60
  process, 60
Theoretical inference, 59–64

Thorndike tradition, 180, 181
  destabilized, 184
Transdomain principles, validity, 79
Transferability, 3
  nomological generalization, 56–57
  observation, 238–239
Treatment, generalizability theory, 29–30
Trends in International Mathematics and
  Science Study, 213

V
Validity, 10, 23–24, 25–27, 67–98
  discourse analysis, 73
  fundamental differences in approaches,
    79–85
  generalizability theory, 21–22
  generalizability forms of arguments,
    271–278
  hermeneutics, 83–85
  inferences, 93–98
  situated and dynamic interpretations,
    80–81
  sociocultural studies, 83–85
  transdomain principles, 79
Videotaping, 9
Vygotsky, Lev Semenovich, 287